DATE DUE

GAYLORD			PRINTED IN U.S.A.

DUMPING: A PROBLEM IN INTERNATIONAL TRADE

DUMPING: A PROBLEM IN INTERNATIONAL TRADE

BY

JACOB VINER

AUGUSTUS M. KELLEY, PUBLISHERS

First edition 1923
(Chicago: University of Chicago Press, 1923)

Reprinted 1991 by
AUGUSTUS M. KELLEY, PUBLISHERS
Fairfield NJ 07004-0008

Library of Congress Cataloging-in-Publication Data

Viner, Jacob, 1892-1970.
    Dumping : a problem in international trade / by Jacob Viner.
      p. cm. — (Reprints of economic classics)
    Reprint. Originally published: Chicago : University of Chicago Press,
    1923.
    Includes bibliographical references.
    ISBN 0-678-01398-5
    1. Dumping (International trade). 2. Dumping (International
    trade)—Law and legislation. I. Title. II. Series.
    HB165.L7413 1991
    382´.3—dc20   90-35119

Manufactured in the United States of America

TO
F. K. V.

PREFACE

Dumping, if not necessarily an "unfair" method of competition, is at least a questionable method. The growing realization of the possible abuses of competition has led to the development of an extensive literature on the general question of unfair competition. Until 1914 the bulk of this literature dealt exclusively with the standards of competition in domestic commerce, and, speaking broadly, only upon occasions of a temporary intensification of the severity of international competition was serious attention given to the methods and practices employed in such competition. The widespread discussion during the war of the allegedly unfair and predatory methods used by Germany to attain world-wide commercial and industrial supremacy has served to heighten and to sustain public interest in the general question of standards of competition in foreign trade. In recent years a number of countries have endeavored to find legislative means of restraining the use of some of the more objectionable competitive methods in foreign commerce. There nevertheless does not exist as yet anything which merits being considered a comprehensive and systematic study of the problem, whether from the economic or the legal point of view. The present study of dumping as a method of international competition, of its economic significance to the dumping country and to the country dumped on, and of the measures, national and international, which have been adopted to restrain its practice, is presented in the hope that it will prepare the way for a study of the broader question of standards of competition in international commerce.

Chapters i to v of the present study are reprinted, with some alterations and additions, from the *Journal of Political Economy* and the *University Journal of Business*. Dr. B. B. Wallace, of the United States Tariff Commission, who read most of the manuscript and who gave me the benefit of his close and penetrating criticism and of his wide knowledge of sources, is responsible for much of what merit this study possesses. For errors of fact and inadequacies of analysis, the author is alone responsible.

J. V.

TABLE OF CONTENTS

CHAPTER   PAGE

I. THE DEFINITION OF DUMPING   I
    Origin of the Term, 1.—The Problem of Definition, 2.—Reverse
    Dumping, 5.—Spurious Dumping, 8.—Exchange Dumping,
    15.—Freight Dumping, 16.—Concealed Dumping, 17

II. THE CLASSIFICATION OF DUMPING   23
    Classification according to Motive, 23.—According to Con-
    tinuity, 29.—Other Bases for Classification, 32.—Allied
    Practices, 33

III. THE PREVALENCE OF DUMPING PRIOR TO 1890   35
    Early Instances, 36.—British Dumping in the United States,
    38.—Other Instances, 48

IV. THE PREVALENCE OF DUMPING SINCE 1890
    I. CONTINENTAL EUROPEAN, CANADIAN, JAPANESE DUMPING .   51
    German Dumping, 51.—Belgian Dumping, 66.—French Dump-
    ing, 68.—Austrian Dumping, 70.—Canadian Dumping, 71.—
    Japanese Dumping, 72

V. THE PREVALENCE OF DUMPING SINCE 1890
    II. BRITISH AND AMERICAN DUMPING   74
    British Dumping, 74.—American Dumping, 80.—Dumping
    resulting from Official Bounties, 90.—Conclusion, 92

VI. THE INFLUENCE OF DUMPING ON PRICES IN THE DUMPING
    COUNTRY   94
    Monopolies and Dumping, 94.—The Effect of Dumping on
    Domestic Prices, 101.—The Effect of Dumping of Primary
    Materials on More Advanced Industries, 107

VII. THE PROFITABILITY OF DUMPING TO THE DUMPER 110
    Sporadic Dumping, 110.—Short-Run Dumping, 111.—Dump-
    ing and the Stability of Production, 117.—Predatory Dumping,
    120.—Long-Run Dumping, 122.—Bounty Dumping, 126.—
    Conclusion, 131

CHAPTER   PAGE
VIII. THE CONSEQUENCES OF DUMPING TO THE IMPORTING COUNTRY   132

The Influence of Dumping on Prices in the Importing Country,
132.—The Effect of Dumping on Producers in the Importing
Country, 137.—Free Trade and Dumping, 144

IX. ORDINARY PROTECTIVE TARIFFS AS SAFEGUARDS AGAINST
DUMPING   148

Ordinary Import Duties as Barriers against Dumping, 148.—
Import Duties as a Cause of Dumping, 157.—Ordinary Import
Duties an Unsatisfactory Antidumping Device, 159.—Anti-
dumping Legislation by Protectionist Countries, 161

X. COUNTERVAILING MEASURES AGAINST OFFICIAL EXPORT
BOUNTIES   163

The Export-Bounty System, 163.—Anti-Bounty Clauses in
Bilateral Treaties, 166.—Bounty-Countervailing Duties, 168.—
The Brussels Sugar Convention, 178.—Recent Developments
in Bounty-Countervailing Legislation, 187

XI. FOREIGN ANTIDUMPING LEGISLATION. I   192

Canadian Antidumping Law, 192.—New Zealand Antidumping
Measure of 1905, 204.—Australian Antidumping Law of 1906,
206.—Union of South Africa Law, 209.—Newfoundland Law,
212.—Proposed French Measure of 1908, 212

XII. FOREIGN ANTIDUMPING LEGISLATION. II   216

British Antidumping Legislation, 216.—Australian Antidumping Law of 1921, 227.—New Zealand Antidumping Law of 1921,
231.—Flexible Tariff Provisions: Japan, New Zealand, Canada,
235

XIII. AMERICAN ANTIDUMPING LEGISLATION   239

DUMPING AND UNFAIR COMPETITION

Sherman Antitrust Act, 1890, 239.—Section 73, Tariff Act of
1894, 240.—Sections 800–801, Revenue Act, 1916, 242.—
Section 316, Tariff Act of 1922, 246.—American Participation
in the International Union for the Protection of Industrial
Property, 254

CHAPTER   PAGE

ADMINISTRATIVE REMEDIES AGAINST DUMPING

Antidumping Proposal of 1913, 257.—Antidumping Act, 1921, 258.—Administration of Antidumping Law, 265.—Section 303, Tariff Act of 1922, 268.—Miscellaneous Provisions, 272

XIV. COMPARATIVE ANALYSIS OF ANTIDUMPING LAWS 274

Classification of Laws, 274.—Type of Import Practice Penalized, 275.—Date of Price-Comparison, 276.—Marginal Allowance before Dumping-Duty Becomes Applicable, 278.—Allowance for Remission of Foreign Taxes, 279.—Allowance for Differences in Conditions and Terms of Sale, 281.—Special Statutory Exemptions of Commodities, 282.—Consignment Sales, 285.—Methods of Determination of Rates, 287.—Notice before Application of Duties, 289.—Cost of Production Provisions, 291.—Methods of Administration, 294

XV. TREATY OBLIGATIONS AND ANTIDUMPING MEASURES . . . 298

Compatibility of Bounty-Countervailing Duties with Most-Favored-Nation Obligations, 298.—Historical Precedents, 303.—Official Arguments for the Validity of Countervailing Duties, 314.—The Opinions of Jurists, 318.—The German-Swiss Flour Duty Controversy, 325.—Compatibility of General Antidumping Duties with Most-Favored-Nation Obligations, 327

SELECTED BIBLIOGRAPHY 331

INDEX 339

CHAPTER I

THE DEFINITION OF DUMPING

It has long been customary to speak of one market as the "dumping-ground" for the "surplus" products of another market when the producers of the latter for any reason sold their commodities in the former at unusually low prices. From this usage it was a natural outcome to speak of selling in a distant market at cut prices as "dumping," but the word used in this sense appears not to have entered into the literature of economics until the first years of the twentieth century. In 1903 and 1904 the tariff question was the dominant political issue in Great Britain, and in the voluminous output of polemical literature which marked the tariff controversy the term became well established and appeared, with or without apologetic quotation marks, in book after book. It has since found its way into the economic terminology of French, German, Italian, and probably other languages. At first, however, it had but a vague and uncertain meaning, and it is still often used indiscriminately for such diverse price-practices as severe competition, customs undervaluation, "bargain," "sacrifice," or slaughter sales, local price-cutting, and selling in one national market at a lower price than in another. In recent years, it is true, the increased use of the term by academic economists, with their commendable tendency toward the exact establishment of terminology, and the development of legislation dealing with dumping and allied price-practices, which made necessary some measure of precision in the differentiation between various price-practices, have both contributed to standardization of usage. But extensive variations in the use of the term, both as to denotation and as to connotation, are nevertheless still current.

As an important element in the analysis of the essential attributes of the practices connoted by dumping, and as an essential preliminary to further analysis, it is necessary to establish a precise definition of the term to be adhered to in the body of this essay.   There follows herewith an attempt to lay down a formal definition, governed by the following considerations: to adhere as closely as is consistent with the other considerations to the usage of the more careful writers; to exclude from the connotation of the term all such price-practices as have already acquired well-defined and sufficiently distinguishing labels; and to strip from the denotation of the term all such attributes as would make of the term nothing more than a vague symbol indicating a slender relationship between various price-practices having little in common.

The term dumping is employed most often, even in careless business usage, to signify selling the same commodities at different prices in different markets.   By business men it is often uncritically extended, however, to cover various types of sales at prices lower than those generally current, even although these low prices are uniform to all purchasers.[1]   Where there is nothing to be said about a low price except that it is low, there is no need to waste a good term on a practice for which another and simpler term is already available and is sufficiently descriptive.   Where the low price is the manifestation of "slaughter" or "sacrifice" sales, or "cutthroat competition," or "price-cutting," or selling below cost of production, in all of which cases all buyers may be receiving uniform treatment, the practices are sufficiently

---

[1] The U.S. Tariff Commission, in response to a questionnaire sent to American business concerns asking for a statement of personally known instances of dumping in the United States by foreigners, received complaints of 146 such instances, of which 146 complaints all but 23 resolved themselves upon analysis into charges of severe competition, threats, deceptive imitation and use of trade-marks, exploitation of patents, imitation of articles, deceptive labelling, or customs undervaluation, and only the remaining 23 instances were alleged cases of price-discrimination. Cf. *Information Concerning Dumping and Unfair Foreign Competition in the United States* (1919), pp. 12–18.

identified by these terms of common use. For the practice of selling at lower prices to some buyers than to others, whether or not accompanied by regional segregation of the buyers who receive, respectively, the lower and the higher prices, the term "price-discrimination" has become fairly well established, especially in the American literature on unfair competition in domestic trade. For the practice of selling at lower prices to buyers in some regional part of a given national market than to buyers in the remainder of that market, the term "local price-cutting" has likewise become customary, especially in American legal usage. When used by careful writers, the term "dumping" now most commonly signifies selling at a lower price in one national market than in another. Of the price-practices considered above, dumping, so interpreted, resembles most closely local price-cutting and is often used so as to include it. But sufficient justification is to be found in the usage of the most authoritative writers and in the considerations of economy and precision of terminology for confining the term dumping to *price-discrimination between national markets.*[1]

This definition, I venture to assert, will meet all reasonable requirements. T. E. G. Gregory, an English economist, in a recent work[2] points out that in current controversy the term dumping is used at one time or another to cover all of the four following practices:

1. Sale at prices below foreign market prices.
2. Sale at prices with which [foreign ?] competitors cannot cope.
3. Sale at prices abroad which are lower than current home prices.
4. Sale at prices unremunerative to the sellers.

[1] When the constituent parts of a loosely related empire, such as the British Empire, are under consideration, there arise the same terminological difficulties in connection with the term dumping as are presented by the terms "foreign" or "international" trade. For the present purpose a convenient, although arbitrary, basis for distinguishing "national" from "local" markets is to include as "national" all political units having separate customs tariffs and to treat all others as "local."

[2] *Tariffs: A Study in Method*, London, 1921, pp. 177 ff.

Failing to find any one essential characteristic which is common to all of these practices, Gregory gives up the attempt to frame a definition. But he demands too much of a definition of a term in common use when he requires it to harmonize all the current usages. Of the four practices cited by him, Case 3 approximates closely the definition of dumping here presented; the others are more or less irrelevant. It is often tacitly assumed because of inadequate analysis that any instance of Case 3 must necessarily be accompanied by one or more of the other cases. This is frequently the situation, but as Gregory points out, it is not necessarily so. The "sale at prices abroad which are lower than current home prices" is properly to be regarded as an instance of dumping irrespective of whether or not the export price is below the foreign market price, or is one with which foreign competitors cannot cope, or is unremunerative to the seller. The one essential characteristic of dumping, I contend, is price-discrimination between purchasers in different national markets.[1] The relations of particular dumping prices to cost of production, to dumper's profits, and to the prices of rival sellers, are often intricate problems which cannot be solved by mere definition, and which in many cases are not susceptible of exact solution. As will be subsequently shown, there are many types and species of dumping and it is always possible logically, although often exceedingly difficult in practice, to distinguish between dumping which is and dumping which is not remunerative to the dumper, and between dumping prices which are and dumping prices which are not lower than the prices of rival sellers.

Dumping when defined as price-discrimination between national markets covers not only the more common form of international price-discrimination, where sales are made at lower

[1] Cf. F. W. Taussig, *Principles of Economics* (3d ed.), I, 207: "The possibility of charging different prices to different purchasers explains the phenomenon of 'dumping'—that is, the disposal of commodities in a foreign country at one price, and to domestic purchasers at another and higher price."

prices for export than in the domestic market, but also the rarer forms, (a) where there is no, or only a meager, domestic market for a particular commodity and the important price-discrimination is between purchasers in different export markets, and (b) where the home market of the seller is made the dumping-ground and higher prices are charged to purchasers in foreign markets. Some types of low-grade, heavily sized cottons are manufactured in England solely for the tropical trade and have no domestic market. An English manufacturer of these cottons may sell at lower prices in China than in India and other markets in order to introduce his product into the Chinese market, or to meet Chinese competition, or for some other reason. In such a case the English manufacturer is dumping in China, even although it is not possible to compare his prices to Chinese purchasers with his home prices. A variant of this form of dumping is to be found where, irrespective of the prices quoted to domestic purchasers, sales are made at lower prices to purchasers in one foreign market than in another. An American consul in Belgium reported some years ago that the Belgian plate-glass syndicate, which disposed of only 5 per cent of its output in the home market, commonly quoted prices lower by 10 to 30 per cent to American than to English buyers, mainly because the English market was the "standard" market for Belgian plate glass, whereas sales could be made to American purchasers only if price concessions were granted.[1] This was an instance of dumping, whether or not the prices to Americans were lower than the prices to Belgian purchasers. The definitions of dumping in some of the laws dealing with this practice cover such cases.

It is often taken for granted that when dumping is practiced it will always be the distant market which is used as a dumping-

---

[1] *Selling Foreign Manufactures in the United States at Prices Lower Than the Domestic Prices*, Report of Secretary of State to Senate (61st Cong., 1st Sess., Sen. Doc. 16), Part I, p. 6. (This report will henceforth be referred to as *Selling Foreign Manufactures in the United States.*)

ground and the near market—especially the domestic market of the dumper—which is charged the higher prices. This is undoubtedly the general rule, but there are important exceptions to it. If the domestic market is relatively unimportant as compared to that distant market and production is carried on primarily for export to that distant market, there may develop what can conveniently be termed "reverse dumping," that is, the quotation of lower prices to domestic than to foreign buyers. Were it not for the fact that the domestic market is often closed to foreign competition by a prohibitive tariff, so that a domestic syndicate can exact monopoly prices behind the shelter of the tariff, the general rule would probably require less qualification if it were formulated with reference to the normal importance of the markets to the dumper, instead of with reference to their distance from his plant. Where dumping occurs, it will generally be found upon investigation that the higher price is charged in the standard or principal market or markets and that the dumping price is effective only in the subsidiary or occasional markets. The position of two markets relative to each other may in this respect be transposed, however, periodically at different seasons of the year, or sporadically as market conditions vary. What is the standard market at one season or in one year may become a subsidiary market in the next season or year. The following comment of an important Canadian miller on the Canadian export trade in flour illustrates the circumstances under which reverse dumping is most likely to occur:

Of the lower grades [of flour] most of the output of Canadian mills is sold abroad, very little of it being used for home consumption. . . . . These grades are on the average sold cheaper in the United Kingdom than in this country; but, at times, one or other of them sells for less in Canada than abroad, because Great Britain, being the big consuming market for such flour, the surplus is disposed of in Canada if there is any risk of breaking the market by exporting the flour abroad.[1]

---

[1] Canada: *Report of the Board of Inquiry into the Cost of Living, 1915*, I, 757.

Reverse dumping may occasionally arise out of other exceptional circumstances. A concern having a world-wide monopoly of its product may be restrained by law, or by fear of inciting hostile legislation or popular resentment, from exacting the full monopoly price from domestic consumers, but may be free from such restraint in its export sales. The German potash industry appears to have been a case in point prior to 1914.[1] A special case is presented by the Canadian ferrosilicon industry. Canada is an important producer of this alloy, but consumes less than 10 per cent of the total output. The remainder is exported, mainly to the United States where under the (Underwood) Tariff Act of 1913 it was dutiable at an ad valorem rate. During 1917 and 1918 the prices for export appear to have run for identical grades from 7 to 70 per cent higher than the domestic prices. An American customs official at Buffalo has testified that the prices for the Canadian market in these years were usually from 20 to 40 per cent below the prices for export to the United States.[2] This instance of reverse dumping was the outcome of an ingenious method of circumventing the American system of levying ad valorem duties. Under the Tariff Act of 1913 ad valorem duties were assessed on the basis of the prices current in the home market of the exporter, regardless of the invoice prices. Since the Canadian consumption is relatively small, it was profitable to the Canadian producers to establish an artificially low price in the domestic market as a basis for the assessment of the American duties upon imports into the United States.[3]

[1] Cf. H. R. Tosdal, "The Kartell Movement in the German Potash Industry," *Quarterly Journal of Economics*, XXVIII, 178.

[2] Abraham Berglund, "The Ferroalloy Industries and Tariff Legislation," *Political Science Quarterly*, XXXVI, 270 ff.

[3] This is Berglund's explanation. Under Section 19 of the Customs Administrative Act of August 11, 1890, as amended by the Act of July 24, 1897, it was specifically provided that duty could not be assessed on "an amount less than the invoice or entered value." This proviso was omitted from the administrative

SPURIOUS DUMPING

In the definition of dumping presented above, the term
"price-discrimination" was intentionally used in preference to
the milder phrase, "sales at different prices." In the growing
literature on unfair competition there are traces of a tendency
to apply the term "price-discrimination" only to such instances
of sale at different prices to different purchasers as are not
readily to be explained by differences in the conditions and terms
of sale governing the different transactions. Given this interpretation, price-discrimination may in fact result from the
quotation of identical prices without adjustment for differences in
the terms and conditions of sale.[1] In international commerce
the sale at different prices to purchasers in different national

---

provisions in the Act of October 3, 1913, which permitted the importer to enter
his goods for duty at such reductions from the invoice value as would lower the
latter to the actual market value in the country of exportation (Sec. III, Par. I).
But as the market value in the country of exportation was defined in the act as
"the price at which such merchandise is freely offered for sale to *all* purchasers in
said markets" (Sec. III, Par. R) it might appear that the customs officials would
be acting within their authority if they refused to permit entry at prices lower
than those at which sales would freely be made to *foreign buyers in the exporting
market*. This reasoning is supported by the definitions in the Tariff Act of 1922,
where the only distinction drawn between foreign value and export value is that
the former is the price offered to *all* purchasers, whereas the latter is the price
offered to all purchasers *for exportation to the United States*. [Sec. 402, (*b*) and (*c*)].
To the layman it seems indisputable that a price which is withheld from purchasers
for exportation to the United States cannot be a price offered to *all* purchasers.
Treasury practice and Court decisions, however, were opposed to this interpretation. There resulted a number of instances of abuse such as that discussed in the
text. The possibility of such evasion of the obvious intent of the customs law
was removed in 1921 by the reinsertion in the Emergency Tariff Act of the old
requirement that duties be levied on the current market value in the country of
exportation or on the export value, whichever was higher (Sec. 301, 2). A similar
provision is embodied in the (Fordney-McCumber) Tariff Act of 1922 [Sec. 402,
(*a*), (1)].

[1] It is not intended here to make the term price-discrimination necessarily
denote unfair competitive practice. Some types of price-discrimination may be
regarded as fair and others as unfair by the mores and the law, but no instance of
a quotation of different prices can conceivably be regarded as unfair unless it also
involves price-discrimination.

markets is to be regarded as price-discrimination, and therefore as dumping, only if the different prices are quoted simultaneously for identical or substantially identical commodities offered for sale under similar conditions and terms, or, where these last are not similar, only if the price-differential embodies what is either more or less than a reasonable allowance for the differences in conditions and terms.

In international commerce the sale at different prices to purchasers in different national markets may occur without involving price-discrimination if the price-differentials are merely adjustments to differences in the size of the unit orders coming from different countries, in the length of the credits, in the extent of the credit risks, in the grades of commodities, in the time at which the sales contracts were made, in the method of conducting the selling operations, or in the treatment of freight and packing charges. Or the differences in prices may result from the grant of export drawbacks in the exporting country on dutiable imported materials re-exported after further manufacture, or from the "temporary admission" of such materials free of duty, or from the exemption from excise duties in the exporting country of commodities destined for export. The sale at different prices to purchasers in different markets, when it is fully explicable on grounds such as these, has a fictitious appearance of dumping and has been aptly termed "spurious dumping" to distinguish it from genuine dumping.

The most important single factor giving rise to spurious dumping is probably the difference in the size of the unit orders which are obtained in different markets. The foreign buyer often gives as a general rule larger orders than the domestic buyer. This may be because the former makes few buying trips and concentrates his purchases into a few weeks of the year, whereas the domestic buyer finds it more convenient to make his purchases in small quantities as he needs new supplies. Or the foreign buyer may be operating in a larger market, or in a market in which the individual concerns are larger than in the domestic market. This applies especially to European sales to American concerns. In many cases, also, export sales are one or more stages less advanced than domestic sales in the process of distribution to the ultimate consumer. The importer typically buys for resale to distributors or to large-scale consumers, whereas in domestic commerce it is often customary for the manufacturer to sell his product direct to the concern which is to use it as material for further manufacture or to the small retailer who is to sell it to the final consumers. For manufactured products, the nearer one approaches to the ultimate consumer, the smaller tends to be the scale of the individual concern, and the smaller, therefore, the normal size of its orders.

The economies to the seller of large-unit orders are fairly obvious. If he manufactures to order and not for stock—and this is the usual procedure in Europe—the larger "run" made possible by a large-unit order will be much more economical than a similar aggregate of sales made up of a number of small orders coming in irregularly, perhaps for varied styles or assortments or sizes. There will also be economies in the clerical work, in the packing and shipping expenses, in the selling costs, involved in large-unit orders as compared to small. Concessions in price to foreign buyers because of the size of their orders are not to be regarded as instances of dumping if similar concessions are made on domestic orders of the same magnitude, or if the sellers would be willing to make similar concessions if such orders were obtainable in the domestic market.[1]

[1] Cf. Memorandum of Confidential Agent of U.S. Treasury, W. E. Bainbridge, March 15, 1909, in *Selling Foreign Manufactures in the United States*, Part 1, p. 41: "Merchandise may be and in fact very frequently is sold for export at lower prices than in the domestic markets. There are various reasons given for this. . . . . [A] reason, especially cogent in the case of goods shipped to the United States, is the much larger orders frequently given by the American importer over those given by the domestic buyer. This is very often the explanation made by the European manufacturer to the Treasury agent of the difference found between his invoice and domestic prices; the statement being generally added that he would be willing to sell to his domestic customers at the same prices for corresponding quantities."

Similarly, if export sales are commonly on cash or short-credit terms, whereas long credits must be given to domestic purchasers; if foreign buyers are safer credit risks than the small-scale domestic buyers; if export grades are of poorer quality or not as well finished or of simpler construction than the domestic grades of similar commodities; if export prices are f.o.b. the factory or a nearby port, whereas domestic prices are prices delivered; if packing is separately charged in the export sale but is included in the domestic prices; under any of these circumstances the sale for export at prices lower than the domestic prices would not of itself necessarily indicate that genuine dumping was taking place.

Foreign buyers often send their agents into the exporting market, where they buy direct from the producer and without solicitation or the mediation of salesmen or advertising. The conduct of selling operations in the domestic market, on the other hand, may involve the employment of traveling salesmen and of advertising, and may require the maintenance of agencies or branch-houses. There was in Canada in 1913 some protest against the admitted practice on the part of the Canadian flour mills of selling certain grades of flour at lower prices in the export than in the domestic trade. The mills defended their practice in part on the ground that the unit selling cost was greater for domestic than for export sales, but their statement also covered a number of the other points made above:

A cable costing 50 cents or $1 sells anywhere from 200 to 20,000 sacks of flour and the miller simply has to load his flour on the car or boat, attach his bill of lading to the draft and the transaction is complete without any additional expense or risk of loss. In selling in Canada, however, it is necessary to keep expensive travellers on the road all the time under heavy expense, the sales run from five bags upwards and the buyers often cancel the orders before the flour is shipped, or refuse the flour when it arrives, or more frequently still ask the miller to hold it for a long time after date for shipment is passed; all of which means additional cost to the miller in selling. But the above are not the worst items, because flour, being sold on time here, bad debts are not infrequent and the miller sometimes has to take 25 cents, 50 cents, or 75 cents on the dollar and occasionally nothing at all, and may lose at times several thousands of dollars on one customer.[1]

Because it is often the practice of foreign buyers to anticipate their needs long ahead, and to give a single order covering their requirements for a substantial period, with deliveries to be made as requested or according to a specified schedule, there frequently occurs a considerable lapse of time between the date of the original purchase and the date of shipment. If during this interval prices rise in the exporting market there will be an apparent manifestation of dumping on the basis of a comparison of export and domestic prices *at the date of shipment.* This is not to be regarded, however, as an instance of genuine dumping if the same prices were available to domestic and foreign buyers *at the date of purchase.* For the purpose of determining whether dumping is taking place, comparison of export and domestic prices should be made as of the same date, and for any particular export transaction the only reasonable date to take is the date on which the export contract was made. This seems an obvious principle, but it is one which existing legislation against dumping in some instances fails to take into account.[2]

[1] Canada: *Report of the Board of Inquiry into the Cost of Living,* I, 752. For similar explanations of differences between domestic and export prices, see *Selling Foreign Manufactures in the United States,* I, 11, 16, 17, 51; *Report of United States Industrial Commission, 1901,* XIII, 726.

[2] The same problem arises in connection with the administration of ad valorem customs duties, where the duties are assessed on the basis of the values in the country of export. In the United States ad valorem customs duties are levied upon the basis of the prices current in the exporting market at the time of exportation. In consequence undervaluation technically occurs in frequent instances because the American importer, ignorant of the fact that prices have risen in the exporting country in the interval between the date of his original purchase and the date of shipment, enters his imports for customs duty at the invoice values. Under such circumstances the importer, although acting in perfectly good faith, was subjected to harsh penalties until the undervaluation provision was modified by the Fordney-McCumber Tariff Act of 1922. Cf. United States Tariff Commission, *Report upon the Revision of the Customs Administrative Laws* (1918), pp. 18, 19; Tariff Act of 1922, Sec. 489.

It has been tacitly assumed in the foregoing discussion that where there are differences in the conditions governing sales to purchasers in different markets such as to call for differences in prices if dumping is not to occur, the higher price will be proper to the domestic sales. Under some circumstances, however, the situation may be reversed and it may be necessary that a higher price be demanded of foreign than of domestic buyers if price-discrimination is not to take place. In other cases there may be differences in the conditions governing sales, not as between domestic sales and all export sales, but as between export sales to some foreign markets or to some particular foreign buyers, on the one hand, and all other sales, domestic and foreign, on the other hand.

The sale at lower prices for export than for the domestic market is likewise not to be regarded as dumping if the difference in price is wholly to be accounted for by the exemption of the exporter from payment of customs duties on dutiable imported materials used in further manufacture for export, whether such exemption is direct or through refund in the form of customs drawback of duties paid on such materials. The drawback system and allied devices confer no special advantages on the exporters in their competition in outside markets with the producers of other countries, but merely mitigate for the export trade one of the special handicaps to which it is subjected by the régime of protective tariffs. It is assumed, of course, that the drawback does not involve a concealed bounty, and is not in excess of the actual amount of duty collected on the imported materials entering into the manufacture of the commodity upon which drawback is granted.[1]

[1] For instances of lower export than domestic prices being explained as due to export drawbacks, see *Report of United States Industrial Commission, 1901*, XIII, 425–27; XVII, 112. Leslie M. Shaw, Secretary of the Treasury from 1902 to 1907, estimated that in 1906, of the total American exports of manufactured products exclusive of prepared foods amounting to $570,000,000, approximately $20,000,000 were manufactured in bond from otherwise dutiable imported raw materials, and

A similar problem arises where the sale for export at lower prices than those current in the domestic market is the consequence of the exemption from internal excise or commodity taxes of commodities destined for export[1]. The domestic manufacturer of commodities subject to excise taxation can obtain the same rate of profit from export as from domestic sales if he sells for export at prices lower than the domestic prices by the amount of the excise tax. Under freely competitive conditions the exemption of export commodities from excise taxation will result in the appearance of a differential between domestic and export prices equal to the amount of the tax. Since the price-differential is the result of a special handicap placed upon domestic sales, and is not due to the grant of a special advantage to export sales, there does not appear to be sufficient ground for regarding it as an instance of price-discrimination or dumping. The remission of an excise duty on exported commodities does not place them in a favored position in competition with similar products produced in the importing country. If there is in that country a similar excise tax, it will be imposed upon the imported and the domestic product alike. If there is no excise tax in that country, the remission of the excise tax in the exporting country will serve merely to place the exported commodity on a parity with the domestic commodity in the importing country. It may be objected that taxes are a normal part of the cost of production of a commodity and that to exempt export commodities from

that $120,000,000 were manufactured in part or in whole from imported dutiable materials upon which a drawback was recovered. He claimed that much of the apparent dumping by American manufacturers was to be explained by these remissions of duty, for "to the extent of this saving in the cost of the finished product, the . . . . manufacturer could reduce his export price and still make the same profit." (*Current Issues*, New York, 1908, chap. xxi.)

[1] For instances of apparent dumping, explained as due to the remission of excise taxes on commodities destined for export, see *Report of United States Industrial Commission, 1901*, XIII, 725–27.

any tax is equivalent to granting indirect bounties to export trade. Where a commodity tax is levied on all or nearly all commodities and is an important source of the government's revenue, there is some force to this objection. The exemption of export commodities from such a tax would mean their exemption from their proper share in the support of government finances. But where the excise tax is levied on only a few commodities, it is to be regarded rather as a special consumption tax, to be paid eventually by the domestic consumers of the taxed commodities, than as a normal element in the cost of production of these commodities. In this connection it should be made clear that the common identification of export bounties, direct or indirect, with dumping, is inaccurate. Export bounties tend to result in dumping to the extent that they enable a producer to accept a lower price for export than would be profitable in domestic trade. But "broadly speaking, grants and bounties may or may not result in dumping. They should be regarded as aids in that direction rather than the practice itself."[1]

EXCHANGE DUMPING

When the currency of a country is on an inconvertible paper basis, there may be for a time substantial divergence between its internal and its external purchasing power. If a currency is undergoing progressive depreciation, it appears to be the normal tendency for the decline in its internal purchasing power to lag behind the decline in its external purchasing power as measured by the foreign exchanges. A depreciating currency will thus tend to operate as a premium on exports by causing export prices, temporarily at least, to be abnormally low in terms of foreign currencies. It has recently become common to apply the term "exchange dumping" to the export of commodities at prices which are abnormally low in terms of foreign currency

[1] U.S. Tariff Commission, *Information Concerning Dumping and Unfair Foreign Competition*, p. 10.

in consequence of the more rapid depreciation of the currency of the exporting country on the foreign exchange market than in the internal commodity markets. This is a practice, however, which is quite distinct from dumping proper. It presents problems of theoretical and practical interest and importance and of considerable difficulty. In many respects it has the same significance for the importing country as dumping proper. But in so far as the exporters in a country whose currency is depreciating do not discriminate in the prices at which they sell, whether in their own or in foreign currency, between domestic and foreign buyers, or between the buyers of different foreign countries, dumping proper does not occur.[1]

FREIGHT DUMPING

In some countries, and especially in Germany until very recently, preferential railroad rates are given to export freight as compared to freight moving in domestic commerce, to transit freight, or to import freight, with the object of stimulating export trade. In the United States preferential export rates are a part of the rate system, but so are preferential import rates, and the object seems to be rather to increase the volume of freight moved by the railroads granting such rates than to stimulate exports for their own sake.[2] But whatever their object, preferential export rates are an artificial stimulus to exports and as such they somewhat resemble dumping. They are not, however, to be identified with commodity dumping. In operation they must tend to act as a restraint on, instead of a stimulus to, the dumping of commodities on foreign markets.

[1] For a discussion of the effects on international competition of divergences between the internal and the external purchasing powers of depreciating currencies, and for a select bibliography, see U.S. Tariff Commission, *Depreciated Exchange and International Trade*, 1922.

[2] Section 28 of the Merchant Marine Act of 1920 attempted to make use of these preferential rates as an aid to American shipping by forbidding rail carriers to quote preferential rates to or from the seaboard on goods exported or imported unless carried in American bottoms. This provision, however, has not as yet been put into operation.

Transportation costs to foreign markets serve as a natural protection to the domestic industries of those markets against outside competition. Anything which reduces these transportation costs tends by so much to increase the ability of exporters to make sales in those markets without making concessions from their home prices. Preferential export rates tend, therefore, to make dumping superfluous as a means of stimulating exports. But such rates may themselves be regarded without an undue stretching of terminology as an instance of dumping, not of commodities, but of freight services. Since the purchaser ultimately pays the freight charges, preferential export rates are equivalent to the sale of freight services at lower rates to foreign than to domestic purchasers.

CONCEALED DUMPING

Just as there may be spurious dumping, so also there may be genuine but concealed dumping. One method of concealment is the charge of the same prices to purchasers in different markets although the conditions and terms of sale differ substantially as between the different markets. Quoting the same prices for export as for the domestic market, but with longer credit terms for export than to domestic buyers, or without charge to foreign buyers for expensive packing or for transportation to seaboard or to the final destination where the charges are borne in the first instance by the exporter, or without extra charge to foreign buyers for better-finished or higher-grade goods as compared with those sold in the domestic market, any of these would be illustrative of actual but concealed dumping. An instance is reported of an American beer-bottling concern which sold for export at the same nominal prices as those quoted to domestic buyers, but concealed its practice of dumping by making its concessions on export sales take the form of omitting any charge for extra boxing and packing and of making its domestic prices f.o.b. factory whereas its export prices were f.o.b. New York.[1] The

[1] *Report of United States Industrial Commission, 1901*, XIII, 726.

Germans are commonly reputed, although probably undeservedly, to have concealed much of their dumping by granting without extra charge much longer credit terms to foreign than to domestic buyers.[1]

In the practices described above, the concealment of the dumping may not be due to deliberate design but may be merely an incidental result of differences in the trade customs governing domestic and export trade, respectively. Exporters who are practicing dumping may, however, have good reason for concealing it from the general public. Open dumping may arouse protest from the domestic consumers of the commodities sold abroad at lower prices. It may provide apparent confirmation of charges that the dumping concerns are exacting exorbitant prices in the domestic market. Domestic manufacturers who buy from them their materials for use in further manufacture may complain that they are handicapped in their competition with foreign producers by the ability of the latter to get their materials at lower prices. Open dumping may lead to a popular demand for the removal of the import duties under whose shelter the higher domestic prices are being maintained. It may excite resentment from competing producers in the countries used as dumping-grounds and may lead to countervailing duties. In some cases the dumper may wish to conceal his practice of dumping in order to evade the existing antidumping legislation of the countries in which he operates.

The most obvious method of deliberate concealment of dumping is to maintain secrecy about export prices, and this is commonly resorted to, especially in the United States.[2] It is often difficult, however, to keep export prices secret, especially if the dumping is practiced by loosely organized industrial combinations. In such cases use may be made of the devices described

---

[1] Cf. p. 65, *infra.*

[2] Cf. *Report of United States Industrial Commission, 1901,* XIII, clviii, and p. 80, *infra.*

above, whereby the dumping is manifested not in a difference in prices but in what is less conspicuous, namely, a difference in the conditions and terms of sale. An ingenious method of concealing export rebates granted in violation of an agreement was resorted to by members of a Belgian iron syndicate in the late eighties of the last century. The agreed export price for members of the syndicate was less than the domestic price by 1 franc per 100 kilograms. For No. 1 iron, for example, the export price agreed upon was $11\frac{1}{2}$ francs per 100 kilograms, *f.o.b. Antwerp*. Some members of the syndicate, desiring to increase their export trade, quoted the agreed price but arranged to have the buyers load the iron on board ship themselves and paid them for this at a rate several times its actual cost.[1]

Even more elaborate devices for concealing dumping have upon occasion been resorted to, especially as means of evading the antidumping or the undervaluation laws of the countries dumped on. The exporting industry planning to dump may deliberately sell a small fraction of its output in a distant section of the home market at an artificially low price in order to establish a fictitious basis for price-comparison with its export prices which will not reveal dumping.[2] Or a producer intending to export at prices lower than those current in the domestic market may refrain from offering for domestic sale commodities identical with those exported at low prices. In this way price-comparison

[1] Arthur Raffalovich, *Les Coalitions de Producteurs et le Protectionnisme*, Paris, 1889, pp. 20, 21.

[2] For example, W. J. A. Donald, *The Canadian Iron and Steel Industry*, Boston, 1915, p. 185, states that the Canadian antidumping law could not be applied against pig-iron dumped in Canada by Buffalo concerns because the latter sold part of their product for delivery to distant points in the United States at "dumping prices." But as the Canadian law provides for the determination of the existence of dumping on the basis of a comparison of (a) the export price and (b) the fair market value in the *principal* markets of the exporting country (*Statutes of Canada, 6–7 Edw. VII*, Vols. I–II, p. 134, and chap. 48, *Revised Statutes of Canada*, 1906, as amended, published by the Department of Customs, 1914, p. 14, sec. 40) it appears to provide adequately for such contingencies.

may be made difficult or impossible, and dumping may even be technically avoided.[1] Even in the absence of special motives, exporters producing also for the domestic market may make discovery of dumping difficult if they export commodities which differ somewhat in shape, form, style, or material from those which they commonly sell in the domestic market.

Another means of concealing dumping is sometimes made available by the use of the consignment method of making sales. This method has often been resorted to illegitimately with the single or main object of circumventing by undervaluation the machinery established for the proper valuation of imports for customs purposes. But it can as readily be used to conceal the practice of dumping by overvaluation in order to evade anti-dumping duties. An exporter to the United States may ship his goods to this country on consignment to commission merchants, who are instructed to sell for the best prices obtainable. The absence of an invoice, and the difficulty of tracing the prices finally realized long after the imported commodities have passed out of the control of the customs, make comparison of domestic and export prices in the exporting country extremely difficult unless special administrative machinery is devised and established. There have been instances where foreign exporters have sold goods directly to American buyers, but with the stipulation that delivery and billing were to be made by American agent-consignees of the exporting concern.[2] In the reported instances this practice had for its object to make it possible for the agent to enter the goods for customs at less than the actual sales price. But it could be used in the same manner to conceal the fact of genuine sales being

[1] Cf. *Selling Foreign Manufactures in the United States*, Part I, p. 36, for an account of the practice of some foreign producers of refusing to sell certain of their products to any but American buyers in order to escape the application of the American undervaluation provisions. This practice would also make difficult the application of antidumping provisions.

[2] Cf. *Selling Foreign Manufactures in the United States*, Part I, p. 37.

made at dumping prices, if the agent-consignee entered the goods at higher prices than those at which they were actually sold.

Such manifestations as have been discussed above, of spurious dumping, of concealed dumping, and of the technical avoidance of dumping, present no very difficult theoretical problems. But they obviously present very serious obstacles to the administration of antidumping legislation in such a manner that it will not at the same time penalize some unoffending transactions and permit other offending transactions to escape penalization through technicalities or by concealment. Antidumping legislation, in its present stage of development, meets these difficulties with only a very partial degree of success.

There is high authority for the definition of dumping as the sale of imported merchandise at less than its prevailing price in the country of export. This is the definition offered by the United States Tariff Commission,[1] and it is also in substance the definition followed in the antidumping provisions of the British Safeguarding of Industries Act, 1921.[2] Some practices which are properly to be regarded as genuine, though concealed, dumping would be held not to be dumping under this definition. The price of imported goods in the importing country normally includes the foreign export price plus: transportation costs; storage, insurance, and interest charges; charges to cover depreciation and wastage; import duties, if any have been paid; and the importer's profit. Under this definition the sale for export at a discount from the domestic price which was uniform for all foreign countries might constitute dumping with respect to sales to purchasers from neighboring or free-trade countries and might not constitute dumping with respect to sales to purchasers from distant or protectionist countries. The higher the

[1] "Dumping may be comprehensively described as the sale of imported merchandise at less than its prevailing market or wholesale price in the country of production." (*Information Concerning Dumping and Unfair Foreign Competition*, p. 9.)

[2] See p. 219, *infra*.

tariff in, or the greater the transportation charges to, a given importing country, the less likely would it be that under this definition the sale for export at prices lower than those pre-vailing in the exporter's domestic market would constitute dumping.   In many instances even the outright gift of valuable foreign goods to American importers would not constitute dumping under this definition, because the transportation, storage, and insurance charges, the import duties, the importer's profits, and the various other costs connected with importation, would in the aggregate make the importer's sale price necessarily exceed the foreign market value if the importer was to derive any gain from the free gift.   It is obvious that the term "dumping" would lose most of its significance if it were so defined, and another term would have to be coined or discovered to signify the practice here defined as dumping.

CHAPTER II

THE CLASSIFICATION OF DUMPING

There are different types of dumping and these may be classified in various ways and from different points of view. The distinctions drawn in the foregoing discussion between open and concealed dumping and between reverse dumping and direct or export dumping are themselves available bases for classification. But for purposes of economic analysis probably the most serviceable bases for classification are according to the motives or the objectives of the dumper and according to the degree of continuity of the dumping. There follows a two-fold classification of dumping according to these two bases:

A CLASSIFICATION OF DUMPING ACCORDING TO MOTIVE
AND TO CONTINUITY

Motive	Continuity
A. To dispose of a casual overstock.....................	Sporadic
B. Unintentional.......................................	
C. To maintain connections in a market in which prices are on remaining considerations unacceptable............	
D. To develop trade connections and buyers' goodwill in a new market.......................................	Short-run or intermittent
E. To eliminate competition in the market dumped on....	
F. To forestal the development of competition in the market dumped on...	
G. To retaliate against dumping in the reverse direction...	
H. To maintain full production from existing plant facilities without cutting domestic prices.....................	Long-run or continuous
I. To obtain the economies of larger-scale production without cutting domestic prices.....................	
J. On purely mercantilistic grounds...................	

A. A producer may find that in a given season sales at the established prices are not running high enough to clear his stocks on hand or in process. The alternative procedures open to him to meet this situation are: (1) to hold over the surplus stocks to another season; (2) to reduce his prices in his standard markets in order to increase sales; or (3) to dispose of his surplus stocks in some distant or unimportant market at the best prices obtainable, even if these are lower than the prices current in his standard markets. He may be reluctant to hold his surplus stocks over to another season, because of the carrying and storage charges, the difficulty of financing an over-large inventory, or the danger of deterioration or of change in style to which his products may be subject. He may also be reluctant to reduce his prices in his standard market. It is probable that it will not be practicable to reduce prices on any portion of his sales in this market without making the reductions general to all purchasers, so that any reduction in domestic price will apply to his entire output. In any case, the demand for his product in his standard market may be inelastic, so that a reduction in price, whether partial or general, will not have a substantial effect on sales. A reduction in price once conceded may make a subsequent re-establishment of the original price difficult or even impossible, or may incite cutthroat competition on the part of rival producers; that is, it may "spoil" his standard market. For any or all of these reasons a producer may choose to unload his surplus stocks at reduced prices in a minor or hitherto uncultivated market.[1]

B. Unintentional dumping can take place only when goods are exported speculatively in anticipation of their sale at a profitable price after arrival in the foreign market, or when goods have been shipped to a foreign market by mistake or for

---

[1] Cf. *Selling Foreign Manufactures in the United States*, Part III, p. 15 (from the report of an American consul in Edinburgh): "A prominent brewer . . . . said: 'I have been dumping ale and beer on foreign markets all my life whenever I have had a surplus. Practically every manufacturer in this country sells his goods abroad for the best price they will bring, when his stock is too heavy to be unloaded at home in a reasonable time without breaking the market.'"

some reason delivery cannot be made to the original purchaser. If such goods were shipped with the expectation that they would eventually be sold at prices as high as those current in the home market, but if they must eventually be disposed of at lower prices, unintentional dumping has taken place. Such dumping is most likely to occur under the consignment system, or under the branch warehouse system, where goods are shipped to be sold after arrival in the foreign market.[1] But such dumping cannot be regarded as unintentional if the goods were shipped with the expectation, or with full realization of the imminent probability, that they would realize upon sale net prices lower than those current in the home market.

C. A producer may find that the prices obtainable in a given market are lower than those at which he can elsewhere dispose of all of his current production, but he may nevertheless meet the prices current in that market to retain his trade connections therewith, if in the long run it affords a valuable outlet for his product. In this case the producer is willing to sell at the reduced prices only because this will serve to retain for the future a market which temporarily has no attraction for him.[2]

[1] Cf. *ibid.*, Part II, p. 18 (from the report of an American consul in Japan dealing with the trade in Japanese raw silk): "There may be cases when shipments are sold in New York at lower rates than the prices prevailing here [i.e., Yokohama]; this arises out of the practice of certain Japanese exporters who ship to New York on consignment and find it necessary to sell at prices under those paid by buyers in Yokohama."

[2] Cf. testimony of E. H. Gary, then president of the Federal Steel Co., before the U.S. Industrial Commission, 1901, *Report*, I, 1001:

A. ". . . . A few days since I told some of our people I thought they had better take an order for quite a large quantity of rails, to be shipped to Japan at a little less price than we were selling here. I think it is trade that we should keep up. . . . ."

Q. "You think it is worth while to encourage that export trade now and hold your market there?"

A. "Yes; we may need that business 2 or 3 years hence. . . . . We want to keep our trade for future business, and there is quite a large tonnage to go to Japan."

D. A producer may for a time sell at reduced prices in a market in which he is endeavoring newly to establish his trade in order to develop therein a demand for his products which will subsequently make possible their sale in that market at prices as high as those current elsewhere.[1]

E. A concern may sell at dumping prices in a given market in order to eliminate its competitors in that market or to bring them to terms. Such dumping may be directed against the domestic producers of the market dumped on, or against competing exporters from the dumper's own country, or against competing exporters from a third country. It may be intended wholly to crush competitors, or it may have the more modest objective of inducing competitors by the threat of destructive competition to follow the prices quoted by the dumping concern, to share the market with it on specified terms, or otherwise to make their operations in the given market conform to the wishes of the dumping concern. This type of dumping is often termed "predatory" or "malignant" dumping.[2] It is the most objectionable form of dumping from the point of view of the country dumped on.

---

[1] Cf. William Smart, *The Return to Protection*, London, 1904, p. 145: "I have known articles sent to India [from England] year after year at half the home price, in order to accustom the natives to the goods, with the view of ultimately raising the price to a paying level."

[2] Cf. *Report of the United States Alien Property Custodian* (1919), pp. 30, 31: "When . . . . in 1910 . . . . the Benzol Products Co. was organized [in the United States] by a group of men interested in the heavy chemical industry to manufacture aniline oil on a large scale, the German hand was immediately shown. The price of aniline oil at the time of the establishment of this company averaged 11½ cents. As soon as its manufacture was fairly under way, the German exporters commenced to cut the price. Apparently no definite prices were made by the Germans, but they adopted the simple policy of offering any customers of the new concern supplies at less than the price he was paying. For example, one of their most important customers refused an advantageous contract at 8½ cents, stating that he had assurance from the Germans that whatever price the Benzol Products Co. made would be met and bettered by them. Accordingly, the new company struggled on, conducting its operations without profit, and only because it was supported by a group of men of exceptional determination and insight was it able to survive until the war gave it an opportunity to establish its business on a firm foundation."

F. A concern which has a monopoly of its product in the markets in which it operates but fears that competition may appear in certain of its markets if it exacts too high a price may quote lower prices in those markets in which competition is most likely to develop in order to forestal such development.[1]

G. If a concern in one country is embarrassed by competition in its home market from products exported to that market by a foreign manufacturer at dumping prices or at unreasonably low prices, it may endeavor to bring such competition to an end by resorting to retaliatory dumping in the principal market of the offending manufacturer. In other words, dumping may not only be used as the offensive instrument of cutthroat competition in international commerce, but it may also be used as a defense against cutthroat competition.[2]

H. If a manufacturer can sell each year in his domestic market a part, but only a part, of his maximum possible output at higher prices than those ruling in outside markets, he may decide to maintain his domestic prices at this higher level and to seek foreign orders at reduced prices for the balance of his potential output in preference to reducing his domestic prices and in preference to operating only to part capacity. By resorting to dumping he may obtain the economies of operation at

---

[1] Cf. *Selling Foreign Manufactures in the United States*, Part III, p. 15: "The British maker of an important machine . . . . although he has no competition, ... quotes the machine to customers in Belgium and one or two other countries on the Continent at 15 per cent less than the price at which it is sold in this country. The reason is that these Belgian and other continental firms will not pay more than a certain amount for it, and he comes to their terms in order to obviate the danger of competition arising from the invention and manufacture of a similar apparatus in Belgium or elsewhere."

[2] Cf. Great Britain, Ministry of Reconstruction, *Report of Committee on Trusts*, 1919 (Cd. 9236), p. 7: "The Chairman of an important [British] metal association stated that: . . . . 'They had a fund, a fighting fund, for the special purpose of subsidising members who found it necessary to sell at less than an economic price in order to cut out foreign competitors. That might be called meeting dumping by dumping. . . . . They had dumped in Belgium as a reprisal against Belgian dumping here.'"

full capacity without surrendering the profits to be derived from
the sale of part of his output in the domestic market at prices
above the foreign level.   A reduction in the domestic prices may
be unprofitable, especially if the domestic demand for his products is inelastic, even in the absence of the possibility of resort
to dumping.   This case closely resembles Case A as presented
above.   It differs from Case A in the one particular that in the
present case the commodities dumped are not merely surplus
stocks which had originally been produced in anticipation of
sale at the full prices but are stocks deliberately produced in
order to be dumped.   It is probable that this is the most prevalent type of dumping, but business men who practice it with
the purpose of maintaining at the same time high domestic prices
and production to full capacity have a readily explicable reluctance to admit it.[1]

I. It is possible that a manufacturer may sell abroad at
reduced prices in order to increase his sales, without reduction
of his domestic prices, to such a rate that it will not only permit
him to maintain full production from his existing plant facilities
but will enable him to extend his plant so as to obtain the economies of larger-scale production.   It is obvious that once the
plant has been extended, further dumping will be illustrative
of Case H.[2]

J. Dumping on purely mercantilistic grounds, that is,
dumping which is resorted to only in order to stimulate export
trade for the sake of the national advantages to be derived
therefrom by the dumper's country, is altogether unlikely to be

---

[1] Cf., however, the *Report of the United States Industrial Commission, 1901*,
XIII, 729:   "A few exporters indicate that prior to 1898 prices were lower abroad
than at home, and that this condition was brought about in order to keep a
stable market in this country, and as one establishment puts it, 'We want the
foreign market to cut our price in, so as not to disturb the domestic market.'
'Naturally enough,' says one correspondent, 'when American mills or factories are
short of orders and trade is at a low ebb, they sell in foreign markets at cheaper
rates in order . . . . to keep their men employed and their works running.'"

[2] I have not been able to find an example clearly illustrative of this type of
dumping, but there is no reason to doubt the possibility of its occurrence.

practiced on purely private initiative. Producers who believe that a country derives some special advantages from exports which are not to be obtained in equal measure from domestic trade are not hard to find, but the producer who will be willing solely on such grounds to sell abroad at lower prices than he can obtain for all of his output at home must indeed be rare. Mercantilistic considerations often play a part in dumping, however, where governments grant bounties on exports. If dumping results from the grant of an official bounty on exports and the establishment of this bounty by the government has for its object the stimulation of exports, the dumping may be said to be the result of mercantilistic motives. The producer who resorts to dumping always does so with the aim of deriving a personal pecuniary advantage therefrom, but he may often find an effective defense of his practice against protests from agencies of his government or from domestic consumers in an appeal to mercantilistic prejudices.[1] It is probable that in most actual instances of dumping no single motive is dominant but that some combination of the ones listed above, all of them concerned with private profit and not national policy, are operative.

There is a commonly used classification of dumping according to its continuity which distinguishes between only two classes,

[1] Cf. the statement of Mr. J. A. Farrell on behalf of the Steel Corporation in *Hearings before the Committee on Investigation of United States Steel Corporation* (1912,) p. 2745: "The practice of the constituent companies of the United States Steel Corporation in the matter of export allowances has been based upon the principle that an export business in all classes of commodities, in which steel is used, should be encouraged, with a view to enlarging the volume of tonnage and to create a basis for an exchange of values, upon which our country's commerce with foreign countries is based."

Cf. also Mr. Gary's defense of the dumping policy of the Steel Corporation: "Of course, we are pressing this export business as far as we can practically for obvious reasons; among others, because we want a place to put our goods, as it so materially affects the employment of our labor and also because it so materially affects the balance of trade. The broad view of this question is that when we can justly do it—when we can fairly do it—we want to bring all the foreign money we can into this country." *Iron Age*, LXXVII, |April 19, 1324, 1906].

"sporadic" and "permanent," and includes under sporadic dumping all dumping which does not continue steadily throughout an indefinitely long period. Steady and systematic dumping recurring throughout every period of business depression and ceasing only at periods of unusual prosperity would under this mode of classification be regarded as sporadic dumping, but in reality it is intermittent or "short-run" and not sporadic. It should be carefully distinguished from genuinely sporadic dumping, or dumping which occurs only in irregularly recurring and scattered instances. Most economists regard what they term sporadic dumping as the most dangerous to the economic welfare of the country dumped on, and permanent dumping as even advantageous. It is not within the scope of this chapter to enter into a thorough analysis of the economic effects of dumping upon the country dumped on, but it will be fairly obvious upon a little consideration that scattering isolated instances of dumping cannot be of much importance for good or ill. But dumping on a steady and systematic scale for several months or years at a time can result in great injury to domestic industry and, unlike permanent dumping, it is without the redeeming feature of providing consumers in the country dumped on with a permanently cheap supply of the commodities which are being dumped.

It appears essential on these grounds to distinguish between three types of dumping according to continuity, namely: sporadic, short-run or intermittent, and long-run dumping. Dumping which is occasional and casual, which occurs only in scattered instances and at irregular intervals, and which is not the manifestation of a definitely established price-policy on the part of the dumping concern, would be typical of sporadic dumping. It would usually not involve deliberate production of commodities with a view to their being sold at dumping prices. An instance of this class would be the sale of a casual overstock in a foreign market at a reduced price in order not to disturb prices in the domestic market. Short-run dumping signifies dumping which is continued steadily and systematically for a period of limited duration, which is practiced in accordance with a definitely established export policy, and which involves the deliberate production of commodities to be dumped. Illustrative of such dumping would be the sale for export at prices lower than those current in the domestic market throughout the depression period of each recurrent business cycle. Long-run dumping signifies dumping which is carried on not merely sporadically nor even intermittently but continuously over a prospectively permanent period.

In the classification of dumping according to motive which has been presented above, Classes A and B, dumping to dispose of a casual overstock and unintentional dumping, would normally be sporadic. Classes C, dumping to maintain trade connections, D, dumping to develop trade connections, E, dumping to eliminate competition, F, dumping to forestal the development of competition, and G, retaliatory dumping, would normally be short-run, continuing steadily and systematically for a period lasting anywhere from several months to several years. Dumping of Classes H and I, dumping to maintain full production from existing plant and dumping to make possible the extension of plant, might be either short-run or long-run, depending in each instance on which of these was necessary for the realization of its objective by the dumping concern. Into what class according to its continuity dumping of Class J, or mercantilistic dumping, would fall would depend usually on the degree of permanence of the system of official export bounties of which it was the outcome. But for all the classes according to motive the continuity of the dumping would be affected by the varying character of the special circumstances governing each particular instance. There is no intent here to suggest that there is any necessary and rigid relationship between the particular motive governing any instance of dumping and the degree of continuity of the dumping.

OTHER BASES FOR CLASSIFICATION

In this study the different types of dumping will be distinguished mainly according to the motive of the dumper and the continuity of the dumping. Some other possible bases of classification, however, will occasionally be referred to and should be mentioned here. Dumping has been distinguished according to whether it was "dumping from strength" or "dumping from weakness." According to this classification dumping is from strength when it is practiced by a large and financially powerful concern either with the motive of capturing control of foreign markets by driving out competitors therefrom by its price-cutting, or because its monopoly position at home enables it to exact in its domestic market prices so high that a reduction therefrom in its export sales still leaves a substantial margin of profit from its export trade. Dumping is from weakness when it is resorted to under the stress of unfavorable business conditions in the home market in order to liquidate an overstock or to reduce the losses from a partial or complete shutdown of its plant. This classification does not introduce any element which is not taken into account to some extent in the classifications according to motive and according to continuity, but it places the emphasis on a phase of the economic situations from which the practice of dumping arises to which the two foregoing classifications do not perhaps give sufficient attention.

For some purposes it is important to distinguish between dumping according to whether or not the dumping price is below the dumper's cost of production, and according to whether or not the dumping is profitable to the dumper. It may appear that classification according to either of these bases will yield identical results, but this depends on how cost of production and profit are defined and determined. Some consideration will be given in subsequent chapters to the relation between dumping and cost of production and to the profitability of dumping to the dumper.

ALLIED PRACTICES

There are certain practices in international trade which do not technically constitute dumping as it is here defined but are so closely related to it in their nature, or in their economic objectives or consequences, as to demand some attention in this study.

The sale of goods for export at prices below their cost of production but nevertheless not below the prices prevailing in the domestic markets of the exporting country does not constitute dumping. But to the importing country the economic signifiance of foreign sales for export at prices below their cost of production is essentially the same irrespective of whether or not these prices are also below the prices at which the same goods are sold for domestic consumption in the exporting country. The marked tendency in the antidumping legislation of recent years to extend to sales for export at prices below cost of production but not below foreign domestic prices the application of the penalties provided against sales of foreign goods for export at dumping prices indicates a widespread realization of the close relationship between these two practices.

Manufacturing plants in one country often have branches in another country which do not carry through the fabricating process from beginning to end but obtain partly manufactured goods from the head plant for completion within the branch plant. In such a case the head plant may invoice materials shipped to the branch plant at the prices current in the country of shipment, but it may nevertheless accomplish the same results as if it were selling them at dumping prices, in so far as concerns the capture, for either its partly finished or its finished product, of the market of the country in which its branch is situated, by permitting the branch plant to sell the finished article at a price which does not fully cover its cost of production. Whether or not a transaction of this sort technically involves dumping is, therefore, mainly a question of internal accounting. The existence of antidumping legislation in the country in which the branch is situated will provide an effective stimulus to the adoption of a method of accounting for the materials shipped to the branch plant which will not establish the existence of dumping.

Where a concern wishes to gain control of a foreign market for its products but the elimination of the domestic producers of that market by predatory dumping would be too expensive because of the necessity of surmounting a tariff barrier, it may achieve the same purpose by establishing temporarily a branch plant in that country and permitting it to sell its products below cost. When its competitors have thereby been forced out of business, the branch plant is closed down or diverted to other uses, and purchasers are forced to obtain their supplies from the foreign plant. Such appears to have been the practice in several instances of German chemical and electrical kartells. Dumping is not necessarily involved in any stage of this practice, but in its objectives, its consequences, and its significance to the importing country, it is substantially identical with predatory dumping.

CHAPTER III

THE PREVALENCE OF DUMPING
PRIOR TO 1890

An attempt to survey the extent to which dumping, or price-discrimination between national markets, is practiced encounters many difficulties. The dumper may have various weighty motives for desiring to withhold from public knowledge the fact that he is selling abroad at lower prices than at home. Even where no deliberate attempt is made to conceal the dumping from the vulgar gaze, it is not likely to be a matter of common knowledge except to those closely interested in the particular dumping transactions. Valuable sources of information are afforded by the publicity which inevitably attends the operations of great industrial combinations and by the numerous governmental investigations into various phases of business activity which have accumulated and made public great masses of more or less detailed data relating to price-policies in international trade. But much of even such material must, unfortunately, be used with great caution. The serviceability of the evidence obtained from business men is prone to be lessened by the intrusion of some element of bias, by the loose use of terminology, or by lack of adequate analysis. Where instances of dumping are reported by others than those directly involved in the transactions, it is often difficult to determine in specific cases whether the reported sales at different prices in different countries are genuine instances of dumping or are to be adequately accounted for by differences in the conditions and terms governing the sales to purchasers in the domestic and the foreign markets, respectively. If the reports of dumping originate with competitors of the dumping concern they are especially to be treated with caution, because of the common tendency of business men to apply invidious terms to any type of competition, however legitimate it may be, which disturbs their chances for profit. These are serious obstacles to safe generalization. In any survey of the prevalence of dumping and the circumstances under which it is most frequently practiced, careful discrimination must be exercised in the acceptance of evidence if exaggeration is to be avoided.

The practice of dumping has long been known, although not by this name, to writers on commercial matters. Adam Smith, for example, not only discusses unfavorably the practice on the part of governments of stimulating exports at prices lower than those current in the domestic market by the grant of official bounties, but gives an instance from personal observation of the grant of bounties on exports by a private combination of producers in order to reduce the supply available for the domestic market.[1] Except, however, as it resulted from the grant of official export bounties, the extensive practice of dumping could not have developed until after the Industrial Revolution brought large-scale production and the active search for wider markets.

England was the first country to undergo the Industrial Revolution. It is therefore not surprising that the first extensive charges of dumping were directed against her manufacturers. It is by no means certain, however, either that actual British practice provided a substantial basis for the charges of dumping, or that fear of or resentment against British dumping, actual or prospective, was the real motive leading to the making of the charges. If foreign manufacturers can be plausibly charged with dumping, an effective argument is made available in support of tariff protection to domestic industries endangered by such puta-

---

[1] *Wealth of Nations*, Book IV, chap. v: "I have known the different undertakers of some particular works agree privately among themselves to give a bounty out of their own pockets upon the exportation of a certain proportion of the goods which they dealt in. This expedient succeeded so well that it more than doubled the price of their goods in the home market, notwithstanding a very considerable increase in the produce."

tively unfair foreign competition. American protectionist writers throughout the nineteenth century made much of this argument for protection, English exporters generally being the ones charged with the resort to dumping. English manufacturers, it was repeatedly alleged, in the early years of American independence not only dumped in the United States but did so with the deliberate purpose of crushing or, in the language of the time, "stifling" or "strangulating" the young American industries. The only supporting evidence possessing any degree of concreteness consists of two or three isolated instances of doubtful authenticity and, even if authentic, by themselves of little general significance. These same instances are cited again and again in the American protectionist literature of the last century.

Alexander Hamilton, in his famous *Report on Manufactures*, declared that the greatest obstacle encountered by new industries in a young country was the system of export bounties which foreign countries maintained in order "to enable their own workmen to undersell and supplant all competitors in countries to which these commodities are sent." He promised to give instances in the course of the report, but the only ones actually mentioned were English government bounties on the export of sailcloth and linens. Hamilton also drew attention to the possibility that unofficial bounties were being given by combinations of producers: "Combinations by those engaged in a particular branch of business in one country to frustrate the first efforts to introduce it into another by temporary sacrifices, recompensed, perhaps, by extraordinary indemnifications of the government of such country, are believed to have existed, and are not to be regarded as destitute of probability."[1] Hamilton's plea for protection to American manufactures, it was later alleged, caused such alarm

---

[1] "Report on the Subject of Manufactures, 1791," in F. W. Taussig, *State Papers and Speeches on the Tariff*, Cambridge, 1893, pp. 31, 32; 92, 93. Hamilton could have cited the unofficial bounty reported by Adam Smith in *The Wealth of Nations*, with which work he was undoubtedly well acquainted. (Cf. E. G. Bourne, "Alexander Hamilton and Adam Smith," *Quarterly Journal of Economics*, April, 1894.)

among English manufacturers that they banded together to dump
their products on the American market with the aim of crushing
their American competitors.[1]

Gallatin, writing in 1810 in opposition to protection, gave
some support to the charge that English manufacturers were
engaging in dumping. Supporting evidence from this source
would have great weight. Gallatin was a conservative writer,
not inclined to make wild and unsubstantiated charges. Moreover, his bias, if he had one, would be in the direction of minimizing or rejecting altogether the accusation that dumping was prevalent because of the aid which such charges lent to the agitation
for high protection. In his *Report on Manufactures*, April 9,
1810, Gallatin wrote as follows:

> It is believed that, even at this time, the only powerful obstacle against
> which American manufactures have to struggle, arises from the vastly
> superior capital of the first manufacturing nation of Europe, which enables
> her merchants to give very long credits, to sell on small profits, and to make
> occasional sacrifices.[2]

It is to be noted that this statement makes no charge of predatory
dumping, i.e., of dumping intended to eliminate competition, and
that only by implication does it suggest the prevalence of dumping in any form.

Soon after the Treaty of Ghent between England and the
United States had made possible a resumption of the trade relations which had been interrupted by the War of 1812, Americans

---

[1] "In the beginning of the year 1792 when the report of General Hamilton, then
Secretary of the Treasury, made by order of the House of Representatives, was published in England, it created such alarm that meetings were called in the manufacturing towns, and Manchester alone, at a single meeting, subscribed 50,000 pounds
sterling toward a fund to be vested in English goods, and shipped to this country for
the purpose of glutting our market and blasting the hopes of our manufacturers in
the bud." (*Address of the American Society for the Encouragement of Domestic
Manufactures*, 1817, cited by G. B. Curtiss, *Protection and Prosperity*, New York,
1896, p. 134.)

[2] Cited by O. L. Elliott, *The Tariff Controversy in the United States, 1789–1833*,
Palo Alto, 1892, p. 148, n.

accused English manufacturers of deliberately dumping their products in the United States in order to crush the new industries which had developed there during the war. What evidence has been presented in substantiation of the charges, although it has been accepted by many writers as full confirmation thereof, is neither by its character nor its quantity such as to bring conviction to an unbiased person either that any of the dumping which occurred was predatory in its motives, or even that there was any intentional dumping. A brief survey of this episode in the commercial relations of England and the United States is worth while both for its historical interest and because it helps to demonstrate the great need for caution in dealing with charges of dumping by biased or uncritical writers.

The cessation of hostilities in 1814 between England and France and between England and the United States reopened to English manufacturers the markets of the world which had been closed to them during the continuance of hostilities, and gave them an outlet for the great stocks of commodities which they had accumulated during the interruption of international commerce. There immediately resulted a wild burst of speculation in the export of commodities, a speculation which was by no means confined to the manufacturers of these commodities. At first, because of the scarcity of English goods in the markets hitherto closed to them by war, and because the speculators, still remembering earlier misadventures in similar enterprises, were restrained in their activities,[1] the exporters realized great profits from the sales of their merchandise. Great quantities of English goods were exported to the Continent and to the United States without waiting for orders and were sold by agents in the ordinary way or at auction for whatever prices they would bring. The first speculative shipments brought very high prices. But the

---

[1] Cf. Thomas Tooke, *Thoughts and Details on the High and Low Prices of the Thirty Years, from 1793 to 1822*, 2d. ed., London, 1824, p. 109; "In 1815 and the early part of 1816 the exports from this country had been made with great forbearance and prudence."

high profits were a stimulus to further speculation and an attraction to new speculators. In the spring of 1816, English· manufacturers and traders again sent out shiploads of merchandise without waiting for orders. They soon discovered to their discomfiture that they had over-reached themselves. An overabundance of supplies led to low prices and tremendous losses to the exporters.[1] To the extent that the prices realized abroad, after deduction of transportation and other incidental costs, were less than the prices current in England, dumping technically occurred. But it was unintentional dumping. The shipments had been made without receipt of orders in the expectation that a profit would be realized. That on the contrary losses were suffered was a source of bitter disappointment. There was nothing novel in the speculative shipment of goods for sale in foreign markets. Such speculative exporting had been engaged in by Englishmen to South America in 1810 upon the temporary removal of the Portuguese government to Brazil, and in 1811 to Portugal upon the expulsion of the French therefrom. Americans had· themselves exported in similar manner to England, in 1810, when the Napoleonic restrictions on commerce were temporarily removed,[2] and again in the very period here under consideration upon the resumption of trade relations after the War of 1812 was terminated.[3]

Moreover, the depression in prices in 1816 was not confined to the export markets but was widespread in England itself, and the prices received in the United States, even when they were below cost of production, were not necessarily lower than the prices received at home.[4] It is difficult to see, therefore, how

[1] Cf. J. B. McMaster, *A History of the People of the United States*, New York, 1907, IV, 323–25, 340.

[2] Thomas Tooke, *op. cit.*, pp. 81–89.

[3] E. R. Johnson, *et. al.*, *History of Foreign and Domestic Commerce of the United States*, Washington, 1915, II, 33.

[4] Cf. Edward Stanwood, *American Tariff Controversies in the Nineteenth Century*, Boston, 1903, I, 166: "The market for manufactured goods both at home [i.e., England] and abroad was completely demoralized [in 1816]."

predatory motives can be attributed to the exporters. The resort by English traders to the auction sale method of disposing of their goods in the United States was especially resented by American manufacturers because of the absence under this sales method of any check to the fall in prices. But the auction sale was used, not because it would bring low prices, but because sales were not readily obtainable in any other way.[1] In so far as the export trade was conducted by traders who were not themselves the producers of the exported commodities, it is inconceivable that they should intentionally have resorted to dumping.

In a famous speech delivered in the British House of Commons on April 9, 1816, and dealing primarily with the prevailing agricultural depression in England, Henry (later Lord) Brougham made incidental reference to the export speculation as a contributory cause of the depression. His words later served a long line of writers as evidence upon which to rest the charge that the primary purpose of the English exports to the United States had been to destroy the newly developed American manufacturing industries. Brougham's reference to the speculation in exports was as follows:

After the cramped state in which the enemy's measures, and our own retaliation (as we termed it), had kept our trade for some years, when the events of spring, 1814, suddenly opened the continent, a rage for exporting goods of every kind burst forth, only to be explained by reflecting on the previous restrictions we had been labouring under, and only to be equalled (though not in extent), by some of the mercantile delusions connected with South American speculations. Everything that could be shipped was sent off; all the capital that could be laid hold of was embarked. The frenzy . . . . descended to persons in the humblest circumstances, and the furthest removed, by their pursuits, from commercial cares. . . . . Not only clerks and labourers, but menial servants engaged the little sums which they had been laying up for a provision against old age and sickness; persons

[1] *Ibid.*, p. 169: "The auction system was resorted to because there was no other way to dispose of the cargoes." It appears, however, that English exporters evaded in part the American customs duties by consigning their merchandise to agents in the United States at fictitiously low values (J. B. McMaster, *op. cit.*, p. 341).

went round tempting them to adventure in the trade to Holland, and Germany, and the Baltic; they risked their mite in the hope of boundless profits; it went with the millions of the more regular traders: the bubble soon burst . . . . . ; English goods were selling for much less in Holland and the north of Europe, than in London and Manchester; in most places they were lying a dead weight without any sale at all; and either no returns whatever were received, or pounds came back for thousands that had gone forth. . . . .

The peace with America has produced somewhat of a similar effect, though I am very far from placing the vast exports which it occasioned upon the same footing with those to the European market the year before; both because ultimately the Americans will pay, which the exhausted state of the continent renders unlikely; and because *it was well worth while to incur a loss upon the first exportation, in order, by the glut, to stifle in the cradle those rising manufactures in the United States which the war had forced into existence contrary to the natural course of things.*[1]

It is to be noted that Brougham ascribed the speculative shipment of exports to the hope of immediate and extraordinary profits and not to the hope of stifling the rising American manufactures. The latter, if it should result, he simply regarded, perhaps somewhat uncharitably, as ample *post facto* consolation for the immediate and unanticipated losses incurred in the trade. Yet with Brougham's speech as their only evidence, writer after writer has accused the English manufacturers of that time of having dumped in the United States with the deliberate object of crushing the new American industries.[2]   In many instances such writers make their case appear stronger than it is by citing, away from its context, only that part of Brougham's speech which is italicized above.[3]

[1] *Hansard*, 1st Series, XXXIII (1816), 1098–99.   These sections of the speech are also to be found in the *Edinburgh Review* for June, 1816 (LII, 263–64.) The italics are mine.

[2] Cf. Edward Stanwood, *American Tariff Controversies in the Nineteenth Century*, I, 168: "Mr. Brougham's words have often since done their duty in firing the protectionist heart."

[3] There is presented herewith what is probably an incomplete list of authors who have charged the English manufacturers of this period with predatory dumping in the United States on a large scale, with the italicized portion of Brougham's speech, given apart from its context, as their only supporting evidence: H. C. Carey,

The Tariff Act of 1816 was the first distinctly protectionist tariff of the United States, and it has been claimed that the threat to American industries from English dumping, and especially Brougham's frank utterance with respect thereto, was an important influence contributing to the enactment of this, as well as of subsequent, protectionist legislation.[1]   There is no doubt that the fear of English dumping, actual or pretended, played a part, although probably a very minor one, in the development of American protectionist sentiment.[2]   In so far as the Act of 1816 was concerned, however, its introduction in Congress preceded the

---

Principles of Social Science, Philadelphia, 1858, II, 128; R. W. Thompson, *The History of the Protective Tariff Laws*, Chicago, 1888, pp. 126–28; G. B. Curtiss, *Protection and Prosperity*, New York, 1896, pp. 135–36; John P. Young, *Protection and Progress*, Chicago, 1900, p. 305; J. L. Bishop, *A History of American Manufactures*, II, 212; Friedrich List, *The National System of Political Economy* (English translation), London, 1904, p. 70; E. R. Johnson, *History of Domestic and Foreign Commerce of the United States*, II, 35.   Edward Stanwood, *American Tariff Controversies in the Nineteenth Century*, I, 166–68, makes the same charge on the same evidence, but quotes more fully from Brougham's speech.   William Roscher, *Principles of Political Economy* (Lalor's translation), Chicago, 1882, II, 437, quotes from Brougham's speech only the section italicized above as confirmation of the exclamation: "How frequently it has happened that England by keeping down her prices for a time has strangled her foreign rivals."   Ugo Rabbeno, *American Commercial Policy*, 2d ed., London, 1895, p. 153, also accuses the English manufacturers of having engaged at this period in predatory price-cutting: "The English manufacturers, to whose merchandise, after years of commercial war, an ample market was finally opened, rushed as if to the attack of a fortress; and it was indeed the weak and badly defended fortress of American manufactures which they wished to conquer, even at the sacrifice of selling under cost-price."   But he makes no reference to Brougham's speech and presents no other evidence in support of the charge.   The italicised portion of Brougham's speech was also repeatedly cited in Congress and in departmental reports.

[1] Cf. R. W. Thompson, *The History of the Protective Tariff Laws*, pp. 126–28; cf. also, Alfred Marshall, *Industry and Trade*, p. 781: "The high Protectionist policy of America, from which England has been a chief sufferer, was largely due to the sedulous spreading among the American people of stories as to her own ungenerous dealings, which had unfortunately some solid foundation."

[2] Taussig's standard *Tariff History of the United States* makes no reference to dumping as one of the factors in the development of protectionism in the United States.

great collapse of prices of imported English goods and preceded also the first arrival in the United States of a report of Brougham's speech.[1]   It does appear, however, that some Americans had foreseen, before it actually developed, the intense and possibly predatory competition to which the new and weak American manufacturing industries would be subjected after the wartime restriction on commerce had been removed, and that this prospect of unrestrained competition from Europe was a factor in the decisions of the committee which drafted the tariff bill of 1816.[2]

While the charge that English manufacturers were at this time carrying on a deliberate campaign of predatory dumping must be regarded, therefore, as unproved, there is less reason to doubt that there were occasional instances of the practice of dumping in less objectionable form, especially in such branches of English industry as were in the control of relatively few individuals or of combinations of producers.   An English work lends support to the charge of dumping, although not of predatory dumping, by English manufacturers, in the statement that "at the beginning of the nineteenth century Lancashire spinners were accused of selling yarns *sub rosa* at miserable prices, that is, of dumping" and that the accusers, apparently English manufac-

---

[1] Cf. J. B. McMaster, *A History of the People of the United States*, IV, 340–41, for statement that British sales in the United States were not at low prices until 1816, and that the framers of the Tariff Act of 1816 had utterly ignored the danger of auction sales as tending toward ruinous prices.   Cf. Edward Stanwood, *American Tariff Controversies*, I, 168: "Mr. Brougham's speech came too late to affect the tariff legislation of Congress."   Brougham's speech was made on April 9, 1816. The tariff act of 1816 was signed on April 27, 1816.   The first American reference to Brougham's speech appears to have been that in *Nile's Register* of December 28, 1816.   An error of List in assigning the speech to 1815, followed by H. C. Carey and others, helped to establish the impression that the Act of 1816 was in part a reaction against Brougham's utterance.   Cf. Friedrich List, *The National System of Political Economy*, p. 70, and H. C. Carey, *Principles of Social Science*, II, 128.

[2] Cf. *Report of the House Committee on Commerce and Manufactures*, February 13, 1816, *Annals of Congress*, 14th Cong., 1st Sess., p. 964: "The foreign manufacturers and merchants will put in requisition all the powers of ingenuity; will practice whatever art can devise and capital can accomplish to prevent the American manufacturing establishments from taking root and flourishing in their rich and native soil."

turers of cotton cloth, made a vain attempt to induce Parliament "to check the practice on the ground that the foreign manufacturers of cotton fabrics were thereby afforded an unfair monopoly."[1]

As has already been indicated, the charge of European dumping played some part in protectionist propaganda in the United States in subsequent years.   Henry Clay, in a speech in Congress in 1824, urged the need of protection to American manufactures because "the unprotected manufactures of a country are exposed to the danger of being crushed in their infancy either by the design or from the necessities of foreign manufacturers."   Apparently this argument had already been losing its effectiveness, for Clay proceeded: "Gentlemen are incredulous as to the attempts of foreign merchants and manufacturers to accomplish the destruction of ours.   Why should they not make such attempts?" But the only evidence he presented to demonstrate the credibility of charges of predatory price-cutting was a reputed offer of an American to carry the mails between Baltimore and Washington for a whole year for one dollar in order to drive a competitor off the road.[2]   That the invocation of the danger of British predatory dumping was no longer seriously regarded as an argument for protection is further suggested by the fact that when John Quincy Adams, writing in 1832, made use of this argument, he did so somewhat apologetically, and admitted that there was a common tendency to exaggerate the losses which British manufacturers were willing to undergo to retain control of the American market.[3]

[1] S. J. Chapman and Lord Brassey, *Work and Wages*, London, 1904, I, 40–41. This is the earliest instance which I have found of a protest against dumping by consumers *in the dumping country*.   Later in the century such protests were common in many countries.   See *infra*.

[2] Speech in House of Representatives, March 30 and 31, 1824; *Annals of Congress*, 18th Cong., 1st Sess., III, 1988–89 (also in F. W. Taussig, *State Papers and Speeches on the Tariff*, p. 295).

[3] *Report of Committee on Manufactures*, 22d Cong., 1st Sess., House Report 481, p. 20: "We may, and probably do, often greatly exaggerate to ourselves the immensity of exertions and of sacrifices made by the British manufacturers to retain and preserve in their own hands the control of foreign markets.   But that such exertions and sacrifices are and will be made by large manufacturing establishments in which extensive capitals are employed, cannot be doubted."

In 1854 a British Commissioner appointed to investigate labor conditions in the British mining districts in the course of his report presented a description of the methods used by British manufacturers in their export trade which, if accurate, would indicate that it was then a common and frequent practice for British manufacturers to resort to cutthroat competition with their foreign competitors in the endeavor to oust them from coveted markets. He did not present this as in disparagement of the British manufacturers, but, on the contrary, made use of it to support his plea to British labor to appreciate more fully the sacrifices which their employers made on their behalf and to realize that by their trade combinations and their frequent strikes they were impairing the ability of the manufacturers to build up the fortunes necessary to cope with foreign competitors. The tenor of the report as a whole indicates that the Commissioner was not a trained or unbiased economic observer, and that his interest was in the main in educational and social and not in primarily economic conditions. It is significant, however, as confirming the impression, obtained from the writings of other men in the first half of the nineteenth century who were themselves neither business men nor trained investigators, that it was a common belief of the time that success in international competition was more a matter of financial ability to withstand predatory price-cutting during times of depression than of relative advantages in productive capacity. There follows a quotation from his report containing his reference to the methods of international competition allegedly practiced by British manufacturers:

I believe that the labouring classes generally in the manufacturing districts of this country, and especially in the iron and coal districts, are very little aware of the extent to which they are often indebted for their being employed at all, to the immense *losses* which their employers voluntarily incur in bad times in order to destroy foreign competition, and to gain and keep possession of foreign markets. Authentic instances are well known of employers having in such times carried on their works at a loss amounting in the aggregate to three or four hundred thousand pounds in the course of as many years. If the efforts of those who encourage the combinations to restrict the amount of labour, and to produce strikes, were to be successful for any length of time, the great accumulations of capital could no longer be made which enable a few of the most wealthy capitalists to overwhelm all foreign competition in times of great depression, and thus to clear the way for the *whole trade* to step in when prices revive, and to carry on a great business before *foreign* capital can again accumulate to such an extent as to be able to establish a competition in prices with any chance of success. The large capitals of this country are the great instruments of warfare (if the expression may be allowed) against the competing capital of foreign countries, and are *the most* essential instrument now remaining, by which our manufacturing supremacy can be maintained; the other elements— cheap labour, abundance of raw materials, means of communication, and skilled labour—being rapidly in process of being equalized.[1]

It would not be surprising if this statement were seized upon by American protectionists as pointing to the need for tariff protection against so ruthless a method of competition, and Marshall, who quotes from it, says that "in earlier decades almost every American had it brought to his notice.[2] He comments on this and similar statements that "Inquiries made in America in 1875 convinced me that the relatively few cases of such practices as had occurred in an earlier generation, had had some considerable influence in checking new industrial experiments, through the effect which they exercised on the imagination."[3]

[1] *Report of the Commissioner . . . . to inquire into . . . . the State of the Population in the Mining Districts*, 1854, p. 20.

[2] Alfred Marshall, *Industry and Trade*, p. 782. I am unable to find confirmation of this statement in American citations of the Report. The only reference to it I have been able to find other than that cited by Marshall is in Roscher, *Principles of Political Economy* (Lalor's translation), Chicago, 1882, II, 437, n., who appears to swallow it whole. Marshall appears to be overanxious to convict the British of dumping in order to minimize the case for the adoption of antidumping legislation by England itself.

[3] *Op. cit.*, p. 783, n. Cf., also Marshall's "Memorandum on the Fiscal Policy of International Trade," *House of Commons Papers*, 321 (1908), p. 26: "English manufacturers, especially in the iron industry, were for more than half a century by far the chief ill-doers in this direction [i.e., of dumping], and the memory of their ill-deeds rankles sorely in American minds."

A more specific complaint against British predatory dumping at about this period came from a French source: "Three times since the commencement of the present century," it was alleged, "have attempts been made in France to spin the wool of the Angora goat. Each attempt has failed; for, as soon as the products appeared in the market, the English spinners lowered the prices from twenty to twenty-five per cent, and rendered competition impossible."[1]

But with the establishment of free trade in England and the development of large-scale manufacturing industries in other countries, complaints of English dumping diminished and charges of dumping began to be directed against the producers of other countries, including the United States. It is said that after the Civil War there was constant complaint by Canadians of American dumping and that in 1872, during a depression in the United States, the complaint "was particularly loud and bitter."[2] Marshall says that inquiries made by him in 1875 convinced him that Ontario manufacturers had real cause for fear of American dumping.[3] The Canadian government in a message to the British authorities in 1879 defended its adoption of a protective tariff policy in part on the ground that protection was needed against American predatory dumping.[4] In the same year Bis-

---

[1] Cited from *Bulletin de la Société Impériale Zoölogique d'Acclimatation*, 2d ser., V, 579, by John L. Hayes, in *Address before the National Association of Wool Manufacturers, Sept. 6, 1865*, Cambridge, Massachusetts, 1865, p. 29.

[2] C. H. Chomley, *Protection in Canada and Australia*, London, 1904, p. 43; the year given should probably have been 1873 instead of 1872.

[3] *Industry and Trade*, p. 783, n.

[4] Despatch of Governor-General to Colonial Office, March 19, 1879, cited in Edward Porritt, *The Fiscal and Diplomatic Freedom of the British Oversea Dominions*, Oxford, 1922, p. 465:" . . . . the present government . . . . desire to point . . . . to the fact that the manufacturers of the United States have established combinations, under such perfect organization, that should any special industry arise in Canada, the Canadian market is at once flooded with a corresponding article of American produce, sold below value, the effect of such combination being equal to that which is produced by a government bounty."

marck, when submitting to the Reichstag the new tariff bill
embodying much higher protection for German manufactures
than had hitherto prevailed, presented as one of the chief arguments in support of the bill the claim that the low German tariff
had hitherto made Germany the dumping-ground (*Ablagerung-
stätte*) of foreign countries.[1] In 1880, the American Secretary
of State, W. M. Evarts, recommended to American manufacturers
of cottons that they dump abroad in order to establish their
trade in foreign markets.[2] The protected industries of Victoria
were reported to have made it a common practice to dump in
the remainder of Australia.[3]

In 1886 witnesses before a British official committee cited
many instances of dumping in England. Most of the complaints were against German and French manufacturers, but in
at least one instance a specific charge of dumping was made
against American manufacturers of cotton goods.[4] A minority
report of the committee recommended a 10 or 15 per cent
ad valorem tariff on imports to countervail dumping and artificial advantages enjoyed by foreign manufacturers in their competition in the English market with English manufacturers.[5] This
minority report was sympathetic with those who advocated the
substitution for England's free-trade policy of a policy of "fair
trade." By "fair trade" they meant placing home and foreign
producers on an equal level with regard to *artificial* conditions

[1] W. H. Dawson, *Protection in Germany*, London, 1904, p. 71.

[2] Cited in U.S. Department of Commerce and Labor, Bureau of Statistics,
Special Consular Reports, XXXVI (1905), p. 45: "We have only to continue the
manufacture of pure cottons; . . . . sacrifice profits for a time, if necessary, to
secure trade standing in the several markets; . . . . and the several roads to universal trade are more open to us today than they were to the British manufacturers
30 years ago."

[3] C. H. Chomley, *Protection in Canada and Australia*, pp. 182, 183.

[4] Great Britain, *Commission on the Depression of Trade and Industry*, 1886;
Final Report (C. 4893), pp. lv, lvi, lvii; *Second Report, Minutes of Evidence*, Part I
(C. 4715), pp. 33, 122, 218, etc.

[5] *Final Report*, p. lxv.

of production caused by such things as export bounties, dumping under protection of a high tariff in the domestic market, and indirect taxation, but not interfering with natural differences in conditions of production. They distinguished the fair trade from the protectionist policy inasmuch as it was the aim of the latter, but not of the former, to offset *natural* differences in conditions of production.[1]

One of the rare instances in the United States of the establishment of a system of private export bounties to facilitate dumping occurred in the 1880's. The American producing capacity for alcohol increased greatly after 1878 because of an increasing export demand. In 1882, however, the German government established a system of export bounties on alcohol amounting to 10 cents a gallon, and this enabled the German producers to drive the American product out of its European markets. The distillers in the United States tried to meet the situation by forming a "whiskey pool," under which all the members were assessed to pay export bounties to such of their members as were selling their surplus stock abroad at a loss. But this method was found expensive and wasteful, and as a consequence the Whiskey Trust was formed in 1887, with the object in part of relieving the pressure on American prices of excessive output by restricting production and by disposing of a part of the output abroad at dumping prices.[2]

[1] Cf. C. J. Fuchs, *The Trade Policy of Great Britain and Her Colonies since 1860*, London, 1905, p. 191.

[2] Cf. 50th Cong. 2d. Sess., House Rept. 4165 (1889), pp. 64, 65; J. W. Jenks, *The Trust Problem*, New York, 1909, p. 244.

CHAPTER IV

THE PREVALENCE OF DUMPING SINCE 1890.
I. CONTINENTAL EUROPEAN, CANADIAN, JAPANESE DUMPING

In more recent times the growth of trusts and combinations in industry has brought with it the systematic and more or less continuous practice of export dumping on the part of many of the important manufacturing industries of the great industrial nations, and especially on the part of such industries as were organized into producers' trusts or combinations. The literature of this period on dumping, much of it a by-product of the study of the operations of industrial trusts and combinations, is voluminous, and it will be possible in the following pages to indicate only the outstanding features of dumping as practiced by the exporting industries of the countries important in world commerce.

GERMAN DUMPING

There is general agreement that before 1914 export dumping was more widespread and was more systematically practiced in Germany than in any other country. The resort to export dumping in Germany was facilitated by the high protective tariff and by the almost complete organization of large-scale industry into kartells, or industrial buying and selling combinations. Both of these factors checked price-competition in the domestic market, the former from outside Germany and the latter among German producers themselves. Combined, they made it possible for many of the kartells to adopt as a definite price-policy the maintenance of domestic prices at the foreign level plus the full amount of the German import duties and the sale for export at the best prices obtainable, even if these should be substantially below the domestic prices. It is obvious that systematic and continued dumping is not likely to arise if the dumping concern must share the higher domestic prices with its competitors and must bear by itself the cost of the export dumping. In Germany the kartell method of combination provided the machinery whereby, without the loss of the individuality of the separate concerns, the benefits and the burdens of export dumping could be equitably distributed among the domestic producers. The protective tariff prevented foreign competitors from sharing in the high domestic prices resulting from the price-fixing activities of the kartells, provided only that the kartells did not endeavor to make the German prices exceed the prices in foreign markets by more than the cost of transportation to Germany plus the duty on foreign imports. The comparative unimportance, in the export trade of Germany, of agricultural products and of raw materials produced under small-scale conditions, commodities which for reasons later to be explained are least likely to be systematically dumped, operated also to make dumping prevalent over a wider range of the export trade of Germany than of other countries in whose exports such commodities were more prominent. Nevertheless, German dumping has received an undue share of attention as compared to that of other countries which have likewise not been backward in the resort to the practice. The greater publicity which necessarily attaches to the operations of loose combinations such as the German kartells as compared to more unified combinations or trusts such as those of the United States, England, or Canada, and also the painstakingly rigorous searching of German commercial methods for evidence of unfair tactics which had been the self-assigned task of many publicists in other countries—and especially in France—even before 1914 and was embarked upon for propagandist purposes by a host of writers after 1914, operated to make prominent the German practice of dumping while permitting the dumping of other countries to remain in the shadow.

Export dumping by German industries, and especially by the iron and steel trade, began far back in the nineteenth century, even before the rise of the kartells.[1]   But systematic and steady dumping on an extensive scale apparently began with the organization of kartells in the late eighties and the nineties of the nineteenth century.[2]

Many, probably most, of those German kartells which engaged in the export trade commonly and systematically sold at lower prices to foreign than to domestic purchasers.[3]   Most of the kartells left the actual handling of the export trade to the individual members.   But if these kartells were anxious that greater quantities of their products should be disposed of outside of Germany than could be sold abroad at the prices established for the German market, it was necessary to exercise pressure on the members, for the individual member concerns would be unwilling to export abroad as long as more remunerative prices were obtainable at home.   In some cases an attempt was made to meet the problem either by requiring the member concerns to export a stated percentage of their output or by setting maximum limits on the amounts which they could dispose of in the domestic

---

[1] "Low export prices have always prevailed in the German iron and steel trade."—Francis Walker, "The German Steel Syndicate," *Quarterly Journal of Economics*, XX (May, 1906), 391.   Cf. also, p. ooo, *supra*.

[2] Cf. Josef Grunzel, *Economic Protectionism*, p. 226.   Arthur Raffalovich, a well-informed and acute student of industrial combinations, as far back as 1889 wrote as follows: "Aux traits caractèristiques des syndicats américains, il faut ajouter ce fait bien connu, c'est que les coalitions en Europe ont ordinairement deux prix, celui pour le marché interieur et celui pour l'exportation."—*Les Coalitions de Producteurs et le Protectionnisme*, Paris, 1889, p. 14.

[3] Cf. *Memorandum on the Export Policy of Trusts in Certain Foreign Countries*, in Great Britain, Board of Trade: *Report on British and Foreign Trade and Industrial Combinations*, 1903 (Cd. 1761), p. 298: "The fact that dumping is a policy habitually practiced by the German kartells is beyond controversy." (This report will henceforth be referred to as *Memorandum on the Export Policy of Trusts*.) Willi Morgenroth, *Die Exportpolitik der Kartelle*, Leipzig, 1907, pp. 15–29, gives detailed comparisons of the domestic and export prices of many of the German kartells.

market. It was difficult, however, to enforce such agreements,
and, moreover, this method failed to take into account the relative
advantages for export which some plants had over others, because
of situation, size, foreign connections, experience in the foreign
trade, or for other reasons. Resulting from these circumstances,
there was general resort among the kartells desirous of practicing
export dumping, either to a transfer of the handling of the export
trade from the individual concerns to a central export agency supported by the kartells as a whole from contributions by the members, or, more generally, to the system of export bounties to
members, granted in proportion to their exports, and supported
by a levy upon all the members in proportion to their productive
capacity or normal output.

Kartell dumping may take place without involving the direct
payment of bounties where the export trade is handled by the
kartell as a whole, or it may result from—or be accompanied by—
export bounties where exporting is left in charge of the individual members. The export bounty method in its simple form of
a specific bounty granted upon each unit of the commodity
exported has the defect from the point of view of the industry
as a whole that it is inelastic and does not adjust itself to changing conditions. An export bounty which at its first introduction
operates to bring about the desired distribution between sales in
the domestic market and sales abroad may soon become too low,
if foreign prices fall or domestic prices rise, to induce the proper
volume of export. Or it may become too high, with the result
that it leads to overexport at low prices or to special profits for
the exporters, with the cost in either case falling on the industry
as a whole. As a result, most, if not all, of the kartells using
export bounties introduced flexible features. The amounts of
the bounties were subjected to periodic revision, and were fixed
at the point estimated to be sufficient to stimulate exports to the
desired volume. In most cases the bounties were paid only upon
proof of exportation, but some kartells, further to protect themselves against abuse, paid bounties only upon proof of exportation

at a price less than the domestic price;[1] some of the kartells did not pay bounties unless the difference between export and domestic prices was substantial.[2]

Some of the kartells appear to have experimented with making the amount of the bounty equal the actual difference between the export and the domestic prices, but to have found this practice undesirable, because it made it a matter of comparative indifference to the exporting concern, within the maximum limits of the bounty, what prices it received on its export sales, and thus led to sales at prices lower than conditions warranted. To eliminate some of the abuses to which the bounty system was subject, many kartells either themselves took over the handling of the export trade, or exercised supervision over the prices at which export orders could be accepted, or granted bounties equal to only a part of the difference between domestic and export prices.

Where the handling of the export trade was transferred to the kartell, this involved a change in the mode of operation of the export bounty system. Under this plan all the producers received the same price for their products whether these were exported or sold to domestic purchasers, but the bounties paid by all the member concerns in the form of assessments remained with the kartell and served to make up the deficit resulting from its export of goods at lower prices than those which it paid to the member concerns, instead of being passed on to individual exporting concerns.

The years from 1900 to 1902 were in Germany, as elsewhere, marked by industrial depression. The decline in prosperity, coming as it did after a period of unprecedented activity, fell with particular severity upon the non-syndicated industries and upon the non-integrated kartells, i.e., those kartells which did not carry the manufacturing process through from the production of their

[1] *Memorandum on the Export Policy of Trusts*, pp. 303, 304.

[2] This was the practice of the *Stahlwerksverband*, or steel kartell, U.S. Federal Trade Commission: *Report on Cooperation in American Export Trade*, 1916, Part II, p. 16. (This report will henceforth be referred to as *Cooperation in American Export Trade.*)

own raw materials to the completion of a manufactured product ready for sale, but purchased their raw material from the primary-material syndicates such as the pig-iron and the coal and coke kartells. The non-integrated kartells attributed their distress in part to certain practices of the raw-material syndicates, and especially to their export policies. In 1901–2, the iron-using industries of Germany protested vigorously against the export-dumping of the pig-iron kartell, on the ground that it was impairing their ability to compete in foreign markets with foreign manufacturers using dumped German iron.[1] Another ground for complaint was that many of the members of the pig-iron kartell were themselves producers for export of more advanced commodities and were therefore in a privileged position, both in the domestic and in the export trade, in their competition with non-integrated German plants which had to pay to the pig-iron syndicate the high domestic prices exacted for their raw materials.[2] It has been claimed, however, that the German dumping of pig-iron in foreign markets did not appreciably lower the prices current there and that the pig-iron kartell was in all probability dumping merely to meet the prices prevailing in outside competitive markets.[3]

Similar complaints had been made by iron and textile industries against the coal syndicate of the Ruhr as far back as 1891, and had resulted in the Prussian government warning the coal syndicate to cease its export dumping. In this instance a careful student gives it as his conclusion that the injury to German industries which was claimed to have resulted from this export dumping "seems to be alleged rather than proved."[4]   Later,

---

[1] *Memorandum on the Export Policy of Trusts*, pp. 307, 308.

[2] Paul de Rousiers, *Les Syndicats Industriels de Producteurs en France et à l'Étranger*, 2d ed., Paris, 1912, pp. 146 ff.

[3] Cf. Robert Liefmann, *Cartells et Trusts*, Paris, 1914 (translated from 2d German edition), p. 102.

[4] Francis Walker, "Monopolistic Combinations in the German Coal Industry," *Publications of the American Economic Association*, 3d Series, V, No. 3, 225.

complaints of the same kind were made against the steel kartell (*Stahlwerksverband*) by German steel-tool makers, machinery manufacturers and shipbuilders and against the German wire syndicate by the German nail syndicate.   There apparently was much better ground for some of these complaints, for the dumping of German steel and wire in Holland appears to have been an important element in the prosperity of the shipbuilding, machinery, and nail industries in that country, and in some cases enabled these industries to compete successfully with German producers in the German market itself.[1]   The local chambers of commerce in Germany, whose membership consisted largely of independent small-scale producers of consumers' goods, repeatedly protested against the export policy of the great raw-material and intermediate-product kartells as injurious to the interests of the domestic manufacturers of finished products.[2]   On these and other grounds, the Reichstag was petitioned in 1902 to institute state regulation of the kartells and the suppression of such of their practices as were dangerous to German industry.   The question of regulating the kartells came up in the Reichstag for debate, and a motion providing that import duties should be lowered on goods produced by syndicates and sold at lower prices abroad than in the domestic market was defeated by only a moderate margin of votes.   The government responded, however, to the growing feeling of hostility to the kartells by appointing a commission to conduct an inquiry into their activities (the *Kartellenquete*).   This commission carried on an extensive investigation lasting over three years.   In the course of evidence given before it, it was "even asserted that manufacturing industries had been compelled to build establishments in foreign countries in order to take advantage of the marketing of raw materials abroad at low

---

[1] Georg Gothein, "La Réglementation Internationale des Droits de Douane sur les Fers," *Revue Économique Internationale*, August, 1904, pp. 509 ff; G. E. Huffnagel, "Fighting Dumping in Holland," *Commercial Holland*, December, 1919, pp. 53–56; February, 1920, pp. 42–44.

[2] André Sayous, *La Crise Allemande de 1900–1902*, Paris, 1903, p. 370.

prices by the German producers' organisations."[1]   The commission nevertheless recommended that there be no government interference with the kartells, on the ground that they had proved advantageous to Germany.

German consumers of pig iron had some time before, in self-defense, organized consumers' kartells.   Either because of the pressure which these kartells exerted, or to forestal a more intensive campaign for governmental interference, or, perhaps, because their high domestic prices were appreciably checking their sales to German manufacturers for the export trade, the pig-iron syndicate in 1902 adopted the policy of granting rebates or bounties to domestic syndicated purchasers of pig iron for use in further manufacture for export.[2]   There had been earlier instances of the occasional grant of such bounties to domestic purchasers: for example, by the pig-iron syndicate itself as far back as 1880, and by the coke syndicate in 1882.[3]   As a systematic practice, it began in the iron and steel kartells and in various metallurgical trades in 1889 or earlier.[4]   After 1902, it was an established phase of the price policy of all of the great kartells which resorted to dumping; domestic purchasers of their products for use in further manufacture for export were given the advantage of the lower export price, or were at least given some concession from the domestic price.

These bounties were sometimes passed on several times in the process of manufacture of a product ready for export.   Thus the coal syndicate gave a bounty on each ton of coke used by the pig-iron syndicate in the making of pig iron either for direct export or for sale to domestic manufacturers for use in further manufacture for export; the pig-iron syndicate gave a bounty on pig

---

[1] Josef Grunzel, *op. cit.*, p. 323.   Cf. also Willi Morgenroth, *op. cit.*, pp. 45–46.

[2] *Cooperation in American Export Trade*, Part 1, p. 207.

[3] Josef Grunzel, *Economic Protectionism*, p. 225; Paul de Rousiers, *Les Syndicats Industriels*, p. 149; Robert Liefmann, *Cartells et Trusts*, p. 111.

[4] A. Raffalovich, *Les Coalitions de Producteurs et le Protectionnisme*, p. 16; Paul de Rousiers, *op. cit.*, p. 149.

iron used in the production of half-finished goods for export or for domestic sale for further manufacture and export; the wire-rolling mills received bounties on their materials used in manufacture for export and gave similar bounties to the wire-tack syndicate, and so on. In each case the bounty received was passed on, often with a further increase at each successive stage of manufacture.[1] The complications of this elaborate system of cumulative bounties necessitated the establishment of some co-operative machinery for its administration. In 1902 the coal, coke, pig-iron, bar-iron, and steel-beam kartells established a clearing-house for export bounties (*Abrechnungstelle für die Ausfuhr*) at Düsseldorf, where counter-claims could be settled and proof of export or of use in further manufacture for export could be examined.[2]

As a general rule, however, the bounties did not reach the domestic manufacturers for export of highly finished commodities, either because these manufacturers were not syndicated, or because the bounty arrangements did not provide for their being passed on through sufficient stages of the manufacturing process to reach them. Even where a domestic manufacturer for export received a bounty, it was often insufficient in amount to offset the difference between the domestic and the export prices of his raw materials. The extension of the bounties to domestic purchasers for use in further manufacture for export did not, therefore, completely succeed in attaining its purpose, if that was to make raw or semi-finished materials available at the export prices to domestic producers for export of finished commodities, and it failed to reconcile these producers to the export dumping policy of the great kartells.[3]

The export dumping of the German kartells had as its predominant objective the maintenance at the same time of full produc-

---

[1] Great Britain, Ministry of Reconstruction, *Report on Trusts*, 1919, p. 42.

[2] Willi Morgenroth, *Die Exportpolitik der Kartelle*, p. 53.

[3] *Ibid.*, p. 58: "Eine weitherzigere Prämienpolitik wäre deshalb sehr am Platze"; p. 113: "Die drohendste handelspolitische Gefahr der Kartelle liegt eben in der Schwächung der Weiterverarbeiter."

tion and stable and profitable domestic prices.   The development of export trade was only a secondary consideration.[1]   Export prices were made lower than domestic prices only when, and only to the extent, necessary to maintain aggregate sales, domestic and export, at near productive capacity.   In boom times, therefore, it was occasionally unnecessary to cut prices in order to obtain export orders in the desired volume.   At other times domestic orders were of themselves sufficient in volume to render unnecessary the artificial stimulation of exports.   At such times the export bounties would be temporarily abolished, or would be greatly reduced.[2]   It is not to be concluded, however, that the dumping was intermittent and recurred only at times of depression in the domestic market.   Dumping was the normal, and the absence of dumping the exceptional situation in the export trade of most of the great kartells.

[1] Grunzel, *op. cit.*, p. 322, even claims that the kartells did not permit an expansion of export sales to lead to an extension of production facilities, the object of the dumping being the stabilization of domestic prices and of production, and not the expansion of the export trade for its own sake.   Cf., also, *Cooperation in American Export Trade*, Part I, p. 206: "For the foreign market the [pig-iron] syndicate has fixed the export quotas of members so as to prevent unnecessary dumping."

[2] Thus the *Stahlwerksverband* stopped its bounties in 1906 because of active sales, but resumed them in the following year. (Robert Liefmann, *Cartells et Trusts*, p. 111.)   The following statistics, which show a great increase in the quantity, but only a moderate increase in the value, of German exports of metal manufactures in the depression years of 1901–3 as compared to the preceding years, suggest that German dumping varied in extent in inverse proportion to the degree of business activity in the domestic market:

GERMAN EXPORTS

YEAR	COARSE METAL MANUFACTURES		OTHER METAL MANUFACTURES	
	Quantity (Thousands of Tons)	Value (Thousands of £)	Quantity (Thousands of Tons)	Value (Thousands of £)
1899	780	8,080	542	16,430
1900	793	8,795	610	18,865
1901	1,235	9,445	675	18,790
1902	1,313	9,170	914	20,845
1903	1,382	10,025	1,018	22,470

(From J. Ellis Barker, *200 Points for Tariff Reform*, London [1910?], p. 167.)

Sporadic or casual dumping, i.e., the occasional export of surplus stock already produced at whatever prices it will bring, was of infrequent occurrence in Germany, partly because such surplus stocks, if they occurred, were disposed of in the course of the systematic and continued dumping, but mainly because German industry is conservative and rarely produces in anticipation of orders, so that overstocks are rare.[1]

Since 1914, the charge has frequently been made by writers hostile to Germany and all her works that much of the German dumping was actuated by predatory motives. Some writers have gone so far as to find in German dumping a manifestation of a deep-laid conspiracy between German government and industry to destroy the competing industries of foreign countries.[2] Such sweeping accusations are to be regarded with skepticism until convincing evidence is presented in confirmation. They are in large part merely one phase of the wartime plague of mendacious propaganda. It is significant that prior to 1914 capable foreign students of the export policies of the German kartells made no such sweeping charges against them.[3]   It is even

[1] Cf. *Selling Foreign Manufactures in United States*, Part I, p. 64.

[2] Cf. Henri Hauser, *Germany's Commercial Grip on the World* (translated from the French by Manfred Emmanuel) New York, 1917, pp. 98 ff.   In the Preface the author says: "Dumping, export bounties, import bonuses, combined sea-and-land transport rates, emigration measures—these are various measures which were employed by Germany not as the normal procedure of economic activity, but as means of strangling, crushing, and terrorising her adversaries."   The translator, in his Introduction, finds the "true *casus belli*" in the belief of the German government that, although economic crises had been repeatedly overcome in the past by export dumping, the crisis which was impending in 1914 could be handled more quickly and cheaply by victory on the field of arms than by dumping and other methods of "economic penetration"!   A comment made upon such charges by a British economist, although written long before the outbreak of the war, is still pertinent: "All the nonsense one hears about dumping as a 'national conspiracy,' is derived from that fallacious idea which thinks of another nation as an industrial unit."—William Smart, *The Return to Protection*, London, 1904, p. 161.

[3] Cf. the British Board of Trade *Memorandum on the Export Policy of Trusts*, 1903, pp. 297–98: "It is of course easy to suppose a state of things in which a Kartell or a combination of Kartells might deliberately export at a low price with the principal or the exclusive aim of injuring and ultimately of entirely ruining and

more significant that within Germany itself opinion was very much divided with respect to the effect on German economic interests of the dumping practices of the kartells. The agrarians, who were most influential in the councils of the government, were almost a unit in opposition to the export dumping of the kartells. Even since 1914, although anti-German propagandists have made much of the menace to the world of German dumping, very little evidence has been published which confirms the attribution to it of predatory motives. Granting the difficulty of discovering and demonstrating the character of the motives behind particular business practices, it still remains true that the preponderance of well-authenticated evidence strongly supports the conclusion that *in general* the German kartells dumped to dispose of surplus productive capacity and not to eliminate foreign competitors.[1]   The kartells, in fact, did their utmost to restrain German exporters from cutting their prices more than was absolutely necessary in order to obtain foreign orders.   The great kartells commonly gave their bounties only to export kartells and not to individual exporters, in order to prevent export prices from being cut as a result of price-competition among the German exporters themselves.[2] The main explanation of the lowness of German export prices as compared to German domestic prices is that behind the shelter of a high protective tariff the kartells were exacting monopolistic

---

bringing to a close a particular industry in a foreign country. But it cannot be said that there is any clear evidence of such action on the part of the German combinations, whose export policy up to the present time appears to be mainly the result of supply exceeding demand in the German domestic markets."

Cf., also, for a post-war opinion, T. W. Page, then chairman of the U.S. Tariff Commission, in *Journal of the American Bankers Association*, XIII (1921), 656: "The present anxiety in regard to dumping appears to have grown out of certain disclosures and allegations about German commercial methods that were given wide notoriety during the war. There is little doubt that the prevalence and gravity of Germany's offenses in this field have been exaggerated."

[1] Cf. Alfred Marshall, *Industry and Trade*, pp. 629, 630.

[2] Cf. Robert Liefmann, *Cartells et Trusts*, p. 112; Willi Morgenroth, *Die Exportpolitik der Kartelle*, p. 11. This refers to bounties to more advanced industries.

prices in the domestic market, and that at these prices foreign business was not obtainable.

There is sufficient evidence, however, to justify the belief that in individual cases where circumstances favored German exporters cut their prices in order to weaken or destroy competitors or to force them to enter into some working arrangement with the German syndicate as to prices and markets.   A. Mitchell Palmer, in his report as alien property custodian, charges German industry in general, and the chemical industry in particular, with predatory dumping intended to crush foreign competition and to establish a German world-wide monopoly.   For so sweeping an indictment the evidence presented is somewhat scanty, but the report cites aniline oil, oxalic acid, and salicylic acid as commodities which had been dumped in the United States with predatory intent, and gives circumstantial details.   Palmer makes the further charge that the German government facilitated the dumping of dyestuffs for military purposes, but he presents no supporting evidence.[1]   Similar charges of predatory dumping were made against the German electrical industry by a British wartime committee.[2]   An American consul reported in 1917 that German hardware exporters had dumped in the Turkish market with the aim of forcing out their French and British competitors.[3]   Long before the outbreak of the war, it was alleged in England that German and American manufacturers of wire nails had dumped their products on the English market until the British producers were driven out of the industry, and had then raised their prices to English purchasers by more than they had previously reduced them.[4]

A well-substantiated and important instance of dumping with the deliberate intent of crushing the domestic industry in the

---

[1] *Alien Property Custodian Report*, Washington, 1919, pp. 30, 33.

[2] Great Britain, Trading with the Enemy Committee, *Report*, 1918 (Cd. 9059), p. 5.

[3] U.S. Dept. of Commerce, *Special Consular Reports*, No. 77, 1917.

[4] *Report of (Chamberlain) Tariff Commission*, Vol. I, *The Iron and Steel Trades*, London, 1904, p. 919.

market dumped on is to be recorded against the *Stahlwerksverband* in its export policy with respect to Italy.[1] A Swiss writer,
in a careful study of the operations of the *Stahlwerksverband* in
the Swiss market, supports in fairly convincing manner his accusation that here also this German kartell quoted extremely low
prices with the main object of forcing out Swiss and English
competitors.[2]

There is no reason to doubt that the German kartells would not
have hesitated to engage in predatory dumping if it promised to
bring results profitable to themselves. The evidence presented
above demonstrates that they did occasionally resort to such
dumping. It is even probable that predatory motives were a
more important factor in German dumping than in the dumping
of other countries. Such evidence as has been published does not
support any more sweeping or dogmatic generalizations. It is
easier to make charges than to substantiate them, and German

[1] Cf. A. D. McLaren, *Peaceful Penetration,* New York, 1917, p. 90: "The
Organisationsgeist has been at work there to oust rivals and competitors in the field
of industry. The most interesting example was the German determination to kill
the iron industry in Northern Italy, which the Italian Government strove so strenu-
ously to foster. The mighty 'Stahlwerksverband' made herculean efforts to 'control' these Italian foundries, that is to say, to make them mere tools in the
hands of the iron and steel magnates of Düsseldorf. Foiled in this attempt, it has
tried to strangle them, as it has already strangled some of those in Scotland and
Staffordshire, **by** dumping on a colossal scale." Cf., also, Maurice Millioud, *The
Ruling Caste and Frenzied Trade in Germany* (translated from the French) Boston,
1916, pp. 104–7. The evidence is convincing that the *Stahlwerksverband* did make
such an attempt. It was finally unsuccessful, however. After tremendous losses
had been incurred on both sides, the *Stahlwerksverband* and the Italian iron and steel
syndicate shortly before the outbreak of the war signed an agreement in which the
former agreed not to sell its products in Italy below certain specified prices. For
an interesting and authoritative account by a representative of the Italian syndicate,
see R. Ridolfi, *Il "dumping," considerato dal lato pratico oppure un caso tipico di
"dumping," La Riforma Sociale,* Torino, XXV (1914), 277 ff. and especially p. 283.
I have not been able to find any confirmation of McLaren's statement that the
Stahlwerksverband had "strangled" Scotch and English steel concerns by dumping.

[2] Eduard Feer, *Die Ausfuhrpolitik der deutschen Eisenkartelle und ihre Wirkungen in der Schweiz,* Zurich, 1918. See, especially, p. 181: "Die Billigkeit des
deutschen Produkts ist deshalb in den meisten Fällen nur als Mittel zum Monopol
zu betrachten."

commercial methods have unquestionably been painted in darker colors than the known facts justify. An instance in point was the accusation, so common during the war, that Germany—or German manufacturers, who in the polemics of wartime were often identified with the German government—was accumulating vast stocks of goods in order to dump them on the markets of the world, with the objects of crushing the new industries fostered by the wartime conditions, re-establishing her foreign commerce, and regaining in the field of economic warfare what she was losing on the military battlefield. These accusations have an interesting parallel in the similar charges brought against England after the Napoleonic Wars and the War of 1812,[1] but they appear to have had even less basis. It has become quite clear that there was not a vestige of truth in the reports of German warehouses bursting with goods ready to be dumped abroad. Germany found herself at the end of the war without goods, financial means, or trade connections for a large-scale dumping campaign.[2]

The Germans have often been accused since 1914 of having resorted on a large scale to "credit dumping," or selling abroad on unreasonably long terms of payment without making proper charges for the deferment of payment. Foreign studies of German export credit practices, however, supply no confirmation for this accusation. The typical German practice of separating the financing of export trade from the exporting itself would make credit dumping difficult to carry out without elaborate arrangements between the export banks and the exporters. Although the Germans, by an efficient organization of the function of financing export trade, were able to adjust the terms of the payment to the needs—or wants—of the different export markets or

[1] See supra, pp. 38 ff.

[2] Indicative of the reliability of wartime literature dealing with German commercial methods was the frequently made claim that the first antidumping law, that of Canada, was intended mainly to meet the menace of German dumping. (Cf. editorial in Chicago Tribune, August 30, 1916, and Walter E. Weyl, American World Policies, New York, 1917, p. 124.) The truth of the matter was that the Canadian law was directed mainly against American dumping.

even of individual customers, they appear as a general rule, if not invariably, both to have charged interest for the longer terms and to have raised their basic prices to compensate for the greater credit risks involved in the longer terms.[1]

BELGIAN, FRENCH, AUSTRIAN DUMPING

The export practices of other continental countries have escaped close and critical examination, so that there is available but scanty material upon which to base conclusions as to the prevalence of dumping in these countries. But the combination of circumstances which especially favored the development of export dumping in Germany on a systematic and extensive scale, namely, the growth of large-scale manufacturing industries operating under unified or syndicated control and enjoying high tariff protection in the domestic market, was not present to nearly the same degree in the remainder of the Continent. In most of the continental countries manufacturing for export was either comparatively unimportant or was largely confined to the production by small concerns of individualized products under conditions not far removed from the handicraft stage. It is not to be expected, therefore, that dumping should be found to be as prominent in the export trade of these countries as of Germany. Such evidence as is available appears to justify the conclusion that in these countries dumping in the export trade was practiced on an extensive scale only by such producers as were operating under conditions closely similar to those governing the syndicated German industries, namely, large-scale machine industry, syndicated control, and a protected domestic market.

In some respects conditions most closely resembling those of German manufacturing industry were to be found in Belgium.

[1] Cf. United States Department of Commerce and Labor, Special Agents Series, No. 62; *Foreign Credits* (1913), pp. 19–34. Cf., especially, p. 20, "American customers, therefore, also receive the benefit of much lower prices in Germany than those quoted by Germans to their over-seas customers requiring long-term credit."

There were in this country many important large-scale manufacturing enterprises, organized into producers' syndicates
closely modeled after the German kartells. But these syndicates
exported so large a proportion of their total output, and the
domestic market in many cases was relatively so unimportant,
that there was little to be gained from an attempt to maintain
domestic prices on a permanently higher level than those prevalent
in the important export markets. Moreover, the Belgian tariff
was too low, and the Belgian market too close to Germany,
France, and England, to permit of the maintenance of prices in
the domestic market substantially higher than the export
prices—often dumping prices—of the producers in these countries.
The conditions were in these important respects unfavorable,
therefore, to the practice by Belgian producers of dumping on a
systematic and substantial scale.[1] Some of the most important
Belgian industries nevertheless found it practicable to resort to
dumping either intermittently or on a permanent basis, and there
were several instances of the grant of export bounties, both
to direct exporters and to domestic manufacturers buying
materials for further use in manufacture for export. Among the
industries which resorted more or less systematically to dumping
were the iron and steel, coal, cement, plate glass, canned vege-
tables, and earthenware syndicates, all of them among the leading industries of Belgium.[2] Because the domestic market was
relatively unimportant for some of these industries, Belgian
dumping occasionally took the form of the sale of Belgian
products at lower prices in distant foreign markets than in other

[1] Cf. G. De Leener, *L'Organisation Syndicale des Chefs d'Industrie*, Brussels,
1909, II, 274, 433. Cf. especially, p. 433: "La Belgique, à défaut de protection
douanière suffisante, présente peu d'exemples caractérisés de la pratique du 'dumping.'"

[2] For evidence of Belgian dumping, see U.S. Dept. of Commerce, *Monthly
Consular Reports*, May, 1905, p. 143; *Co-operation in American Export Trade*,
Part I, pp. 180, 222, 307; *Selling Foreign Manufactures in the United States*,
Part I, pp. 10, 11, 13; G. De Leener, *op. cit.*, I, 80–85; II, 430–34; L. Van Isegehm,
"Le 'Dumping' et les Mesures Prises ou Préconisées pour en Combattre les Effets,"
Revue Économique Internationale, III, (1921), 328.

export markets which were closer by and were "standard" markets for Belgian products.[1]

The greater part of the export trade of France consists of articles made by hand, or if made by machine, manufactured on a small scale in varied styles and designs and without much utilization of expensive plant or machinery. In many cases the exports are artistic specialties and novelties made to individual patterns and are not subject to keen competition from other countries on a price basis. Under such conditions of manufacture, the labor cost and the cost of materials together comprise nearly all of the total cost, and these are not favorable conditions for the development of dumping on a comprehensive scale.[2] But it would be reasonable to infer, from the general situation in other countries under like circumstances, that the few French industries which are organized into producers' syndicates, which are

---

[1] The following account of the export price methods of the Belgian plate-glass industry, taken from *Selling Foreign Manufactures in the United States*, Part I, pp. 10, 11, illustrates the practice of price-discrimination between different export markets:

"The Belgian home market is exceedingly small. I estimate its consumption to amount to less than 5 per cent of the Belgian production—and your purpose will probably be more equitably served by a comparison between the syndicate prices for the United States and those for England, which latter country, because of its free trade and its very large consumption, is the recognized standard market for Belgian plate glass. . . . . The discounts granted on the same for shipment to the two markets are respectively:

Polished Plate Glass, Ordinary Thickness (¼ Inch)	England	United States
	Per Cent	Per Cent
Cut sizes, silvering quality, all sizes...............................	20	30
Cut sizes, glazing quality, above 20 and up to 100 square feet........	30 and 2½	50 and 5
Stock sizes, glazing quality, 4 to 7 square feet......................	15 and 2½	30

"The difference in the selling price between the two markets, although quite noticeable, is far from what it has repeatedly been at previous times, when the outlet to the United States had to take care of a surplus production. At present the entire production of the syndicated factories is being reduced 60 per cent through mutual understanding, which makes aggressive selling prices on the United States market less urgent, as long as the present policy is considered expedient."

[2] Cf. H. O. Meredith, *Protection in France*, London, 1904, pp. 103–8.

protected in the domestic market from foreign competition by high import duties, and which engage in the export trade, do resort to dumping either intermittently or continuously. Little evidence of such practice is to be found in French literature, but this is not conclusive. The voluminous French literature dealing with the policies and practices of trusts and industrial combinations enters into great detail in its discussions of the abuses of German kartells and American trusts but finds little or nothing to criticize in the practices of the French syndicates.[1] Most French writers on the export policies of trusts and kartells either are silent on the question of the practice of dumping by French syndicates or deny it outright. One writer, a member of the Chamber of Deputies and prominently identified with the formulation of French tariff policy, has even gone so far as to deny the legal possibility, under the Civil Code, of dumping by French producers.[2] Another French writer claims that if instances of dumping by French syndicates are discovered, they will be found upon investigation to consist merely of the sporadic sale at sacrifice prices of casual overstocks, "un expédient essentiellement accidentel et passager," and not part of a systematic and continuous policy.[3]

In spite of these disclaimers, however, French syndicates have at times resorted to systematic dumping, sometimes on a substantial scale. In 1886 witnesses before a British official

[1] This may perhaps be explained by the fewness of powerful industrial combinations in France and by the greater measure of secrecy which surrounds business activities in that country as compared to Germany and the United States. (Cf. *Cooperation in American Export Trade*, Part II, p. 94.)

[2] Jean Morel, in France, Chambre des Députés, Commission des Douanes, *Rapport Général* (1908), p. 93. He bases his argument on the assumptions that dumping is possible only on the part of a concern or combination which has a monopoly of its domestic market and that Article 419 of the French Civil Code prevents the establishment of monopoly. But the French courts have shown reluctance to enforce this article and have interpreted it very liberally. (Cf. U.S. Department of Commerce, Bureau of Corporations, *Trust Laws and Unfair Competition*, pp. 269 ff.)

[3] Charles Longuet, *Des Syndicats d'Exportation en France*, p. 25.

commission complained of French dumping in the English market.[1]   The French iron and steel syndicates were established with a view to raising prices in the domestic market by restricting the amounts of their products offered for domestic sale, the balance of their output to be marketed abroad for whatever it would bring.   The dumping which resulted led to the complaint by a French writer that France was being taxed to supply other countries with cheap iron and steel.[2]   In more recent years the pig-iron syndicate has commonly dumped its surplus output abroad during periods of depression in the domestic market, and the flax, hemp, and tow-yarn syndicates and the cotton-yarn syndicate have facilitated dumping by their members by granting them export bounties.   The coal syndicate has not only granted export bounties to its own members, but it has extended them to the French manufacturers of metal and glass products upon purchases of coal for use in manufacture for export.[3]

In Austria export dumping, if the report of an American consul is to be accepted without reserve, has been the customary and normal practice of manufacturers engaged in the export trade.[4]   The practice of dumping has been specifically attributed

[1] Great Britain: Commission on the Depression of Trade and Industry, 1886, Second Report, Minutes of Evidence (C. 4715), Part I, pp. 218, 286.

[2] Georges Villain, Le Fer, la Houille et la Métallurgie à la Fin du XIXᵉ Siècle, Paris, 1901, as cited by E. D. Jones, Journal of Political Economy, X, 304. (The original was not available.)

[3] Cooperation in American Export Trade, Part I, pp. 227, 261, 262, 332; Albert Aftalion, "Les Kartells dans la Région du Nord de la France," Revue Économique Internationale, I, (1908), 120 ff., 131 ff.; II (1911), 289 ff.

[4] Selling Foreign Manufactures in the United States, Part I, p. 9: "In the Vienna consular district, as in all other parts of Austria, the practice prevails of granting lower prices for export in goods that compete in the world's markets. This practice is regarded as essential for the development and maintenance of export trade, and applies to all foreign trade, including that with the United States. So-called "export prices" are recognized as legitimate in Austrian commercial circles and are lower than can be obtained by domestic purchasers. Austrian manufacturers state that they can not meet the competition of the manufacturers of other nations in foreign markets unless they grant prices lower than those prevailing in the home market."

to the wire-tack, enamelled ware, and petroleum-refining syndicates.[1] The *Hauptkartell* in the iron and steel industry facilitated exporting by its members at reduced prices by exempting exports from the production quota or limits assigned to the member concerns. The subsidiary kartells further facilitated dumping by granting export bounties to their members.[2] The oil and the cotton-spinning kartells also granted export bounties to their members.[3] The dumping policy of the Austrian iron kartell was subjected to bitter criticism in the Austrian Parliament.[4]

For other continental European countries, only a few reports of the practice of dumping have been found. Export bounties were used to facilitate export dumping by the cotton textile syndicates of Spain[5] and of Italy,[6] and by several syndicates in the iron and steel industry in Russia.[7] Dumping was also commonly practiced by some Polish syndicates.[8]

CANADIAN DUMPING

In Canada export dumping is not widely prevalent, for the chief exports are the products of the extractive industries, which are typically produced on a small scale by thousands of scattered and unorganized individuals and are therefore not readily subject to systematic price-discrimination. This does not hold true of most of the products of the mining industry, which are produced under large-scale conditions and in some cases are under what approaches monopoly control, but there does not appear to be any reason to believe that these products are

[1] *Report of United States Industrial Commission*, 1901, XVII, 111 ff.

[2] *Cooperation in American Export Trade*, Part I, p. 230.

[3] Josef Grunzel, *Economic Protectionism*, pp. 227, 228.

[4] Maryan Glowacki, *Die Ausfuhrunterstützungspolitik der Kartelle*, Posen, 1909, p. 19.

[5] *Selling Foreign Manufactures in the United States*, Part I, p. 109.

[6] *Cooperation in American Export Trade*, Part I, p. 263.

[7] *Ibid.*, p. 234.

[8] Maryan Glowacki, *op. cit.*, pp. 19 ff.

sold in Canada at higher prices than abroad.[1] Although there have developed in Canada under the shelter of a high protective tariff important manufacturing industries operating under highly concentrated control, few of these industries are able to compete outside their domestic market, even by resort to dumping, with the manufacturers of other countries. Export dumping has been a common practice, however, on the part of the flour-milling industry,[2] and the agricultural implement manufacturers.[3] The leading interest in the iron and steel industry from 1908 to 1910, while receiving production bounties from the Canadian government, sold rails abroad at lower prices than in Canada. Protests were made to the government against this export dumping by various persons in Canada, and also by an English rail mill which suffered from what it regarded as unfair Canadian competition, and the government withdrew its bounties on rails not sold in Canada.[4] The United States Tariff Commission, in the course of an investigation of the prevalence of dumping by foreigners on the American market, received a number of complaints of dumping by Canadian producers of harness leather, sole leather, and lumber.[5]

JAPANESE DUMPING

In so far as reported instances are concerned, Japanese dumping appears to have been confined to the export trade in cotton yarns. But until very recent years there were few other Japanese industries which were operating under the conditions

[1] Cf. *supra*, p. 7, for the practice of Canadian producers of ferrosilicon of maintaining in their domestic market prices *lower* than those obtaining abroad (i.e., "reverse dumping") in order to establish an artificially low base for the assessment of the American ad valorem import duties.

[2] Canada: *Report of the Board of Inquiry into the Cost of Living*, 1915, I, 750 ff.

[3] Edward Porritt, *The Revolt in Canada against the New Feudalism*, London, 1911, pp. 100 ff.

[4] Edward Porritt, *op. cit.*, pp. 111, 133–36, 139; W. J. A. Donald, *The Canadian Iron and Steel Industry*, Boston, 1915, p. 153.

[5] *Information Concerning Dumping and Unfair Foreign Competition*, 1921, pp. 13, 15.

which lend themselves to the practice of dumping, namely, large-scale, machine production under monopolistic control and receiving high tariff protection. The Japanese Cotton Spinners' Association has at different times resorted to a variety of dumping practices in its endeavors to develop its exports to the Chinese market. In 1890 a report of a committee of this association submitted a plan for exporting at a loss for five years with a view to gaining a hold on the Chinese market, the loss to be shared by all the member mills whether or not they took part in the export trade. The plan, apparently, was either at once rejected or was soon abandoned. In 1902 a system of export bounties, payable at six-month intervals, was established, but it broke down in fifteen days, mainly because the export houses demanded cash instead of deferred bounties. In 1908 the Association made a short-lived experiment with the novel device of introducing a lottery element into the export trade. Lottery tickets were inclosed with each bundle of yarn exported, and drawings were scheduled at periodic intervals, the prizes to the winning ticket-holder consisting of bales of yarn, with consolation prizes of "beautiful paintings or sets of fancy post cards to be presented to all lots remaining uncalled." All the mills were to share the expense of the lottery in proportion to their total production of yarn. Drawings were held according to schedule in 1908, but the scheme was not successful in stimulating exports and was abandoned in the same year. In 1909 the cash export bounty system was established, and it continued in effect until early in 1912. The bounties were at first granted only upon exports of yarn, but after protest from Japanese exporters of cotton textiles they were extended to exports of cotton cloth made from Japanese yarn.[1]

[1] U.S. Dept. of Commerce, *Special Agents Series*, No. 86 (1914), "Cotton Goods in Japan," pp. 88–103. This section of the report concludes as follows: "A study of the way in which Japanese mills have cooperated to promote their export trade is not only interesting but may not be without value in its suggestions to mills in other countries, especially when they are faced with a surplus on a dull home market."

CHAPTER V

THE PREVALENCE OF DUMPING SINCE 1890. II.: BRITISH AND AMERICAN DUMPING

BRITISH DUMPING

Sporadic dumping, or the export at reduced prices of casual overstocks, is infrequent in England, because British manufacturers do not in general produce for stock in anticipation of orders not already on hand.[1] Nevertheless, there were in Great Britain, as in other countries, occasions when stocks did accumulate, and on such occasions British producers were as likely as the producers of other countries to dispose of their surpluses in foreign markets at reduced prices in order to protect their domestic prices.[2]

In Great Britain until very recent years monopolistic combinations of producers have not been either numerous or important, but of late the world-wide trend toward such combinations has been evident in that country on a more comprehensive scale.[3] Partly because of the absence in general of such combinations, partly—probably mainly—because throughout a wide range of those British industries which produce from expensive plant and

[1] Cf. *Selling Foreign Manufactures in the United States*, Part III, p. 18: "Manufacturing is carried forward in this country [i.e., Great Britain] with greater reference to immediate demand than in the United States, and there is not, therefore, the accumulation of surplus stocks which periodically occurs in America, and which may induce the manufacturer, in order to secure a ready market, to sell abroad at a lower price than at home."

[2] Cf. the reported remark of an Edinburgh brewer, *ibid.*, p. 15: "I have been 'dumping' ale and beer on foreign markets all my life, whenever I have had a surplus."

[3] Cf. Great Britain, Ministry of Reconstruction, *Report of Committee on Trusts*, 1919; *Cooperation in American Export Trade*, Part I, pp. 77–98, and chapter v; G. R. Carter, *The Tendency towards Industrial Combination*, London, 1913.

with high fixed charges the British domestic prices are normally low enough to permit of a steady and prosperous export trade without resort to lower export prices, and partly because of the absence of protective duties on imports, there has been in recent times very little resort to or occasion for systematic and continuous export dumping on the part of British producers.

This reasoning, however, may be carried too far. It is often taken for granted that the free trade policy of Great Britain makes impossible, or at least unlikely, the development either of industrial trusts or combinations able to charge monopoly prices to the English consumer or of export dumping on a systematic and continued scale. The possibility of importing free of duty the competing products of foreign countries, it is argued, makes it impossible for a trust to raise English prices above the competitive level in outside markets. It is similarly argued that the possibility of reimportation free of duty by British merchants of any products sold abroad at dumping prices makes continued export at prices lower than the domestic prices impossible.[1] That there is some flaw in this reasoning is apparent from consideration of the evidence that there has been in late years a quite extensive development of producers' combinations, although probably not nearly to the same degree as in Germany and the United States, and that export dumping on a systematic and continued scale has been known to occur on the part of some of these combinations. The explanation, however, is not far to seek. If a British industry is, prior to combination, operating on a lower cost basis than similar industries outside of Great Britain, a monopolistic combination of the British producers may be enabled even under free trade to raise

[1] Cf. F. W. Hirst, *Monopolies, Trusts and Kartells*, New York, 1906, pp. 106–7: "The consequence [of England's free trade policy] is that . . . . we have hardly any cases of combinations strong enough to fix prices above their natural level; and none in which an English firm has made its price to the home consumer perceptibly higher than the price at which it sells the same article to foreign purchasers. For at the moment that such a policy were established it would pay English merchants to re-import the article from abroad."

prices to the British consumer by the difference between (a) the British cost and (b) the lowest foreign cost plus the transportation cost to the British market. In the absence of import duties a British monopoly may also be able as a continuous policy to sell abroad at prices lower than its domestic prices by the costs of transportation *to and from* the foreign market, including interest and insurance charges, plus an allowance for a reasonable profit to the original purchaser in the foreign market, before it need fear the reimportation of its dumped commodities.[1] For expensive commodities and for commodities sold in nearby markets an appreciable difference between the domestic and the export price will usually not be feasible. But for bulky commodities, especially if they are sold to distant markets, there must be a substantial margin of difference between the domestic and the export price before the possibility of reimportation will become a real restraint on the practice of dumping. That the dumping of the German kartells was not always dependent upon the possession of a protected domestic market is demonstrated by the fact that among the most systematic and persistent of the German dumpers were the producers of shipbuilding materials, which were admitted free of duty into Germany.[2]

The real restraint on export dumping in a free trade country is probably not so much the danger of reimportation of the dumped commodities as the fact that systematic and continuous dumping is generally a concomitant of the exaction from domestic purchasers of more or less exorbitant monopoly prices, and that in a free trade country the possibility of exacting such prices

[1] Cf. S. J. Chapman, *Outlines of Political Economy*, London, 1911, p. 179: "A monopolist may sell abroad at any price which differs from the home price by cost of carriage between the foreign market and the home market, if the monopolist produces in a free trade country. . . . . Were the foreign price to drop below this level, the goods would be sent back to earn a profit out of the high home price." This agrees with the statement made in the text if the export price is understood to be the c.i.f. and not the f.o.b. price, and if allowance is made for an extra profit for the foreign purchaser who re-exports.

[2] Cf. Robert Liefmann, *Cartells et Trusts*, p. 110.

is generally closely limited by the potential competition of similar foreign commodities. As a matter of fact, many writers have been too ready to take for granted that wherever import duties are levied they are imposed alike on foreign products and on reimported domestic products. The American tariff laws prior to the present act (i.e., the Fordney-McCumber Act of 1922) and the Canadian tariff legislation prior to the 1907 revision permitted the reimportation of domestic goods free of duty if they had not been subjected to further manufacture while abroad.[1] Similar provisions are probably a common feature of protective tariff legislation.[2]

There is evidence to show that there were some British manufacturers who found it possible to engage in systematic dumping even under the free trade policy of Great Britain. A witness before the Chamberlain Tariff Commission claimed that the "English [cotton] spinners frequently sell their yarns

[1] Cf. U.S. Tariff Act of October 3, 1913, par. 404, and Canada, *The Custom Tariff*, 1906, Sec. 14. The Canadian revision of 1907 limited the reimportation of Canadian goods free of duty to articles "returned to the exporter thereof" (6-7 Ed. VII, chap. 11, Tariff item 709), thus protecting Canadian exporters against the return to Canada of goods which they had dumped abroad, although I have no evidence which indicates that this was the purpose of the change. The Fordney-McCumber Tariff introduces a similar provision into American tariff legislation. Paragraph 1514 of this act limits the free admission of American goods to goods "imported by or for the account of the person who exported them from the United States." The new clause appeared in the bill as it passed the House, and neither the Congressional debates nor the tariff hearings give any indication that it attracted any attention. Its immediate object probably was to check the reimportation into the United States at very low prices of the great quantities of army supplies which had been sold in France at sacrifice prices. The House in 1921 passed a bill imposing a prohibitive import duty of 90 per cent on army goods reimported into the United States, but the Senate failed to take action on this bill. (See *Christian Science Monitor*, September 2, 1921.) But the Tariff Act of 1922 contains in Sec. 322 a provision making reimports of automobiles and parts exported for military use subject to a duty of 90 per cent.

[2] Cf. G. M. Fisk, *International Commercial Policies*, New York, 1907, p. 137: "The commercial policy of modern industrial nations generally provides for the free re-importation of certain exported domestic goods which are returned in an unaltered form."

in foreign markets at less price than they would accept at home, to the detriment of the English merchants."[1]   The Scotch Steel Makers Association regularly quoted in the trade papers lower export prices for steel plate than those offered to domestic buyers. They had little cause to fear the reimportation into the domestic market of their dumped exports, because their export trade in these commodities was mainly with distant countries, and the dumped commodities, being bulky, could not bear the freight costs of the double shipment.[2]   English steelmakers also dumped in foreign markets.[3]   An American investigator reported in 1909 that English manufacturers of machinery sold their products to the continent at lower prices than in the domestic market and to prevent reimportation required of foreign purchasers that they obligate themselves not to ship any of their English purchases back to Great Britain.[4]   An English manufacturer of structural steel complained to a British wartime committee investigating the steel trades that British steel manufacturers commonly quote lower export prices for steel, the differential under domestic prices at times reaching 20s. per ton, but that they refuse to make any rebate on steel sold to English manufacturers of steel products, even when it is proved that the steel is to be used in

[1] Tariff Commission, *Report on the Cotton Industry*, London, 1905, par. 602.

[2] Hermann Levy, *Monopoly and Competition*, London, 1911, pp. 229 ff.   Cf. also *Cooperation in American Export Trade*, Part I, p. 220.

[3] *Economist* (London), November 16, 1907, pp. 1967, 1968.   In 1906, E. H. Gary, chairman of the United States Steel Corporation, in the course of his defense before a Congressional committee of the Steel Corporation's dumping policy, presented data which if accurate would indicate that English manufacturers of steel products far exceeded the Steel Corporation in the extent of their dumping and the margin between their home and export prices.   (See *Iron Age*, LXXVII [April 19, 1906], 1324.)   But similar data which he presented with reference to the prices charged at home and abroad by the German Stahlwerksverband were promptly repudiated by the latter.   (*Iron Age*, LXXVIII [September 20, 1906], 744.)   And his evidence in general showed that he had been misinformed about the extent of European dumping and its degree of dependence upon official bounties.

[4] C. M. Pepper, *The British Iron and Steel Industry*, 1909 (61st Cong., 1st Sess., Sen. Doc. 42), p. 23.

the manufacture of products for the export trade.[1]   The British
salt producers' combination has been charged with export
dumping.[2] The British alkali combination during the war was
reported to have endeavored to secure contracts with South
American importers to handle its caustic soda exclusively, with
the object of shutting out the American companies as soon as
the British wartime prohibition of exportation was removed.
The British combination "in consideration of this exclusive
contract" guaranteed "that the British prices will be lower than
any that might be offered by the Americans,"[3] a type of guaranty
which must tend to lead to predatory dumping.   The British
Committee on Trusts, in its 1919 report, stated that there was
a general agreement among representatives of combinations
who had appeared before it that "one of the beneficial results
of the formation of Associations sufficiently powerful to control
and maintain prices in the Home market was that it enabled
British Manufacturers to extend their output by selling their
products at a lower price, or even at a loss, in foreign markets."[4]
The chairman of an important metal combination admitted to
the Committee that his association had a "fighting fund, for
the special purpose of subsidising members who found it necessary
to sell at less than an economic price in order to cut out foreign
competitors," but he did not make clear whether this price-
cutting was practiced in the domestic or the export trade.   This
witness also said that members of his association "had dumped
in Belgium as a reprisal against Belgian dumping here."[5]   British
syndicated producers of linoleum have resorted to dumping to
drive Belgian and French competitors out of the Turkish market.[6]

[1] Great Britain, Board of Trade, *Report of the Committee on the Engineering Trades*, 1918 (Cd. 9073), pp. 9, 10.

[2] Hermann Levy, *op. cit.*, p. 246.

[3] *Cooperation in American Export Trade*, Part I, p. 179.

[4] Great Britain, Ministry of Reconstruction, *Report of Committee on Trusts*, 1919 (Cd. 9236), p. 7.

[5] *Ibid.*   [6] *Cooperation in American Export Trade*, Part II, p. 135.

Export dumping on a continued and systematic scale has been a common practice of American manufacturers since at least the late eighties of the last century. The mass of evidence available in various official and non-official sources is conclusive in this regard, and demonstrates beyond question that a substantial fraction of the American export trade in manufactured commodities had, before 1914, been developed and maintained on the basis of the sale at dumping prices. The abundance of evidence is all the more significant because American exporters who resorted to dumping generally endeavored to conceal their export prices from the American public. Export price lists and export price quotations were carefully kept out of domestic circulation. In 1902 a committee of the Democratic party seeking campaign material succeeded in obtaining from a foreign subscriber a copy of the discount sheet of an American export journal which contained the lowest export prices only after offering $100 for it.[1] Some years before a trade journal had stated that advertisers had withdrawn their patronage because it published quotations of export prices lower than domestic prices.[2] A New York Tariff Reform Club pamphlet published in 1890[3] presented many instances of dumping. In the same year, J. M. Rusk, Secretary of Agriculture in the Harrison cabinet, protested publicly against export dumping on the part of the American Harvester Company as unfair to the American farmer, and as injurious to the popularity of the protectionist policy.[4]

A publication of the Department of Commerce in 1900 warned the steel manufacturers that their dumping was retarding

[1] Cited by Byron W. Holt, "Home and Foreign Price of American-made Goods," 1906, a New York Tariff Reform Club pamphlet, reprinted in *Congressional Record*, Vol. 40, Part 8, pp. 8024 ff. (p. 8029).

[2] *Engineering and Mining Journal*, August 26, 1890. Cited by Byron W. Holt, *op. cit.*

[3] "Protection's Home Market," New York, 1890.

[4] Byron W. Holt, *op. cit.*, p. 8025.

the American shipbuilding and perhaps other industries, and was thereby lending strength to agitation for the lowering of the American tariff on foreign goods.[1] By this time, the Democratic party had, in fact, already found in the general practice by protected American manufacturers of selling abroad at lower prices than at home a powerful argument against the tariff policy of their political opponents, and were making much of it. Evidence as to the prevalence of dumping was becoming abundant. The Industrial Commission, in the course of its investigation of 1900 and 1901 into industrial conditions, made some inquiry, both by the questionnaire method and by personal examination of witnesses, into the practice of dumping by American manufacturers. The Commission sent its questionnaire to 2,000 concerns, of whom 416 replied and 75 admitted that they sold abroad at lower prices than at home.[2] As the

[1] "The Iron and Steel Trade of the United States," *Monthly Summary of Commerce and Finance of the United States*, August, 1900, p. 250: "The progress of work on shipbuilding in the United States has likewise been retarded, because makers of steel materials required a higher price from the American consumers than they did from the foreign consumers for substantially similar products. Of course American exporters have to get foreign contracts in competition with foreign plate makers, who are excluded from our domestic market. In addition to this, American export plate makers are interested in preventing the establishment of plate manufacturing in their customer nations abroad, and to that end bid low enough to discourage foreign nations from entering the field for producing their own plate at home. The progress of domestic manufacturers of iron and steel goods may likewise be handicapped by the sale of iron and steel in their unmanufactured state at so much lower a price to foreigners than to domestic consumers as to keep the American competitor out of foreign markets generally. The natural limit to such a policy of maintaining a higher level of prices for these materials at home than abroad is found in the restriction of domestic consumption and in the import duty. If restriction of consumption at home does not operate to prevent the shortsighted policy of discrimination against domestic development of manufacturing industries, the other contingency is more or less sure to arise, namely, the demand for a reduction of the tariff on unfinished iron and steel, in order to equalize the opportunity of makers of finished products in foreign markets. To this policy the domestic consumer is usually ready to lend himself, thus making a powerful combination of interests to set limits to the rise of domestic prices of iron and steel materials."

[2] Cf. the minority report of Mr. T. W. Phillips, United States Industrial Commission, *Final Report*, XIX (1902), 663.

replies to the questionnaire were not compulsory, however, it is reasonable to suppose that among those concerns which failed to reply there were many who practiced dumping, and that those concerns who did practice dumping were less likely to reply than those who did not. Most of the concerns commonly referred to as "trusts" failed to reply. Even of those who replied that they did not practice dumping, it would be credulous to accept the denials at their face value.[1]   Nevertheless in the replies to the questionnaire which admitted the practice of export dumping and in the evidence given before the Commission there was presented an important body of data which demonstrated that a large number of important exporters of manufactured products commonly sold at lower prices to foreign than to domestic buyers.   That the Industrial Commission was impressed by this evidence is indicated by the fact that one of the recommendations which it made in its final report was that import duties should be remitted on goods of a kind exported by American producers at dumping prices, in order to protect the American consumer against the exorbitant domestic prices which the practice of dumping appeared to imply.[2]

In 1902, and again in 1906, a committee of the Democratic party collected for its campaign books considerable evidence of the practice of dumping by American exporters, which made an impressive exhibit in support of their contention that the tariff policy of their political opponents enabled the protected interests to charge exorbitant prices in the domestic market. In 1906 a pamphlet of the New York Tariff Reform Club listed

[1] Cf. Great Britain, Board of Trade: *Memorandum on the Export Policy of Trusts*, 1903 (Cd. 1761), p. 310: "It is also to be remembered in considering the value to be attributed to these answers, that the firms who supplied them had an interest in concealing or minimizing the extent to which they export goods at lower prices than those charged at home, in view of the unpopularity of such a policy among the American working-classes, and the enemies of trusts generally." Cf. also, to the same effect, the minority report of Mr. Phillips, in the *Final Report*, XIX, 663.

[2] *Final Report*, XIX, 651. Similar proposals have frequently been made in the American Congress and in the legislative bodies of other countries, but have nowhere been put into effect.

several hundred commodities, covering a wide range of industries,
which were being commonly sold for export at prices lower than
those current in the, domestic market.[1] The Republicans at
first made some endeavor to minimize the extent of the practice,
and to explain away such instances of export sales at reduced
prices as had incontestably occurred as being cases of spurious
dumping resulting from the refund on exported commodities
through the drawback system of the duties paid upon the
importation of the materials from which these exported commodities were manufactured.[2] But the accumulation of evidence
of dumping was becoming too impressive to make this a satisfactory explanation even on the political platform, especially
as very few industries were in a position to take substantial
advantage of the drawback privileges. In 1906 the Republican
campaign book indicated a change in tactics, for it proclaimed
that if American manufacturers had gained foreign markets
through resort to dumping "it is to the glory and honor of every
American manufacturer who has done it that he has increased
the sales of his wares abroad, thereby increasing the volume of
his output, the employ of labor, and the wages of his men."[3]

Dumping continued to be practiced by American manufacturers on a substantial scale until the outbreak of the war.
Since 1914 there has been first a period during which American
manufacturers found it unnecessary to make reductions from
their domestic prices in order to obtain export orders in the
desired volume and subsequently a period during which such
orders were difficult to obtain at any price. But dumping is
undoubtedly being practiced to-day by some American exporters,

[1] Byron W. Holt, *op. cit.*

[2] Cf. especially Leslie M. Shaw, Secretary of the Treasury from 1902 to 1907,
in his book, *Current Issues*, New York, 1908, chap. xxi.

[3] Cf. J. G. Parsons, *Protection's Favors to Foreigners*, 1909, reprinted as government document, 61st Cong. 1st Sess., Sen. Doc. 54, p. 13: "The wide publication
of the official and authoritative admissions and other evidences of customary
lower prices for export have made it practically impossible for any Republican or
protectionist declaration to continue the former denial."

although probably on a very limited scale as compared to the pre-war period.[1]

In the United States the systematic and continued practice of dumping appears to have been largely confined either to the dominant concerns in the staple industries or to manufacturers of specialties. In other countries, and especially in Germany, even the smallest concerns participated in the exportation at reduced prices through their membership in kartells or producers' combinations and through the use of the system of export bounties. The illegality in the United States of associations for the control of prices prevented the development of producers' associations with common funds used to grant export bounties to member concerns. The small producer of a staple commodity had no motive for continuously selling abroad on his own initiative at prices lower than those obtainable in the domestic market, since he could not appreciably affect domestic prices by any reduction in the amount of his own product which he disposed of at home. Even the large producer who sold abroad at dumping prices bore alone the burden of the reduced prices, but shared with the remainder of the industry the beneficial effect of his increased exports on domestic prices. Only for concerns controlling a very large fraction of the total American production—and even then only if there was no keen price-competition in the domestic market—was any conceivable gain to be derived from the systematic export of a part of their output at prices lower than those current in the domestic market. And only a concern which had very nearly monopoly control of its product in the domestic market or else was governed in its business practice by altruistic—i.e., non-business—principles could afford to grant indirect export bounties or rebates, of the type common to the European kartells, to domestic purchasers of its products for use in further manufacture for export. For as long as there continued to be substantial competition in the

---

[1] Cf. the evidence of Mr. H. E. Miles, in *Hearings before the (Senate) Committee on Finance on the Proposed Tariff Act of 1921*, pp. 5368, 5392, 5395, 5398.

domestic market, there would be a struggle on the part of each producer to obtain the higher-price orders and to avoid the necessity of accepting the lower-price orders, with the consequence that both types of orders would move toward a parity of prices. It is not surprising, therefore, that there should be only a single recorded instance in the United States of the systematic practice of granting indirect export bounties or rebates, nor that the United States Steel Corporation, with its dominant position in its industry and its practical freedom from substantial price-competition in the domestic market, should be the one concern in a position to use the system of indirect export bounties.[1]

The United States Steel Corporation was most prominent among the American concerns which systematically dumped

[1] *Government Suit against the United States Steel Corporation, in the United States District Court of New Jersey,* 1913, pp. 3835, 3836, evidence of J. A. Farrell, President of the Corporation. Mr. Farrell stated that there were 158 American manufacturers to whom rebates had been granted and that the Steel Corporation sold about $30,000,000 of materials annually at special discounts from the current domestic prices to American manufacturers who used these materials in further manufacture for export. Cf. also *Hearings before the (H.R.) Committee on Investigation of the United States Steel Corporation,* 1912, pp. 2753, 2754, where the evidence of Mr. Farrell makes it appear that the practice of granting export rebates was not confined to the U.S. Steel Corporation: "The Government pays such drawback to the exporters when satisfactory proof is presented under Government regulations, and it is the practice of *manufacturers who make export allowances* to require their customers to furnish similar proof of export before allowances are made." (Italics mine.) Cf. also the evidence of Mr. Schwab before the Industrial Commission in 1901: "I think you can safely say this, that where large export business is done, for example, in the line of iron or steel, nearly all the people from whom supplies are bought for that purpose give you a good price for all the materials that go into export." *Report,* XIII, 454.

In 1918 the Federal Trade Commission issued an "unfair competition" order against the United States Gold Leaf Manufacturers' Association on the ground that they were "engaging in a concerted movement to unduly enhance the prices of gold leaf and to maintain such prices, through meetings, correspondence, etc., and by pooling their surplus products and selling the same abroad at a less price than such products are being sold in the United States at the same time, assessments being made to cover losses on foreign sales when made below cost, the effect being to curtail supply, restrain competition, and enhance prices, in alleged violation of Section 5 of the Federal Trade Commission Act." United States Federal Trade Commission, *Annual Report* (1918), p. 65; *Decisions,* I, 173.

their commodities in foreign markets. Not all· of its products were commonly sold abroad at prices lower than the domestic prices; but the list of commodities which were dumped was ordinarily a long one, the resort to dumping had been in effect for many years, and in many cases the difference between the domestic and the export price was substantial.[1] Dumping in Canada by the Steel Corporation was the original cause of the enactment by that country in 1904 of the first general antidumping law.[2] Its dumping of tin plate in Canada, with the alleged intent of ousting the Welsh product from the Canadian market, led to the inclusion of that commodity in 1908 in the list of articles coming under the protection of the antidumping clause in the Canadian tariff, although it was removed in the following year.[3] The usual concomitant of export dumping of raw or half-manufactured materials, namely, protests by domestic users of such materials for further manufacture for export that the dumping export prices were handicapping them in their export trade by affording an artificial advantage to their foreign competitors, was not prominent in the United States. Several such instances of protest, however, did occur, and were directed mainly against the steel industry. In 1906 the National Association of Agricultural Implement and Vehicle Manufacturers initiated a protest against the export dumping of iron and steel products on the ground that it hurt their export trade by making

[1] Cf. evidence of President Schwab before the Industrial Commission in 1901 (Vol. XIII, pp. 454–55):

Q. "Would you say that when business is in a normal condition the export prices are regularly somewhat lower than home prices?"

A. "Oh, yes, always."

For more recent years see *Government Suit against the United States Steel Corporation, United States District Court of New Jersey*, 1913, Defendant's Exhibits, II, No. 41; and *Hearings before the (H.R.) Committee on Investigation of the United States Steel Corporation*, 1912, pp. 2726 ff.

[2] Cf. Edward Porritt, *Sixty Years of Protection in Canada*, London, 1908, p. 406.

[3] W. J. A. Donald, *The Canadian Iron and Steel Industry*, Boston, 1915, p. 185.

raw materials cheaper to their foreign competitors than to them-selves, but upon the solicitation of some of the members of the association, the protest was apparently withheld from publica-tion.[1] At the hearings of the Merchant Marine Commission, held in 1904, witnesses claimed that the export dumping of shipbuilding materials by the steel trust was one of the important factors checking the development of the American shipping industry and that the steel trust obtained compensation for the low prices charged to foreign purchasers by charging excessively high prices to domestic purchasers. An instance was cited of the sale by the United States Steel Corporation of steel ship-building materials at $32 per ton f.o.b. Pittsburgh to domestic purchasers as compared to $24 a ton, c.i.f. Belfast, to British shipbuilders.[2] Shipbuilding materials to be used in the con-struction of vessels built to engage in foreign commerce were admitted into the United States free of duty, but vessels built from materials imported free of duty under this provision of the tariff law were not permitted, except to a narrowly limited extent, to engage in the coasting trade of the United States. Witnesses stated that under the conditions then existent in the American shipping industry no American would take advantage of this provision and build ships which could not escape unfavor-able conditions in foreign shipping by being diverted to the nationally monopolized coasting trade. The provision had, in fact, only been utilized once up to 1904 and only because excep-tional circumstances were present. The Commission in its report

[1] J. G. Parsons, *op. cit.*, p. 46. For protests on similar grounds, made over fifteen years earlier on behalf of the American steel-using industries, vide *The American Machinist*, September 26, 1889, and the *Engineering and Mining Journal*, March 15, 1890.

[2] *Report and Hearings of Merchant Marine Commission*, 1905 (58th Cong. 3rd Sess., Sen. Rep. 2755), pp. 565, 813–14. The Chairman of the Commission, Senator Gallinger, commented on this evidence that "if the situation is as has been described, it is a great outrage." (*Ibid.*, p. 814.) In justice to the Steel Corpora-tion, it should be said that E. H. Gary later denied that there was any truth in this charge. (See *Iron Age*, LXXVII, 1324.)

condemned the practice of export dumping and recommended a fuller extension of the privilege of the coasting trade to vessels built from foreign materials entered under the free admission provision of the tariff.[1]

From 1902 to 1905 the Steel Corporation induced its employees to enter into an agreement to accept about 20 per cent lower wages upon tin plate made for ultimate export than on work for domestic orders, on the plea that it could not otherwise afford to accept the orders of the Standard Oil Company for tin plate for containers for export oil.[2] The latter company, by virtue of the drawback system, was able to purchase Welsh tin plate to be used in making containers for its export products on virtually a free import basis. In order to obtain such orders, therefore, it was necessary for the Steel Corporation to meet the Welsh prices on a competitive non-tariff basis. By a later agreement between the employees' unions and the American tin plate companies 3 per cent was deducted from the wages of all employees and placed in a trustee fund. This fund was used to reimburse the tin plate companies to the extent of 25 per cent of the union scale of wages on all domestic plates which they sold for use in export trade in place of foreign plates subject to drawback of import duty upon re-export. The companies were to use this subsidy to defray the cost of making special rates on plates sold for export.[3]

American export dumping had before the war given rise in foreign countries to more vigorous protest and to more countervailing legislation than the export dumping of any other country. It has already been indicated that the first general antidumping law, that of Canada enacted in 1904, was directed primarily against American dumping. From 1899 on, protests against

[1] *Ibid.*, pp. ix, x.

[2] Byron W. Holt, *op. cit.*, *Congressional Record*, LXXX, 8025, 8028.

[3] *Tariff Hearings*, Committee on Ways and Means (1908–9), VII, 7401 ff., where the text of the agreement is given in full.

American dumping, especially of steel products, were conspicuous in European journals, and in 1902 prominent European statesmen belonging to four different countries, Witte of Russia, Luzzati of Italy, Goluchowski of Austria, and Gothein and Posadowsky of Germany, apparently without collusion with each other, simultaneously proposed the formation of a European union along the lines of the Brussels Sugar Convention as a means of defense of their joint economic interests against the objectionable practices of American trusts and especially against their dumping of American goods in European markets.[1] In 1905 New Zealand, in response to complaints from British and domestic manufacturers of agricultural implements that the "American Harvester Trust" was dumping in the colony in order to suppress competition with certain of its products, passed an act authorizing the imposition of countervailing duties or the grant of bonuses to domestic or British manufacturers to meet unfair competition in agricultural implements on the part of foreign manufacturers.[2] Joseph Chamberlain's campaign of 1903 for the adoption by Great Britain of a protective tariff was based in part on the alleged need of British industry for protection against German and American dumping.[3] The antidumping provisions of the Australian Industries Preservation Act of 1906, according to the sponsor of the bill, the Australian Minister of Trade and Commerce, were intended to provide a means of defense for Australian industries against dumping and other allegedly unfair practices of American trusts.[4] It is not without significance that each of the three laws enacted by as many countries

[1] W. F. Notz and R. S. Harvey, *American Foreign Trade*, Indianapolis, 1921, p. 385: Wilhelm Feld, "Anti-dumping, Prämienklausel und Ausgleichzölle," *Archiv für Sozialwissenschaft und Sozialpolitik*, XLIV, 476.

[2] U.S. Tariff Commission, *Colonial Tariff Policies*, 1922, p. 775, n.; G. H. Scholefield, *New Zealand in Evolution*, London, 1916, pp. 326, 327.

[3] Cf. C. W. Boyd (editor), *Mr. Chamberlain's Speeches*, Boston, 1914, II, 173-74, 199-200; Josef Grunzel, *Economic Protectionism*, p. 149; Geoffrey Drage, *The Imperial Organization of Trade*, London, 1911, pp. 138 ff.

[4] Commonwealth of Australia, *Parliamentary Debates*, June 14, 1906, p. 247.

prior to 1914 to meet the menace of dumping was directed mainly against American export practices.

When American governmental agencies have found occasion to protest against export dumping by American concerns, it has always been the high domestic prices and not the low export prices which they found objectionable, except as it was presumed that the low export prices were a cause of the high domestic prices. Such for example was the position taken by the Department of Commerce in 1900, by the Industrial Commission in 1901, and by the Merchant Marine Commission in 1905.[1] The Report of 1907 on the Petroleum Industry of the Commissioner of Corporations presented considerable evidence to the effect that the Standard Oil Company exported at prices lower than its domestic prices, in some instances in order to eliminate competitors in foreign markets.[2] The Commissioner condemned this practice, but not because it was unfair to the foreign competitors of the Standard Oil Company: "It is not so much the low prices in foreign markets as the exorbitant prices in the domestic market which require condemnation."[3]

DUMPING RESULTING FROM OFFICIAL BOUNTIES

Dumping is as likely to result from an official or government export bounty as from a private bounty. Official export bounties were a common, if minor, feature of the mercantilistic system. But in most countries they had been wholly or largely eliminated by the early part of the nineteenth century, and in European countries what few instances had hitherto survived were, with rare exceptions, repealed during the free trade movement of the 1860's. The beet sugar industry, however, received in this respect exceptional treatment. In several European countries an elaborate system of export bounties on beet sugar

[1] Cf. *supra*, pp 80, 81, 87.   [2] Part II, pp. 317, 360, 372–77.

[3] Part II, p. 427. Cf. also p. 431 for the charge that the Standard Oil Company "practically makes the people of the United States very largely bear the cost of its policy of domination in the world's markets."

developed unintentionally out of a clumsily contrived system of excise taxation, and from these countries it spread to other European countries, which adopted the bounty system either in defense of their export trade in beet sugar or out of a feeling of international rivalry. It involved a heavy drain on state treasuries, and was subjected to a severe blow when the United States in the tariff laws of 1894 and 1897 imposed countervailing duties on bountied sugar. The final blow came in 1902, when Great Britain, the only remaining important export market for beet sugar, threatened to impose penalizing duties on bountied sugar in the interests of its sugar-refiners and the cane-sugar growers in its colonies. In 1902 most of the important European beet-sugar growing countries agreed in the Brussels Sugar Convention—not unwillingly in most cases—to end the unprofitable competition in export bounties by suppressing the system. A few countries, among which was for a time Russia, continued, however, to grant export bounties on beet sugar. The only other instances of open official export bounties which were in effect in recent years were in France, on cured fish, in Venezuela temporarily after 1910 on a considerable list of natural products, in Australia on combed wool and silver, and in several tropical countries on miscellaneous commodities.[1] Dumping arising from the open grant of official export bounties does not, therefore, present an important problem.

Official export bounties still survive in numerous instances, however, in concealed or indirect form, mainly through the grant of drawbacks on import duties in greater amounts than the import duties of which they are presumably a refund, or by making the right to drawback of import duties transferable from the original importer to other persons, or from the original commodities imported to other similar, or even different commodities. Such regulations were effective prior to the war in Germany, in France,

[1] Cf. Josef Grunzel, *Economic Protectionism*, pp. 200 f., and Great Britain: *Reports of H.M. Representatives Abroad on Bounties*, 1904 (Cd. 1946).

and in other European countries.¹   There appear to have been only two instances in American history of the grant of official export bounties, in˙one instance open and in the other concealed. Under an act of July 29, 1813, which appears to have remained in force until 1845, an open bounty was paid on the export of pickled fish derived from American fisheries.²   In the 1880's the drawback of the import duty on raw sugar granted to American refiners was for a time excessive and concealed so substantial a bounty as to lead to the charge that New York refiners could profitably sell their product in London at a price lower than that which they had originally paid for the raw sugar.³

CONCLUSION

Dumping has by no means been confined to staple manufactured commodities.   Raw materials, the immediate products of extractive, and especially of mining industries, have been as conspicuously subject to dumping as manufactured products, where these raw materials were produced on a large scale, and where the utilization of expensive machinery and equipment has made the maintenance of full production financially urgent. Pig iron, coal, raw sugar, crude mineral oil, lumber, all of these have been, at different times and by producers in different countries, dumped abroad on a systematic and continued scale. Nor have manufactured specialties, patented and trade-marked articles, been altogether immune from dumping.   Sewing machines, safety razors, cash registers, typewriters, watches, fountain pens, have all been sold abroad by American exporters at lower prices than at home.   Foreign consumers have not been willing to pay the prices to which American purchasers had become accustomed, or American manufacturers who could rely

¹ *Ibid.*   Cf. also, Ludwig Dan Pesl, *Das Dumping, Preis-Unterbietungen im Welthandel*, Munich, 1921, pp. 5–20.

² 53d Cong., 3d. Sess., *Sen. Misc. Doc.* 52, p. 4.

³ *United States Foreign Relations*, 1888, I, 690; Great Britain, *Commercial No. 3*, 1888, pp. 110, 125; *Commercial No. 15*, 1888, p. 156.

on the operation of the business man's code or on the individuality of their products to protect them from keen price-competition at home, have found that they could not obtain export orders unless they met the prices of competing foreign articles.

No attempt has been made here to estimate quantitatively the proportion of export sales which are made at dumping prices. For the United States estimates have run from as low as one-half per cent to as high as 20 per cent of the total exports of manufactured commodities, but there is no possible means, short of an extensive governmental investigation, for checking these estimates or even for making an approximate guess. It has been shown, however, that dumping is a practice of long standing in international trade, that it has wide prevalence in most of its possible forms, and that it presents a problem in international competition comparable in importance with the problems of standards of competition in domestic trade. Because dumping is an international matter, moreover, there becomes attached to it a factitious importance to which intrinsically it has no claim. Men are less tolerant of questionable methods of competition, or even of any methods of competition, to which they or their fellow-citizens are subjected, when the agents are foreigners. What they accept as reasonable when done to them by a fellow-citizen, or even as laudable when done by a fellow-citizen to a foreigner, they bitterly resent when done to one of themselves by a foreigner. National animosities, international jealousies, mercantilistic prejudices and ambitions, are prone to influence discussions of international competition, and serve too often to convert what began as scientific and dispassionate analysis into strident and belligerent invective. This makes it all the more important that the economic consequences of dumping, its relation to the question of unfair competition, and the available methods of controlling or suppressing its possible abuses, be carefully, calmly, and disinterestedly studied, in order that exaggerated fears may be set at rest, and that legitimate interests may be properly protected.

CHAPTER VI

THE INFLUENCE OF DUMPING ON PRICES IN THE DUMPING COUNTRY

MONOPOLIES AND DUMPING

In the course of the preceding summary of the export dumping practices prevalent in various countries, it was made apparent that dumping on other than a sporadic basis was typically, if not invariably, confined to monopolistic producers' combinations. This conforms with the theoretical expectations.[1]   First, dumping is most likely to appear to be profitable in the case of industries using large plant and expensive machinery, so that the fixed charges are an important part of the total costs of production. For such industries maintenance of output at near maximum capacity is most urgent on financial, and sometimes on technological, grounds.   It pays such industries to accept additional orders at any price which more than covers the direct costs, if these orders are not otherwise obtainable and if full production cannot be maintained without them.   But it is in industries having these characteristics that, apart from natural and legal monopolies, monopolistic organization is most likely to be attempted, mainly in order to escape the danger of destructive competition.

Once monopoly control has been achieved in the domestic market, it may pay, if domestic orders do not fully occupy the productive facilities, to bid for orders in other markets at prices lower than those exacted at home.   If cutthroat competition results from this policy, it will at least be confined to markets

[1] Cf. F. W. Taussig, *Some Aspects of the Tariff Question*, p. 208: "Sales at lower prices are made to foreigners, not only sporadically, but for long periods and systematically. This phenomenon would seem to be explicable only on [the] ground . . . . of monopoly."

in which the dumping organization is not vitally interested. The mere fact of monopoly control in the domestic market will make it probable that the prices exacted in that market will be above the competitive level in outside markets, and that foreign orders will be obtainable only if the prices quoted to prospective foreign purchasers are lower than the domestic prices. Monopoly in the domestic market would appear for another reason to be essential if continued dumping is to be profitable. If there is competition in the domestic market, the concern which dumps a portion of its output in foreign markets in order to reduce the supply and maintain or raise the prices in the domestic market must bear by itself all the sacrifice involved in the export at reduced prices and must share with all its domestic competitors the advantage accruing from the reduction in the domestic supply. Under these circumstances a concern will have as much—or nearly as much—to gain from price-cutting in the domestic market as from export dumping. It is only to a monopoly that export dumping has attractions greater than those of moderate domestic price-cutting.

It is on grounds such as these that it has been held by many economists that dumping as a systematic and continued practice must normally be confined to monopolies. A study of the practice of export dumping by European industries offers no basis for doubting the validity of this reasoning. But when attention is directed to the extensive, systematic, and continued practice of dumping by American exporters some interesting questions suggest themselves. Are we to conclude from the prevalence of dumping that a large part of the manufacturing industries which are important in the American export trade are in monopolistic control of the domestic market?[1] As far as

[1] Cf., however, the following statement of the Federal Trade Commission, which sets forth the claim that the American prohibition of combinations in restraint of trade has been an effective barrier to American dumping: "Probably the most prominent example of a country which has followed the policy of pushing its foreign trade by making export prices lower than its home prices is Germany. But

open and avowed monopoly is concerned, certainly not. But in Europe, in Japan, in practice if not in legal theory in Canada, monopolistic combinations are not harried by adverse legislation and hostile regulatory bodies, and even receive some measure of governmental sanction and encouragement. It is not necessary for them to operate under cover, and they can without fear of consequences openly adopt forms of organization, such as the kartell, which disclose their monopolistic character to the public. In the United States, however, should monopolistic combination exist concealment thereof would be highly expedient, both to forestal the intervention of government and to avoid arousing popular antagonism. It might seem, therefore, a plausible inference from the theoretical expectations that the prevalence in the United States of systematic and continued dumping on a widespread and extensive scale proves the existence of at least as widespread and extensive monopolistic control in the domestic market.

If the term monopoly is to be taken to mean 100 per cent control, there are, with the exception of natural and franchise monopolies, few if any instances in the United States. But between the "perfect competition" and the absolute 100 per cent monopoly of the classical economics, there is a wide area in which is to be found the greater part of modern manufacturing

---

Germany freely permits combinations in its home market. This facilitates the exaction of high prices in its domestic market, which is one of the principal conditions enabling such combinations to sell at very low prices in export trade. The fact that the law of this country prohibits such combinations in the home market not only safeguards against artificially maintained prices at home, but also gives substantial economic guaranties that American export prices will not, in general, be lower than American domestic prices. Where the domestic prices are kept on a competitive basis there is little margin left to enable the exporter to sell goods abroad at lower prices" (*Cooperation in American Export Trade*, Part I, pp. 377, 378). As the American prohibition of monopolistic combinations has *not* been an effective barrier against American dumping, it would follow from this reasoning that it has also failed to be an effective barrier against monopolistic combinations!

and mining industry. Although the prevalence of dumping in the export trade of the United States is not to be explained by the existence of absolute monopoly control in many industries, it is to be attributed in large part to the absence of keen price-competition in the domestic market for manufactured and other products produced under large-scale conditions. Whether this absence of keen price-competition in the domestic market is due to tacit or concealed agreements, or to interlocking directorates, or to the dominance in the respective industries of single, great concerns whose domestic price lists are accepted with or without an understanding of some sort as the standard to be adhered to by all producers in these industries, is not material to the present study. But this absence of keen price-competition operates to facilitate export dumping substantially as would complete monopoly organization. It makes it dangerous, or at least inexpedient, to attempt to stimulate sales by cutting domestic prices. Through the comparative inflexibility of domestic prices, it brings about for long periods a lack of adjustment between the volume of domestic orders and productive capacity. It confines to the export trade the opportunity for experimenting with price reductions as a means of bringing about expansion or outmaneuvering rival producers. It may even result in intensive price-competition in the export trade between American producers, so that their dumping is directed against each other rather than against foreign competitors. It is a form of industrial organization which tends to stimulate export dumping under circumstances in which it would be repressed by completely monopolistic organization, for it tends to divert to the export trade the execution of all those impulses leading to cutthroat competition, which formal or informal agreement, or the commercial mores, or the fear of dire consequences, have suppressed in the domestic market.

That monopolistic combination may lead under certain circumstances to the suppression instead of the stimulation of dumping is at first sight a surprising conclusion. But it can be supported, not only by a priori reasoning, but by citations of instances where the suppression of export dumping was both the original motive for monopolistic organization and one of the rules of the organization once established. If a given country produces all or a very substantial proportion of the world supply of a commodity, it is in the interests of its producers that there be no intensive price-competition among themselves whether in the domestic or in the export trade. One of the factors leading to the establishment of the Stahlwerksverband was the desire of eliminating competition in export markets among German producers of steel.[1]   The china manufacturers of Austria agreed, as in their mutual interests, to refrain from cutting prices in foreign markets below the domestic level.[2]   Governments have even intervened to enforce monopoly upon a domestic industry,[3] to assume monopoly control themselves,[4] or to prohibit export dumping by statute,[5] in order to prevent domestic producers who in combination could dominate the world market from cutting prices to foreigners below a profitable level through competition among themselves in the export trade.[6]

[1] *Cooperation in American Export Trade*, Part I, p. 213.

[2] *Selling Foreign Manufactures in the United States*, Part I, p. 6.

[3] The cacao association of Ecuador, which is semi-official in character, is a case in point. Cf. *Cooperation in American Export Trade*, Part I, pp. 189 f.

[4] For example, the Brazilian valorization scheme for coffee, *ibid.*, p. 190.

[5] For example, the German law of May, 1910, with regard to potash: "The German Government has enacted a law which fixes the quantities of potash sold both in export and domestic trade and forbids the sale for export at prices below those fixed for the domestic market," *ibid.*, Part I, p. 8.   Cf. also H. R. Tosdal, "The Kartell Movement in the German Potash Industry," *Quarterly Journal of Economics*, November, 1913, p. 186: "Except for very short periods export prices have been higher than domestic. *Having a monopoly of the products*, there has been no necessity for a resort to the 'dumping' which has been a practice of the steel and coal Kartells." (Italics mine.)

[6] Cf. also U.S. Dept. of Commerce, Bureau of Corporations, *Trust Laws and Unfair Competition*, 1916, p. 189, with reference to Brazilian coffee, Argentine quebracho, Chilean iodine, and Ecuadorian cacao: "The combination of the

In recent years international combinations have made their appearance, whose purpose it was, by apportioning markets or by fixing prices for common markets of member concerns, to extend the area in which monopoly prices could be exacted beyond the national boundaries of the countries in which the member concerns had their producing establishments.[1]   Such associations are combinations of combinations, and cannot be organized unless there already is monopolistic organization in the various producing regions.   Their purpose is in part to eliminate the danger of competitive dumping in markets not controlled by any one national combination.

In the United States the campaign among business men for the passage of legislation legalizing combinations in the export trade, such as was finally embodied in the Webb-Pomerene Act of April 10, 1918, was based in part on the argument that in the absence of combination among American producers they would compete with each other in foreign markets, with the result that foreigners would obtain lower prices than domestic purchasers. If export combinations were legal, they could operate to prevent such dumping abroad.[2]   It was also argued that there existed abroad combinations of buyers of American commodities, who forced the export prices of these commodities below the levels current in the United States.[3]   These arguments were accepted

---

producers of each of these commodities is the result of their attempt to take advantage of a great natural resource, largely peculiar to their own country, and through combined effort to secure the maximum return for their product in the markets of the world."   The recent developments in the rubber industry are also a case in point.

[1] Cf. William Notz, "International Private Agreements in the Form of Cartels, Syndicates and other Combinations," *Journal of Political Economy*, XXVIII, 658-79.

[2] Cf. *Official Report, First National Foreign Trade Convention,* 1914, p. 163; *Cooperation in American Export Trade,* Part I, pp. 7, 297, 373, Part II, p. 374.

[3] Cf. the evidence of John D. Ryan before the Federal Trade Commission with respect to copper: *Cooperation in American Export Trade,* Part II, p. 261.   Cf. also the pamphlet, *Report of Special Committee on Trust Legislation,* Chamber of Com-

by the Federal Trade Commission.[1] There is implicit in both of them the acknowledgment that where they apply there is operative among American manufacturers keen price-competition in the export trade which is absent, or is not present in the same degree, in the domestic market, for otherwise the price-cutting would not be confined to the export trade. The Federal Trade Commission, on the other hand, also presented as an advantage of export combinations their ability to dump abroad in order to meet the dumping of foreign producers:[2] "The ability to adjust and fix export prices would be a great advantage in dealing with underselling in foreign markets by foreigners. An American combination could afford to make lower prices and sustain losses rather than relinquish markets abroad to foreigners who were dumping there." But the conflict between these two positions is more apparent than real. Producers' combinations have been organized to facilitate export dumping and to check it, and occasionally the same organization has at different times, as circumstances changed, operated with first the one and later the other object in view.

In the discussion in this and the immediately following chapters of the economic effects of dumping it will be assumed throughout, except in the case of sporadic dumping or where the contrary is expressly indicated, that the dumping is being practiced by concerns or combinations in substantial monopoly control of their domestic markets. There is adequate reason

---

merce of the United States, Dec. 1, 1914: "In the foreign trade, however, a combination of buyers beyond the reach of control by the United States may practically dictate the prices at which American goods may be sold in foreign markets, in the absence of authority to American manufacturers and exporters to co-operate to maintain prices abroad."

[1] *Cooperation in American Export Trade*, Part I, p. 7. Cf. also Part I, p. 298: "By fixing an export price [an American export combination] could prevent the quotation by foreign buyers of one American producer against another and could eliminate harmful price competition among Americans themselves in foreign fields."

[2] *Ibid*, Part I, p. 298.

to suppose that with the exceptions noted this assumption is in close harmony with the facts.

Dumping can affect consumers in the dumping country only as it affects domestic prices. The effect of dumping on domestic prices is often summed up by critics in the formula that dumping means undercharging the foreigner in order to overcharge the home purchaser, or that dumping means selling dear at home in order to sell cheap abroad. The problem is not so simple, however, and no one formula exhausts all the possibilities. It is necessary once more to distinguish between the various types of dumping and the different circumstances under which dumping may arise.

Where the commodities which are dumped were not produced to be dumped but were produced in consequence of an over-estimate of the amount which could be disposed of in the domestic market at the established prices, the disposal of the overstock abroad at reduced prices will generally obviate the necessity of reducing the domestic price either to some or to all domestic purchasers. Of sporadic dumping of this sort, and of such dump-ing only, it can be truly said that the export at reduced prices necessarily makes domestic prices higher than they would otherwise be. But it is scarcely conceivable that such dumping should result in any serious injury to domestic consumers. At its worst it merely deprives some domestic consumers of the benefit of a "bargain sale."

Where dumping is practiced for a short period with the object of maintaining connections with a foreign market during a period of depression of prices in that market, or to facilitate the intro-duction of the dumper's product into a new market, or to elimi-nate or subdue foreign competitors or to forestal the development of competition in a foreign market, there is no apparent reason why domestic prices should be affected in any way by such practice, unless the dumped commodities would, in the absence of the dumping, have been produced for the domestic market.   If the dumped commodities are an additional output which it would not have been profitable to produce for the domestic market, domestic prices will obviously be unaffected by their export. Only if maximum output would have been reached even in the absence of dumping, and if every article exported means one article less to be sold at home, will such dumping, by lessening the domestic supply, operate to raise domestic prices.   It is unlikely, however, for such a situation to occur, for it involves the deliberate sale of a portion of the output at lower prices than were obtainable for that portion at home.   Only if the advantages anticipated from the realization of the objective of such dumping were very great is it conceivable that producers would resort to it as long as they could freely dispose of their current output at higher prices at home.[1]

Where the object of dumping is to maintain full production without reducing domestic prices below the point of maximum profit, the situation is essentially the same.   It is assumed throughout that the concern which is contemplating resort to dumping is already charging in the domestic market the price which yields the maximum profit from domestic sales, and that it will take no action which will reduce the profit yield of its total operations.   Resort to dumping will not make any change in the domestic price profitable.   The domestic price which would yield the maximum return from domestic sales in the absence of dumping will continue to be the most profitable domestic price after dumping is resorted to.   With respect to this type of dumping, probably the type of widest prevalence, there is, therefore, no ground for maintaining that it causes domestic prices to be higher.   *There is no conceivable combination of demand*

---

[1] Stated more precisely, in order that such dumping shall result in an increase in the domestic price, it is necessary that the output for domestic sale after resort to dumping shall be less than the output which would yield the maximum current profit from domestic sale by all or a substantial part of the portion dumped abroad.

*schedule and cost curve having any relation to actual conditions which
can render profitable an increase in the domestic price which was
not equally profitable before resort to dumping of this type.*[1]

If it be granted, as has been maintained above, that resort to
dumping, unless it involves the sale abroad of a portion of the
output which could have been sold at home at the current
(higher) domestic prices, does not make it profitable to make
any change in the domestic price, there is also thrown out of
court the standard defense of dumping concerns against domestic
critics of their practice, namely, that dumping, through the
increased volume or the steadier production which it brings
about, makes the domestic price lower than it would otherwise
be. If systematic dumping and keen price-competition in the
domestic market were conceivable together, resort to dumping,
to the extent that it made the operations of the dumping concerns
more profitable, would provide a wider profit margin in which
competition could operate to bring down domestic prices. But
it has been so far assumed and shown to be probable that when
systematic dumping is practiced, prices in the domestic market
are under monopolistic or quasi-monopolistic control. Given the
power to exact in the domestic market the prices which will
yield the maximum profit from domestic sales, the dumping
concerns will not find that their resort to dumping of itself makes
any change in these prices, upward or downward, profitable.

There are, however, several qualifications of a practical nature
which must be made. The resort to dumping, by increasing
profits, may make it financially *possible*, even though not *profitable*, for the dumping concern to reduce its domestic prices, and

---

[1] It is assumed, of course, that no change occurs in the basic conditions except
such change as is specifically due to the resort to dumping. There is probably no
way in which this proposition can be directly demonstrated except by resort to
subtle mathematics. The reader can test the position taken in the text, however,
by endeavoring to find a hypothetical arithmetical illustration which will demonstrate the profitability after resort to dumping of an increase in the domestic price
which was not profitable before.

thus may weaken the ability of a monopolistic concern to withstand legislative or consumers' attacks on its high domestic
prices. The higher profits resulting from the dumping may
increase the attractiveness of the industry to potential domestic
competitors, and the dumping concern may feel forced to make
a reduction in its domestic prices as an insurance premium against
the stimulation of new competition. If, with or without dumping in either case, a domestic price X yields a greater total profit
than a lower domestic price Y, but if the domestic price Y *with*
dumping yields a greater total profit than the higher domestic
price X *without* dumping, downward pressure on domestic prices
from hostile public sentiment or from a hostile legislature, or
from potential competition, is more likely to succeed in forcing
a reduction in domestic prices from X to Y if dumping is practiced
than if it is not practiced.

The consumers in the dumping country, except where
overstocks already produced are disposed of by export at reduced
prices, have, therefore, no valid ground for complaint against
export dumping. It is true that dumping prices in the export
trade are often accompanied by exorbitant prices in the domestic
market, but the export dumping in such cases is often the
effect, rarely if ever the cause, of the high domestic prices.
Producers who are in position to exact in the domestic market
prices substantially higher than those current in outside markets
must reduce their prices for the export trade if they are to receive
any export orders. The domestic consumer may have a sufficient
cause for complaint against the exorbitant domestic prices, and
the tariff policy and monopolistic control which give rise to them,
but he is not prejudicially affected by the lower export prices.
As has been shown above, if the practice of dumping increases
the profits of the dumping concern, it may even increase its
willingness to reduce its domestic prices or weaken its power of
resistance to a popular demand for such reduction.

This reasoning, it must be admitted, runs counter to the body of authoritative doctrine with respect to the effects of dumping on the consumer in the dumping country. All writers appear to be agreed that the domestic consumer is either favorably or prejudicially affected by dumping. It has been conceded above that the dumping concern may under certain circumstances lower its domestic prices in consequence of its receipt of increased profits because of its resort to dumping. But such reduction in domestic prices will be due to fear of hostile legislation or popular resentment or to forestal the development of new competition, and not because dumping will of itself make lower domestic prices profitable. The counter argument that dumping leads to higher domestic prices than would be current in its absence has been presented by a number of writers, most forcibly by Professor Taussig. He makes the point that all the advantages that are attributed to dumping are obtainable in equal measure by a reduction in the domestic prices, and he appears to imply that resort to dumping offers an alternative to the reduction in domestic prices which otherwise would be either necessary or profitable:

It is often maintained that lower prices to foreigners are in no way disadvantageous to the domestic consumers; they enable the business to be carried on continuously, keep the working force intact and employed, lessen the overhead charges per unit, and so on. The reasoning is specious, but not tenable. All these same desirable results would be attained if the reductions in price were made to favored domestic purchasers, not merely to foreigners. Yet if made to a special knot of domestic purchasers, the question would at once be asked, why not equally to all? Why not lower the price for everybody, to the extent needed in order to dispose of the whole output? Then there would also be continuous operation, steady employment of workmen, reduction of overhead charges, and so on.[1]

To the consumer, it is true, a reduction in domestic prices will bring all the indirect advantages which result from contin-

[1] F. W. Taussig, *Some Aspects of the Tariff Question*, p. 209.

uous operation, steady employment of workmen, and so forth, and it will bring in addition the direct advantage of lower prices. To the producer, also, the reduction of his domestic prices may bring the advantages of continuous employment, lower average costs of production, and so forth, which he seeks to derive from dumping. It may at the same time bring bankruptcy, and it *will* bring reduced profits, if his original domestic prices were already fixed at the point of maximum yield from domestic sales. Granted that his domestic prices have been fixed at this point, the producer will not reduce his domestic prices if dumping is prohibited, but he will reduce his output. If his domestic prices have been above this point, it is in his interest to lower them, dumping or no dumping.

There is one type of monopoly organization, however, to which this reasoning does not apply, and that is a combination of producers for export purposes but with the continuance undisturbed of free competition is so far as the domestic market is concerned. It may be profitable for the producers in a given industry by agreement to reduce their output and thus obtain higher prices in the domestic market for their product, whereas it may not be profitable for any one or more producers acting of their own accord to restrict their output or raise their prices. Under these circumstances monopolistic organization would be profitable to the industry, the main object of such organization being to secure an increase in price through a restriction of output. But it may not be feasible to secure such organization. If the producers consent to enter into an export combination, the exporting to be done at dumping prices if necessary and the deficit to be met by assessment on the members in proportion to their total output, the amount of output available for the domestic market may in this way be reduced and an increase obtained in the domestic price. In such a case the dumping will result in an increase in the domestic price, but this will be due to the fact that, in the absence of the export combination and of a complete monopoly organization, the producers had not reduced their output for domestic sale to the point of maximum profit yield to the industry as a whole.   There are undoubtedly frequent instances of the establishment of export combinations with such a purpose in view.   Many of the German kartells were essentially export combinations rather than domestic monopolistic combinations.   In the United States the whiskey pools of the 1880's and the Gold Leaf Manufacturers' Association against which the Federal Trade Commission issued a restraining order in 1918[1] were intended to make possible an increase in the domestic prices by reducing the amount of their output available for domestic sale through export dumping.   But such export combinations are a less effective means of achieving their objective than outright combination for both domestic and export trade.   Their dumping may be unprofitable as compared to a restriction of output such as could be accomplished through complete establishment of monopoly organization.   It is not surprising, therefore, that they have sometimes been merely a preliminary to such complete monopoly organization.

THE EFFECT OF DUMPING OF PRIMARY MATERIALS ON MORE ADVANCED INDUSTRIES IN THE DUMPING COUNTRY

In countries where raw and partly manufactured materials, such as coal and iron and steel, are commonly sold for export at lower prices than to domestic purchasers the more advanced industries which use these materials in further manufacture frequently protest against such dumping on the ground that it is injurious to them.   Their dissatisfaction is often rather with the high domestic prices than with the low export prices, but the low export prices may conceivably be a just cause for complaint under some conditions.   The low export prices on raw materials may give an artificial advantage to foreign competitors of the more advanced industries in trade with foreign markets, and they

[1] Cf. pp. 50, 85 n., *supra*.

may also enable foreign competitors to contest the domestic market with the more advanced domestic industries who are obliged to pay the higher domestic prices for their raw materials. There have unquestionably been instances where the dumping of raw materials has in this way inflicted injury on more advanced industries in the dumping country. In previous chapters several such instances have been mentioned. The shipbuilding industries in both Germany and the United States appear to have been retarded by the practice of the steel combinations in these countries of selling shipbuilding materials abroad at much lower prices than at home, although other retarding factors were also operative and were undoubtedly more important. An interesting situation was present in the tin plate industry, where an integrated steel trust striving for world-dominance of the tin plate industry, the United States Steel Corporation, nevertheless helped its strongest competitor to survive by providing it with raw materials at dumping prices.

Claims of injury of this sort, however, readily lend themselves to exaggeration, and they should be treated with caution. The handicap under which, according to such complaints, more advanced industries suffer in their competition with foreign producers is that their competitors obtain their raw materials at lower prices than are available to them. As has been shown, however, there is little likelihood that the high domestic prices are caused by dumping. High import duties, a domestic monopoly, or unfavorable producing conditions in the home country are with more justice to be blamed for the high domestic prices for raw materials. Unless, therefore, the dumping is responsible for the low prices abroad, the handicap of higher costs for materials is not to be attributed to the dumping. It is conceivable that the foreign prices are appreciably lower because of the dumping, but it is not probable. It is more likely that the export prices of the dumping concerns, lower though they are than their domestic prices, are not lower than the prices which are prevailing abroad and which would substantially continue to prevail even if they should cease to dump. Dumping means undercutting domestic prices on export sales, but it does not necessarily involve undercutting the prices current in the markets dumped on. The dumping concern ordinarily endeavors to obtain the highest prices possible on its export sales, and only as its attempt to gain a share of the foreign trade and its addition to the supply seeking purchasers there operate to force foreign prices downward does it contribute, by its dumping, to a widening of the already existent margin between domestic and foreign prices. Where the dumper of raw materials extends the benefit of its lower export prices to domestic purchasers of its products for use in further manufacture for export it helps instead of hindering them to overcome the handicap of higher costs of materials. In the absence of dumping the materials would cost domestic purchasers more instead of less, and their admission to the privilege of making purchases at the export price puts them on a parity with foreign competitors which they could not otherwise attain.

CHAPTER VII

THE PROFITABILITY OF DUMPING TO THE DUMPER

SPORADIC DUMPING

There is general agreement that under certain rather limited circumstances there is a clear case for the profitability of dumping to the dumping concern. When a producer, because of an over-estimate of prospective demand, is left with an overstock which he cannot immediately dispose of in the domestic market without making a substantial reduction in his prices, it may be sound policy for him to make no change in his domestic prices and to dispose of his surplus stock at reduced prices in foreign markets. The domestic demand for his product may be inelastic, and even a drastic cut in his prices may not stimulate domestic sales to a sufficient degree to absorb the surplus. Even if a moderate reduction in the domestic price will clear the surplus stock, he will incur the loss of the difference between the original and the reduced price, not only on the additional sales which result from the reduction in price, but also on the sales which could still be made without a reduction in price. Moreover, the reduction in price may not be as temporary as he would wish, and it may be difficult for him to re-establish his original price after the surplus stock has been disposed of. If the industry is competitive, his reduction in price may be met by other producers, with the consequence that the benefit to his sales will be slight and even that cutthroat competition may ensue. He may be able, however, to dispose of his surplus in a distant market, at a low price, it is true, but at a price which is not so much lower than that at which it can be disposed of in the domestic market as to more than offset the effect of a reduction in domestic price on *all* domestic sales still to be made.   Even if all his supply can be disposed of at home at a higher price than that at which the surplus can be disposed of abroad, dumping may still be profitable because it lessens the need for price-cutting in the domestic market, with all its attendant disadvantages.

SHORT-RUN DUMPING

In the case of dumping to dispose of a casual overstock, the dumped commodities were already in stock or in process, and were not deliberately produced to be dumped.   A somewhat different problem is presented by the question of the profitability of producing commodities to be dumped.   In certain types of short-run dumping, the probability that the dumping will be immediately unprofitable is fully foreseen and resort is nevertheless made to dumping in the expectation that after the objective of the dumping is realized the losses will be recouped.   If a concern finds that, owing either to unusual prosperity at home or unusual depression abroad, orders at the prices prevailing in its important export markets are not acceptable from the point of view of immediate profits, it may nevertheless decide to meet the prices of its competitors in foreign markets in order to retain its connections with these markets.   A concern may sell at dumping prices in a hitherto uncultivated market in order to develop trade connections and buyers' good-will as a preliminary to eventual trade at profitable prices.   A concern may cut its export prices in order to eliminate or subdue competition in its export markets, or to forestal the development of competition in these markets, or to retaliate against dumping in the reverse direction.   In all of these instances a temporary loss is accepted as a means to securing a long-run gain.   Whether or not such dumping will in the long run prove to have been profitable will depend in each instance on whether its objective has been successfully realized and on whether its realization was worth its cost.   The case for the profitability of such dumping is analogous to the case for the national protection of a young industry; each of these can be justified on economic grounds only by its results, which will not be predictable beforehand and not always ascertainable even after the event.

Whether dumping resorted to in order to make possible without a reduction in domestic prices the maintenance of full production can be profitable is a problem of much greater complexity and one about which there is considerable difference of opinion among economists. Assume that at the domestic price which will yield the maximum profit from domestic sales there will be sold at home either temporarily or for the duration of the existing plant facilities less than can comfortably be produced from these facilities and that at this price no export sales can be made. Is it profitable to dispose of the surplus producing capacity by selling for export at dumping prices? By hypothesis full production cannot be maintained unless either dumping is resorted to or the domestic price is reduced. By hypothesis, also, the domestic price is already at the point of maximum yield from domestic sales, and it has been argued here that no reasonably possible circumstances are conceivable under which the point of maximum yield from domestic sales will become either higher or lower solely because of resort to dumping. Unless this last contention is erroneous, it follows that under the circumstances given the problem resolves itself into the question of the relative profitability of, on the one hand, no dumping and the utilization of plant only to part capacity and, on the other hand, resort to dumping and the complete—or more nearly complete—utilization of plant.

If the domestic price which will yield the maximum return from domestic sales is substantially above the average cost of production, and if the dumping export price, although lower than the domestic price, is also above the average cost, it is clearly profitable to accept the export orders. Only one qualification of little importance need be made. If the industry is subject to increasing cost per unit as output is increased—which is highly improbable if production from already existent plant is alone under consideration—it may not be profitable to accept the export orders even at a price above the average cost of the total increased output, because of the effect such increase in output would have on average cost.   This is illustrated by the following hypothetical example.   In Case B resort to dumping is not profitable, although the dumping price, $4.50, is above the average cost of production of the increased output.   In Case C, where the rise in the average cost of production as output is increased is not so sharp, dumping is profitable.

TOTAL OUTPUT	AVERAGE COST OF PRODUCTION	PRICE		SALES		TOTAL PROFIT
		Domestic	Export	Domestic	Export	
(A) 100,000...	$4.00	$5.00	$5.00	100,000	0	$100,000
(B) 200,000...	4.30	5.00	4.50	100,000	100,000	90,000
(C) 200,000...	4.20	5.00	4.50	100,000	100,000	110,000

What is more often denied, however, is that it can ever be profitable systematically and for some time to sell for export at a price which is not only lower than the domestic price but which is also lower than the average cost of production.[1]   If production

[1] Cf. G. Armitage Smith, *The Free-Trade Movement and Its Results*, London, 1898, pp. 117, 118: "No doubt in many trades there is occasional over-production, and surplus goods, unsaleable at home, are then shipped off to find a market in other countries at any price.   But manufacturers making a large profit at home are scarcely to be credited with organizing their industries so as to secure a permanent loss by steady over-production.   The passion for underselling will not lead to a regular business of an utterly unprofitable character."   (The context shows that systematic dumping is meant by the "regular business of an utterly unprofitable character.")   Cf., also, H. W. Macrosty, *The Trust Movement in British Industry*, London, 1907, p. 342: "It has been demonstrated by abundant German experience that dumping does not pay and that it is more advantageous for a domestic trust or kartell that export trade should be so regulated as to yield the maximum of profit."   The first proposition of Macrosty is highly debatable; the second is an outright begging of the question.

is under conditions of decreasing cost as output is increased, it is
readily demonstrable that dumping at a price lower than the
average cost of production not only of the original output but
of the output as increased by the resort to dumping *may* be profitable.   An additional profit will be obtainable from export sales
at prices lower than the average cost of production if the reduction in average cost of production per unit resulting from the
increase in output multiplied by the total output before resort to
dumping is greater than the excess of the average cost of production after resort to dumping over the export price multiplied by the number of units sold at the dumping price.[1]   This is
illustrated by the following example.   In Case B dumping is

Total Output	Average Cost of Production	Price		Sales		Total Profit
		Domestic	Export	Domestic	Export	
(A) 100,000...	$4.00	$5.00	$5.00	100,000	0	$100,000
(B) 150,000...	3.50	5.00	3.00	100,000	50,000	125,000
(C) 150,000...	3.80	5.00	3.00	100,000	50,000	80,000

profitable; in Case C it is not.   In Case B the reduction in
average cost of production resulting from the increased output,
$0.50, multiplied by 100,000, the total output before resort to
dumping, or $50,000, is greater than 50,000, the number of
units sold at the dumping price, multiplied by $0.50 (the excess
of the new cost of production, $3.50, over the export price,

---

[1] For a different presentation of this formula, cf. A. C. Pigou, "Pure Theory
and the Fiscal Controversy," *Economic Journal*, XIV (March, 1904), 32: "If the
foreign sales are effected at prices, which though not monopolistic, yet yield normal
profits when a proportionate share of the cost of production is debited against them
they are an obvious advantage to the monopolist. . . . . When they are effected
at prices lower than this they are still an advantage to the monopolist if their selling
price does not fall below the average full cost of production which holds good when
they are being produced, by more than the difference between this average full
cost and that which would rule if they were not being produced, multiplied by the
ratio of the quantity sold at home to that sold abroad."

$3.00), or $25,000. In Case C the second product is greater than the first.

It is not essential for the profitability of dumping in an industry subject to decreasing cost per unit as output is increased that the domestic price in the absence of dumping should be substantially above the average cost of production. In fact, dumping may conceivably convert a net loss into a net profit. In the example used above to illustrate the possibility that dumping may be profitable, the profitability of dumping would be equally demonstrable if the most-profitable domestic price were $4.05, or $3.90, instead of $5.00, other things remaining the same.

Dumping in order to maintain full production without reducing domestic prices may continue for only a short period or it may persist throughout the life of the existing plant facilities. A concern which commonly produces both for the domestic market and for export may find that the price situation in its export markets necessitates a temporary reduction in its export prices if it is to receive any export orders. Or a concern which commonly produces only for the domestic market may encounter a temporary lull in its domestic sales but may be able to obtain export orders if it reduces its export price. These are both instances of short-run dumping, and are most likely to be prevalent only during depression periods either in the export market, or in the domestic market, or in both. Such dumping, it has been contended above, may be profitable from the point of view of immediate returns. Moreover, such dumping, to the extent that it permits of steadier and fuller operation of plant, makes possible the steadier and fuller employment of labor, and this may be a weighty consideration both on sentimental grounds and because it will facilitate the maintenance intact through depression periods of the working organization. But the value to the dumper of such dumping has occasionally been questioned on the ground either that it leads to some undesirable after-effects or that it is unlikely to attain its objectives. Professor Taussig, for instance, appears to be skeptical of the practical soundness of such dumping—which he terms sporadic—but he apparently assumes the existence of competitive conditions in the dumping industry. If short-run or intermittent dumping by monopolistic concerns is alone being considered, his discussion does not demand any modification of the conclusions here presented. Taussig cites, it is true, two instances of "shrewd business men" who "have questioned whether it is good policy"[1] but these instances, if closely examined, will be found to have little bearing on the question at issue.

A member of Lister & Co., a famous British silk manufacturing concern, raised the specific objections against "occasional sales for export at lower than home prices" that (a) it causes irregular work, and (b) it tends to spoil reputation because quality and costs are cut keenly.[2] It is not evident how dumping which is resorted to only at times when sales would in its absence fall short of full capacity can make work less regular than it would be in the absence of dumping. It would seem obvious that the reverse must be true. The second point is irrelevant to the issue. Impairment of quality and the losses resulting therefrom have no essential relationship to the question of dumping. If it is meant that the necessity of price-reduction presents an irresistible temptation to skimp on quality, the loss of reputation resulting therefrom will be less damaging if the reductions in price and the consequent impairment of quality are confined to commodities sold in a distant country which is not sought as a permanent market than if they are extended to the standard market.

The other citation is from testimony given in 1913 by Mr. Farrell, then president of the United States Steel Corporation, in the course of the government suit against that corporation. Mr. Farrell characterized dumping during a depression period

---

[1] *Some Aspects of the Tariff Question*, pp. 207, 208.

[2] *Report of the* (Chamberlain) *Tariff Commission*, London, 1904, II, Part 6, 3326.

as "an uneconomic practice, and one that does not develop continuous business." The context shows, however, that it was only because such dumping did not develop continuous business that Mr. Farrell found it objectionable.[1] Dumping in markets sought as permanent markets "spoiled" those markets. The inference is not that short-run dumping is unprofitable, but is rather that it should be confined to markets not sought as permanent markets. Moreover, Mr. Farrell's evidence, coming as it did from a representative of the foremost short-run dumper in the United States, if not in the world, should be taken *cum grano salis*.

DUMPING AND THE STABILITY OF PRODUCTION

Although there is no basis for the position that the resort to dumping during periods of depression in the home market in order to stabilize production will have the reverse effect of making production more irregular, the degree to which dumping may be used to stabilize production may easily be exaggerated. It is probably true that defenders of dumping—especially on behalf of the German kartells—have overestimated its efficacy as a

[1] *Testimony in U.S.A. v. U.S. Steel Corporation and Others*, District Court of the United States for New Jersey, 1913, pp. 3842, 3843:

Q. "Mr. Farrell, what advantage is possessed by a corporation doing a continuous foreign trade as distinguished from one that does foreign business for dumping purposes or does business in a sporadic way in foreign countries?"

A. "It is impossible to develop a foreign business unless it is done continuously. Buyers will not patronize people who are not in a position to give them a continuous source of supply. . . . ."

Q. "Will you explain what you mean by 'dumping,' Mr. Farrell?"

A. "Prior to the formation of the United States Steel Corporation some manufacturers in this country at times, during depressions here, would ship large quantities of materials to markets, principally to producing markets, such as Great Britain. The result was that prices were broken down."

Q. "What you mean by 'dumping,' then, is that sort of practice?"

A "Yes. It is an uneconomic practice, and one that does not develop a continuous business. It is a sporadic business, and was indulged in owing to the exigency of manufacture at the time."

For similar reasoning, cf. also, Eliot Jones, *The Trust Problem in the United States*, pp. 523, 524.

stabilizing device for the dumping industry.   On the other hand, critics of dumping have unduly minimized its possibilities in this direction.   Professor Marshall makes the point that in so far as the object of dumping is to maintain an even rate of production, it will be successfully realized only if the depression is localized in the dumping country, so that full production for domestic sale can be maintained only at extremely low prices, whereas export sales can be stimulated by moderate price reduction.   But Marshall claims that depressions are typically not localized, so that dumping is of little value as a stabilizing device.[1] To the extent, however that the depression is localized, or to the extent that it is more severe in the domestic market than abroad, dumping may still prove an effective stabilizing device for the dumping industry.   It is probable, moreover, that Marshall overestimates the extent to which depression tends to be world-wide, especially in so far as depressions affecting particular industries are concerned.   Even if a given depression is world-wide, it may affect different industries in different countries. Moreover, a particular industry in one country may be undergoing a period of depression when industry as a whole in that country and this particular industry in other countries are prospering.[2]   Marshall supports his argument by the claim that in Germany, where dumping was extensively practiced before the war, prices and industry were less stable than in England, where there was little dumping.   It would be at least as valid to explain the greater stability of English prices and industry by the argu-

[1] Alfred Marshall, *Industry and Trade*, London, 1919, p. 631.

[2] Cf. evidence given by Mr. Farrell, *loc. cit.*: "It seldom happens that there is a world-wide depression.   The advantage of the foreign market is that our business might be good in Australia; there might be good crops in Australia, and the wheat crop in Argentina might fail, and we would probably do little business there. Business might be good in South Africa and very bad in the Balkan States, and so it goes throughout the whole of the kaleidoscope of the world and its markets."
Q. "Has it sometimes happened that business was very much depressed in this country while good in other countries?"
A. "It has happened frequently.   It happened in 1910 and 1911, and in 1903 also, and I know in 1897."

ment that free trade tends to promote such stability, protection to destroy it, and that in a protectionist country the stabilizing influence of dumping will not be sufficient wholly to offset the counter-influence of protection. On the lines of Marshall's reasoning, why would it not be proper to argue that the greater stability of industry in Germany than in the United States, both protectionist countries, was to be explained by the more wide-spread resort to dumping in Germany than in the United States?

A noted German economist, Professor Dietzel, has conceded that dumping during depression periods exerts a certain degree of stabilizing influence, but he claims that free trade is a better means of stabilizing industry than a high protective tariff plus export dumping in times of depression.[1] This is probably sound doctrine, and was a needed rejoinder to the exaggerated claims of some of the German proponents of the price-policies of the kartells. But the real issue is not whether free trade is more effective than protection plus dumping as a means of stabilizing industry. What is in question is, given protection, or given free trade, will production be more stable with than without resort to dumping? And as Professor Pigou pointed out in reply to Dietzel, to the extent that dumping exercises a steadying influence on production, and to the extent that protection facilitates the resort to dumping, the stabilization of production is indirectly due to protection. He argues that it is conceivable in certain cases that the steadying influence of dumping, facilitated by protection, may outweigh the otherwise disturbing influence of protection.[2]

Pigou elsewhere argues, however, that it is necessary to distinguish between the effect of dumping on the stability of production in the dumping industry and its effect on industry as a whole in the dumping country. He concedes the possibility that the

---

[1] H. Dietzel, "Depression und 'Exportdusel,'" *Nation*, Berlin, 1902, No. 11, p. 12.

[2] "Professor Dietzel on Dumping and Retaliation," *Economic Journal*, XV (1905), 439 ff.

dumping industry may gain in stability of production through resort to dumping, but he claims that the dumping may unsteady the more advanced industries of the dumping country which use the products of the dumping concern as materials for further manufacture and must pay the full domestic prices for them at the same time that prices of materials are falling in the markets of their foreign competitors.[1]   But he assumes that the dumping of the materials is responsible for the disparity in their price to domestic and to foreign users.   As has been argued above, not only is it unlikely that dumping is responsible to any significant extent for this disparity in prices, but if the dumping concerns extend the benefit of their lower export prices to domestic purchasers for use in further manufacture for export, the resort to dumping will operate to remove such disparity in so far as the export trade of the more advanced industries is concerned.

PREDATORY DUMPING

It is sometimes argued that there is a strong presumption against predatory dumping being successful in its objective of eliminating competition, and that such dumping is consequently not likely to be resorted to.   In order to benefit from the elimination of domestic competition in the market dumped on, the argument runs, a world-wide monopoly must be established.   In the absence of world-wide monopoly, the dumping concern will have to share with rival concerns in its own country or in other foreign countries the benefit accruing from the destruction of the native industry in the country dumped on.[2]   There are, however, suffi-

---

[1] *Protective and Preferential Import Duties*, London, 1906, pp. 76 ff.

[2] Cf. A. C. Pigou, *ibid.*, pp. 23 ff.: "Destructive dumping into England from abroad does not take place, and for a very simple reason.   The only purpose of that policy is to secure the control of the supply, and therewith the power to exact monopoly prices. . . . . In the British market, if a German Kartel or an American Trust kills British competitors, what advantage has it?   It is still prevented from reaping its reward by the presence of sellers from other foreign countries.   It will not, therefore, be worth its while to 'dump' unless it has not merely an American or a German, but a world-embracing monopoly."

cient instances of trusts and combinations, many of them international in their membership or affiliations, that are within reach of a world-wide quasi-monopolistic control of their industry, to make the danger of predatory competition a real one even if this reasoning is unqualifiedly accepted. What is more to the point, this reasoning has only a limited degree of validity, and it would be hard to reconcile it with the well-authenticated instances where predatory dumping has been practiced in the unquestioned absence of even an approach to world-wide monopoly.

The explanation is not far to seek. Because of geographical conditions, transportation costs, tariff walls, there is often not one unified world-market for a given commodity, but a series of more or less independent markets. Competition in iron and steel products in Canada, for instance, is virtually confined to the Canadian, American, and British producers, although the steel industry of the world is by no means wholly in their hands. For western Canada, but excluding the Pacific Coast, competition is practically confined to Canadian and American concerns. All other producers are effectively excluded from the market by transportation costs and import duties. If one American concern is in monopoly control of the American market, it need only crush its Canadian competitors to obtain similar monopoly control of the western Canadian market, and it need only eliminate Canadian and British competition to win monopoly control of the entire Canadian market. In every important manufacturing industry a substantial fraction of the world output is produced by concerns who survive only under the shelter of high tariff protection in their domestic markets, and are not in a position to contest foreign markets. Of the relatively more efficient concerns in any industry, there are often comparatively few who can offer effective competition in any given market; it is the competition of such concerns alone which needs to be eliminated if a producer is intent upon gaining monopoly control of that market.

Predatory dumping, moreover, may have for its objective additional non-predatory results. And even if dumping is motivated by purely predatory objectives, it may nevertheless have a less ambitious aim than the establishment of completely monopolistic control. A producer may engage in export dumping primarily with a view to maintaining full production during a period of depression in the domestic market, but he may at the same time deliberately manage his dumping so that it will inflict as much injury as possible upon his foreign competitors. Moreover, the predatory dumper may not expect that he will succeed in wholly eliminating the competitors against whom he is dumping, but he may be content if his dumping so weakens them that they will thereafter refrain from contesting his prices or from extending their activities into his special markets.

LONG-RUN DUMPING

There has so far been considered the profitability of only such dumping as is continued during periods not long enough to permit of the reduction of existent production facilities through the withdrawal of part of the invested capital. Some writers who have conceded the possible profitability of a dumping policy if limited to such periods have denied that dumping can ever be profitable as a permanent policy, unless both the domestic and the (lower) export prices are substantially above the average cost of production of the total output. The question at issue appears to be, can it ever be profitable to add to productive facilities if the consequent increase in output must be disposed of abroad at prices not only lower than the domestic prices but lower also than the average cost of production of the increased total output?

If comparison between the average cost of production of the total output and the export price is made the sole test of the profitability of permanent dumping, it will appear that dumping under the circumstances indicated will necessarily be unprofitable. This appears to be the position taken, for instance, by Professor Taussig in the following statements:

The domestic price (higher than the export price) may or may not be a "fair" or normal price, that is, such a price as would bring the usual rate of profit, and would be maintained under competitive conditions. If it is a fair price, then the foreign price being lower, is less than fair. In the long run, the business as a whole then would prove a losing one; the domestic business just pays, the foreign business does not pay.[1]

In the long run, and as a matter of permanent policy, every part and parcel of the output should bear its due share of the total cost of bringing it to market. If in the long run it does not so bear its due share—if it is sold in such a way that the overhead or general expense is not properly debited against it—then sooner or later the rest of the output must bear *more* than its due share of the general expense. The overhead must be paid for somehow. No part of a business really pays which fails to pay its proportionate share of the expenses of conducting it. This is no less true of foreign trade than of domestic trade; no less true for the country at large than for a separate business.[2]

It has already been shown, however, in connection with the discussion of the profitability of dumping to maintain full production from existing plant, that a simple comparison between average cost of the entire output and export price does not provide an adequate basis for the determination of the profitability of dumping. If an increase in the volume of output brings a decrease in the average cost of production, what is lost in the sale of a portion of the output at less than the average cost may be more than made up by the reduction in the average cost for the remainder of the output. Instead of comparing export price with average cost of the total output, it is necessary to compare the additional cost resulting from the additional output with the increase in gross revenue which it produces.[3] No fundamental

[1] *Some Aspects of the Tariff Question*, p. 210.

[2] *Free Trade, the Tariff, and Reciprocity*, New York, 1920, p. 110.

[3] Cf. William Smart, *The Return to Protection*, London, 1904, p. 148, note: "The expression 'at or under cost' may very well be objected to. Total Cost in a producing unit includes, roughly, Fixed Charges and Running Expenses. A manufacturer, unless he is selling in agreement with others at a fixed price list extending over all markets, very seldom distributes his fixed charges proportionally; he adds to some goods, or in some markets, more of the fixed and less of the running expenses, and he may, indeed, lay the whole of the fixed charges on certain

change is made in the character of the problem where what is at issue is the profitability of enlarging the scale of production in order to dump instead of increasing production from already existent plant. In both cases the profitability of dumping is generally due to the existence of a tendency for cost per unit to decrease as output is increased. Whether this tendency is due to fuller utilization of existing plant or to an increase in the capacity of the plant, i.e., the "economies of large-scale production," is not material, except as it affects the degree of reduction in costs and therefore the profitability of additional sales at reduced prices.[1]

It will be profitable to enlarge a plant, if the added output must be sold abroad at a price lower than the average cost of production of the increased output, only if the volume of export sales multiplied by the excess of the average cost of the increased output over the export price is less than the domestic sales multiplied by the average reduction in cost resulting from the increase in output. That the domestic price, although necessarily a monopoly price if permanent dumping is to take place, is not necessarily an exorbitant price if such dumping is to be profitable, is demonstrated by the following hypothetical example. If

---

goods, or certain markets, selling in the others at what is usually called Prime Cost. So, if a manufacturer sells some goods at high prices and others at low it may be questioned if he is selling 'under cost,' so long as, in the price of his total output, he covers all his cost, fixed and running, and has his profit over." Cf. also, J. A. Hobson, *International Trade: An Application of Economic Theory*, London, 1904, chap x.

[1] It is probable that the trend of average costs is more likely to be downward as output is increased through fuller utilization up to maximum capacity of existing plant than when output is increased through enlargement of the plant. As output is increased from existing plant the trend of costs is reasonably certain to be downward until near maximum capacity is reached, and is reasonably certain to be substantially downward if the fixed charges are important. An increase in the general scale of production, on the other hand, is not so likely to bring with it the so-called "economies of large-scale production," and even if they are present, they are not so likely to bring a substantial reduction in average cost.

100,000 units are the maximum output before the plant is
enlarged, and 200,000 units are the maximum output after the
plant is enlarged, the enlargement of plant and the export of the
increase in output at a dumping price (Case B) will be more
profitable than either the continuance of the original situation
(Case A) or the enlargement of plant and the reduction of the
domestic price until the domestic sales are sufficient to provide
for the increase in output (Case C).

Total Output	Average Cost of Production			Price		Sales		Total Profit
	Indirect	Direct	Total	Domestic	Export	Domestic	Export	
(A) 100,000..	$1.00	$3.50	$4.50	$4.75	$4.75	100,000	0	$ 25,000
(B) 200,000..	0.80	2.80	3.60	4.75	3.50	100,000	100,000	105,000
(C) 200,000..	0.80	2.80	3.60	3.70	3.70	200,000	0	20,000

In the example above it is intentionally assumed that
within that part of the range of demand which is of practical
significance in the determination of price a reduction in price
would be less effective in stimulating increased sales in the
export than in the domestic trade. It has been demonstrated,
therefore, that dumping may conceivably be profitable even
though a reduction in domestic price is more effective in stimulating sales than a corresponding reduction in export prices alone.
But the greater the elasticity of domestic demand, and the
greater the reduction in export prices necessary to secure the
desired increase in export sales, the greater will be the probability
that it will prove more profitable either to leave prices unaltered
or to lower prices to all purchasers than to resort to dumping.
The extent to which dumping is likely to prove profitable is
limited, therefore, by the extent to which producers find export
sales more responsive than domestic sales to reductions in price.
But concerns having a monopoly of their domestic market but
meeting competition in their export markets are likely to find

that such is the situation for their products. Under the conditions stated, a reduction in domestic price will increase sales only as it increases the total domestic consumption of the particular commodity concerned. A reduction in the export price, on the other hand, may not affect consumption at all, since it may only serve to bring the dumper's price into line with the price already prevailing in outside markets. But the reduction in export price may nevertheless operate so as sharply to increase export sales because it may win away sales from competing concerns, where before the reduction in price nothing at all was sold. A reduction of say 10 per cent in the domestic price may, for a monopoly commodity with an inelastic demand, have no appreciable effect on the volume of domestic sales, but a reduction of the same amount in the export price may conceivably increase the export sales from zero to the maximum capacity of the plant. The greater the importance as consuming markets of the outside world as compared to the domestic market, the more likely is this to be the case.[1]

BOUNTY DUMPING

If dumping results from the grant of export bounties, whether these bounties are given by the government or by private trusts or combinations, the reduction in the export as compared to the domestic price will to that extent offset the benefit of the bounty to the exporter and will leave him in the same position as if there were no bounty. If there is active competition among the exporters who receive bounties, the normal tendency will be for the export price of the bountied article to be less than the domestic

[1] It is to be noted that what is important is not the relative degree of elasticity of the domestic and the foreign demand for the particular product concerned, but the relative amounts of increase in the domestic and the export sales of the given producer which will result from a given decrease in price, a quite different thing. Consumers' demand may be less elastic in the foreign than in the domestic market, but a given reduction in price may nevertheless bring a greater absolute increase in export than in domestic sales to a given producer.

prices by the amount of the bounty. Bounties are likely, however, for a substantial period after their introduction to stimulate exports more than they stimulate production. Where this is the case, the grant of bounties will result in a reduction in the supply of the bountied article available for the domestic market, and will cause domestic prices to be higher than they would be in the absence of the export bounty. The export price under competitive conditions will then be lower than the domestic price by the full amount of the bounty, but it will not be lower by the full amount of the bounty than the domestic price which would have prevailed in the absence of the bounty. Under these circumstances a bounty-receiving firm will gain, therefore, both from the higher prices at which its domestic sales are made and the greater receipts per unit, including the bounty, on its export sales. The production of bountied products will thus yield for a time an extra profit both on export sales and on non-bounty domestic sales, but domestic consumers of the bountied product will suffer correspondingly.

The reasoning of the preceding paragraph rested on the assumption that production was carried on under conditions of constant cost per unit as output was increased. If unit costs increased as output under the stimulus of the bounties was increased, as would be likely to be the case for extractive industries, the increase in cost of production might more than offset the increase in receipts per unit from domestic sales and from export sales after the addition of the bounty. The grant of the bounty might trap producers into a less profitable situation than if there were no bounty. If, on the other hand, as output was increased costs per unit decreased, as might often be the case in industries with production facilities hitherto utilized only to part capacity or in industries subject to the economies of large-scale production, the reduction in unit costs resulting from the increase in output might check the tendency toward higher domestic prices while still permitting the industry to profit from the export bounties through the savings in costs attributable to their influence on the volume of production.[1]

In the long run, however, the export bounty system should be expected to result in the industry being expanded up to the point at which the returns to producers, including the bounties, are again at their normal equilibrium with the returns in other,industries, so that no special gain will any longer accrue to the bountied industry from the bounties. Production will increase until either the increase in unit cost of production or the decrease in the domestic and export prices wipes out all the extra profit resulting from the bounty. It is to be remembered, however, that it was assumed that there is free competition between the producers entitled to bounties. If there is not free competition between the bounty-receiving producers, or if the grantors of the bounty place maximum limits on the amounts which are to be exported, the export prices may not fall below the domestic prices, or may fall below them by an amount less than the amount of the bounty. Where this is the situation, the exporters may be able to pocket as an extra profit all or part of the bounty. Where limits are put on the amount that may be exported subject to bounty, there may be no fall in export prices as compared to domestic prices, and the bounty system may not give rise to dumping.

But the bounties themselves do not fall from the heavens, and must be paid for. Where the bounties are granted by the government, the burden of financing them will ordinarily fall upon the general body of taxpayers. In so far as the community is concerned they will be a net loss, unless the bountied industry is operating under conditions of decreasing cost as output is

[1] This reasoning is essentially the same as that which maintains the possibility that protection to industries subject to decreasing costs may result in a fall instead of in an increase in domestic prices. Cf. T. N. Carver, *Principles of National Economy*, Boston, 1921, p. 456. Cf., however, the practical limitations of the argument pointed out by Alfred Marshall, *Principles of Economics*, 6th ed., London pp. 464, 465.

increased so that the bounty is offset or more than offset by the reduction in costs which result therefrom. Most of the authoritative writers on this and allied topics would maintain that in the case of a bounty to any industry which was general and was not confined to exports, the bounty in the long run would be a net loss to the community. Even if the industry was one subject to conditions of decreasing costs as output was increased, they would argue, there was no reason to suppose that the industry would not through individual initiative reach the stage of maximum profit without the bounty, and with the bounty the industry could profitably—for itself—advance beyond the point at which an increase in the scale of production still yielded economies. But where the bounties are confined to production for export, there appears to be a possibility that there will be a compensating return in higher profits—or lower domestic prices—for the burden of the bounty. The same reasoning applies here which was used in connection with the discussion of dumping in general. An increase in production which cannot be made with profit to the industry if all the output is to be sold in the domestic market may be profitable if the increase in output is exported at reduced prices. It may be argued here, also, that if dumping is profitable it can safely be left to individual initiative, and that government subsidizing of exports will tend to result in more dumping than is profitable. It has been pointed out, however, that the absence of competition in the domestic market is essential if dumping is to be profitable for the individual producer as a systematic practice. For highly competitive industries, the only way in which dumping can be practiced so as to be profitable for the industry as a whole is through governmental subsidy of dumping by means of export bounties. Such bounty-dumping may be profitable to the industry as a whole, even though through special taxation it is made to bear the full cost of the bounties.

But even in such cases there is a strong presumption against the economic profitability to the community of export bounties.

A monopolistic producer can adjust his export policy to meet the special circumstances of the moment, and can make the practice of dumping correspond in the volume of commodities dumped and the extent of the price-differential to the changing conditions of the market. But government bounties are inevitably arbitrary and inflexible, and therefore will only by accident result in just that volume and degree of dumping which would be economically justifiable.[1]

In the case of bounties granted to their members by producers' combinations, the situation is different in several respects. Since the burden of the bounties is borne by the industry as a whole, the bounties are merely an internal transfer of funds from one group to another. The real issue here is in the reduction of export prices which presumably results from the bounties, and we thus are back once more to the fundamental question of the profitability of dumping. Between direct dumping by a single monopolistic concern, and dumping through the grant of bounties to its members by a producers' combination, there is, however, this practical difference, that it will be difficult to give to the bounty system the flexibility, the close adjustment to varying conditions, which are feasible in the export policy of a single concern.

---

[1] Professor Taussig, it appears to me, takes a position with respect to export bounties which is properly subject to some theoretical modification, when he says that "Only if we accept the old and long discarded notion that any foreign sale whatever is profitable, can we conceive of export bounties as being advantageous to a nation" (*Free Trade, the Tariff and Reciprocity*, p. 104). Aside from the conceivable possibility that long-run dumping which would be profitable to the nation as a whole will not take place because of competitive conditions unless stimulated by an official export bounty, there is the possibility that a temporary export bounty may be economically justifiable, as a means of introducing a new commodity into foreign markets. Moreover, I would take issue with the statement that "If an export bounty is paid, you must reckon as part of the total cost of the exports not merely the labor directly applied to them, but also that which is involved in the export bounty" (*ibid.*). The bounty is not to be added to the cost of production of the exported commodities. It is merely a reimbursement to the producer of part of his cost.

CONCLUSION

There is a theoretical possibility that virtually every conceivable type of dumping may under the proper circumstances be profitable to the dumping concern, and there is good reason for conceding that circumstances favorable to the profitable practice of dumping on a systematic and continued basis are likely frequently to be present for monopolistic concerns operating in a protected domestic market under conditions of decreasing cost as output is increased, especially if the foreign demand for their products will be much more responsive than the domestic demand to reductions in price.   There is no reason to suppose, except in the case of dumping to dispose of a casual overstock, that the resort to dumping where the dumping concerns have already been charging in the domestic market the prices which yield the maximum possible return from domestic sales will result in any change, upward or downward, in the domestic prices.   For the country as a whole, therefore, the profit to the dumping concern from dumping is not offset by a resulting burden to the domestic consumer.   Nor is there to be added to this profit an additional gain to the community in the form of a reduction in domestic prices.   These conclusions, however, take no account of the equally possible circumstances (a) that monopolistic producers who are unwittingly exacting domestic prices higher than are justifiable from the point of view of maximum profit yield may be stimulated to do this by the possibility of disposing of surplus product in foreign markets, or (b) that the added profits resulting from the profitable resort to dumping may give rise to forces which will make the dumping concerns, against their wishes and against their immediate economic interests, lower their domestic prices.   Bounty dumping, whether through official or unofficial bounties, is less likely to be profitable than direct dumping, because of the difficulty of devising a system of bounties which will be flexible and elastic enough to permit of rapid and accurate adjustment to changing market conditions.

CHAPTER VIII

THE CONSEQUENCES OF DUMPING TO THE IMPORTING COUNTRY

THE INFLUENCE OF DUMPING ON PRICES IN THE IMPORTING COUNTRY

The significance of dumping to the country dumped on may likewise be considered from the divergent points of view of consumers and producers. Dumping can affect the interests of consumers in the country dumped on only as it affects the prices prevailing there. To the consumers of the dumped commodities dumping always tends to be advantageous while it lasts, because it always tends to make prices to them lower than they would otherwise be. It is to be remembered, however, that dumping does not necessarily, and probably does not usually, involve selling in the foreign market at prices lower than those prevalent there. The dumper often resorts to dumping only in order to bring his export prices down to the level prevailing in his export markets. But even where the dumper does not accept lower prices than those currently demanded by his competitors in the market dumped on, his added competition in supplying the demand of that market will tend to force down the prices of his competitors and to necessitate a still further reduction of his own prices. Where the dumping is intended to introduce a new product to the consumers of a foreign country, or to establish new trade connections, it will, however, necessarily involve the establishment for the time being of a price-level lower than would have been current in the absence of dumping. Where the dumping is predatory, or where it is the outcome of keen price-competition for the trade of a given foreign market by rival producers all of whom are in other countries, it clearly determines the level of prices which will prevail in the importing country at least for the time being, and makes it lower than would be the case in the absence of dumping.   If these types of dumping are successful in achieving their objectives, the temporary gain to the consumer in the country dumped on may in the long run be more than counterbalanced by the higher prices which their resort to dumping will eventually enable the foreign producers to exact.   Predatory dumping, it is true, will often fail to attain its objective of complete or partial monopoly control over prices; even if the original competitors are eliminated or subdued, new competitors may spring up to take their place and it may become necessary to persist in the process of selling at artificially low prices or to abandon the aim of gaining monopoly control.   It is nevertheless unquestionable that only in the case of long-continued dumping will there be a substantial and unqualified gain to the consumer in the country dumped on.

The nature of the problem makes it difficult to find clear and indisputable evidence of the profitability of dumping to the consumer in the country dumped on.   If dumping necessarily or normally involved sale at prices lower than those simultaneously prevailing in the importing country or even necessarily resulted in all sales, whether by the dumper or by other producers, being made at prices lower than those which would prevail if dumping were not practiced, the mere occurrence of dumping would be sufficient proof of gain, for the time being at least, to consumers in the market dumped on.   But the influence of dumping on prices is obscured by the ordinary practice of dumpers of selling at the prices prevailing in their export markets. In order to demonstrate under these circumstances a clear—even if only temporary—gain to the consumer, it would be necessary to show that prices in the country in which the goods were dumped were lower than they had been previous to the resort to dumping, and that this reduction in price was not due to some other factor operating at the same time.[1]

[1] This statement obviously ignores some of the possibilities.   Dumping may conceivably involve a relative, but not an absolute, reduction in prices; it may not

This would be a difficult inductive task under any circumstances and very nearly an impossible one in the absence of abundant statistical data as to general market conditions and prices before and during the resort to dumping. It is generally agreed, however, that the price of sugar in the sugar-importing countries was substantially lower, during the period in which the export-bounty system was in force in Europe, than it would have been if the bounties had not been granted or if they had not resulted in dumping. For many years, while the bounties were in effect, the price of sugar was abnormally low in England. Upon the suppression of the bounties by the Brussels Sugar Convention of 1902, the price of sugar in England rose sharply, although by less than the full amount of the terminated bounties.[1] But the difficulty of demonstrating statistically the accrual to the consumer in the importing country of a gain from dumping does not appreciably weaken the force of the a priori expectation that such gain is likely to occur and may conceivably be substantial in amount.

Where the dumped commodity is a raw material or a product in a partial stage of manufacture so that the immediate "consumers" thereof are purchasers for use in further manufacture, the gain from dumping to the consumer can generally be more objectively and convincingly demonstrated. The great development of the British sugar-using industries in the latter part of the nineteenth century was clearly due in large part at least to the abnormally low price of sugar in England consequent upon the bounty-dumping of European beet sugar and the necessity on the part of the producers of cane sugar of meeting the dumping prices of beet sugar if they were to be able to sell their product in

---

cause prices to be lower than they were previous to the resort to dumping, but it may prevent a rise in prices from taking place which would have occurred in the absence of the dumping. The principle involved is, however, the same in all of these possibilities, and it will be sufficient to work out the problem in its simplest form.

[1] Cf. U.S. Tariff Commission, *Colonial Tariff Policies*, 1922, p. 699.

their most important market. The European sugar-bounty systems stimulated the dumping not only of raw but also of refined sugar. Under the pressure on the one hand of the dumping of refined sugar and the stimulus on the other hand of the artificial cheapness of both raw and refined sugar, the British sugar-refining industry was unprosperous and declining, but the manufacture of biscuits, confectionery, jams, and pickles flourished. These last-named industries continued to prosper, although not in the previous proportions, even when the bounties were abolished; the financial strength, the commercial predominance, and the technical development which they had acquired during the continuance of the bounty régime were potent advantages in industrial competition which tended to persist even after the termination of the artificial situation of which they were a product.

The prosperity of the iron and steel industries of Rotterdam was commonly attributed to the availability of German raw materials at dumping prices. An investigator for the British Board of Trade reported in 1903 that British manufacturers using steel as their raw material had greatly profited from the availability of German and American steel at dumping prices, and at some times were able to operate successfully only because of purchases of dumped materials.[1] A curious case of this sort was that of the Welsh tin-plate industry. Driven out of the Canadian market, and perhaps out of other markets, by its inability to compete with the dumping prices at which the United States Steel Corporation exported its tin plate, the Welsh industry was able to hold other markets and to strengthen its position in its domestic market because of the availability at low prices of its important raw material, steel, which the United States Steel Corporation also produced, and which it dumped in South Wales.[2]

[1] *Memorandum on the Export Policy of Trusts*, pp. 308, 326.

[2] William Smart aptly says of this phase of the export policy of the United States Steel Corporation that "It reminds one of a besieging army smuggling ammunition and food into the beleaguered town" (*The Return to Protection*, p. 152).

The importance of the British entrepôt trade was attributed many years ago to the fact that other countries commonly dumped their products in England, with the result that consuming countries found it more advantageous to buy these products in England than in the country of origin.[1]

If there could be assured to the purchaser of dumped commodities that the dumping would be permanent, there could be, from the consumer's point of view, no valid objection to dumping, and any reduction in price which resulted from the dumping could be counted as so much clear gain.   Where the consumer is a final consumer and the commodity which is dumped is a consumers' good, the ever present danger in connection with dumping that it will suddenly cease would scarcely be sufficient of itself to make dumping objectionable from the point of view of the consumer.   He could ordinarily afford to take the chance that the low prices were merely a part of the process of establishing a situation in which he could be mulcted of abnormally high prices.   To the manufacturer the opportunity of obtaining his materials at dumping prices is a much more questionable advantage.   The possibility of a sudden cessation of dumping would not be a matter for serious concern to him, if he had not newly embarked on his enterprise or extended his investment therein under the stimulus of artificially low prices for his materials, and if he could be assured that if the dumping ceased he could return to his original source of supply under conditions not less favorable than those which would have prevailed if dumping had never taken place.   But the dumper may gain monopoly control of his product by means of his resort to dumping, and once he has established such control may exact so high a price as to more than counterbalance the temporary advantage of the cheap dumping prices.   The cessation of the dumping may render valueless the capital invested in enterprises which can be profit-

[1] Great Britain, Commission on the Depression of Trade and Industry, 1886, *Second Report, Minutes of Evidence*, Part I, p. 218.

ably operated only if materials are obtainable at dumping prices. An industry rests on an unstable foundation if its existence is dependent upon the continuance of artificially cheap prices for its raw materials.

If the interests of consumers were alone to be considered, it would nevertheless be unwise to restrain the importation of dumped commodities, and it might even reasonably be maintained that such importation should be encouraged. The refusal of a concrete and immediate gain because of the fear that its acceptance might in the indefinite future result in a greater loss would in effect constitute the payment of an excessive insurance premium to avoid incurring a minor risk. The competing producers of another importing country, less timorous as to the future, might take full advantage of the temporary cheapness of the dumped materials and might during the continuance of the dumping gain thereby a position of mastery in the world's markets from which they could not easily be displaced even if the dumping should cease. Here the history of the sugar-using industries of England again affords an apt illustration. England's sugar-using industries gained more from the artificial cheapness of dumped sugar than did the sugar-using industries of other countries because England's manufacturers, under her free-trade policy, could take fuller advantage of cheap imports than could the manufacturers of protectionist countries.

THE EFFECT OF DUMPING ON PRODUCERS IN THE IMPORTING COUNTRY

If the dumped commodity is not produced in the country dumped on and is a consumers' good, the dumping is a clear gain to the importing country, provided only that it does not eventually result in the establishment of a monopoly able to exact monopoly prices, or that it does not prevent the introduction of a new industry to which the importing country would be well adapted under normal conditions of international competition.

But if the dumped commodity competes with a domestic product of the importing country, the injury to the domestic producers is to be set against the gain to the consumers. It should not be necessary to elaborate on the proposition that a gain to the consumer is by so much a gain to the country as a whole, and that cheap imports are an advantage to the importing country provided the injury to domestic industry is not as great as the gain to the consumer. That the cheapness of the imported goods is produced by artificial means, is not a normal cheapness, does not in any way impair its benefit to the consumer except as it makes it probable that the cheapness will only be temporary. From the point of view of the importing country as a whole, there is a sound economic case against dumping only when it is reasonable to suppose that it will result in injury to domestic industry greater than the gain to consumers. Only on the crudest of protectionist reasoning can it be argued that the desirability of allowing the importation of dumped goods should be decided with reference solely to its effect on domestic producers and without taking into account its benefit to consumers.[1]

Where the dumping is certain to continue indefinitely, or at least for a very long period, the advantage of the dumping to the consumer in the importing country must be accepted as in the long run more important than the injury to the domestic producer. If the domestic industry cannot compete with the dumped imports, it will be to the national interest that it shift its capital and labor to the production of other commodities, expensive though this shifting process may be. The case against the interference with permanent dumping is fundamentally the same as the case against interfering with imports in general because these are sold at prices with which domestic producers cannot compete. That the comparative cheapness of the foreign products is due to artificial causes and not to a fundamental

[1] For an excellent statement of the advantages of permanent dumping to the country dumped on, see F. W. Taussig, *Free Trade, the Tariff and Reciprocity*, pp. 10 ff. Cf. also H. Dietzel, "Free Trade and the Labour Market," *Economic Journal*, XV (1905), 4: "In truth it is a strange sort of dread, the dread of cheapness."

difference in production costs arising out of comparative advantages in sources of supply of raw materials, technical efficiency, cheaper or more effective labor, or climatic advantages, does not affect the issue if it is reasonably certain that the artificial advantage of the foreign producer will persist indefinitely.

But the evil of dumping from the point of view of the importing country is its uncertain duration. Even if the dumping appears to be permanent the case will be rare where there will be certainty of its permanence so that producers and consumers in the importing country can adjust themselves to the indefinite continuance of the dumping prices. Only in the case of dumping resulting from the existence of a system of official export bounties which is strongly intrenched in national policy would it appear to be safe for individuals in the importing country to plan their business for the future on the assumption that the dumping will continue indefinitely and may not suddenly cease. In the case of bounty-dumping alone can an importing country accept the benefits of presumably long-run dumping without at the same time assuming an imminent risk that the dumping will transpire to have been only short-run. There is no practical means whereby an importing country can discriminate beforehand between dumping which is destined to continue indefinitely and dumping which will cease after a few months or years. In general the presumption must be that any instance of dumping will prove after the event to have been short-run, if not sporadic.

Casual or sporadic dumping, corresponding to the bargain sale in internal commerce, is relatively unimportant either in its advantages to the consumer or in its injury to the domestic producer. Such dumping may prove to be troublesome to the domestic producer in so far as his profits are concerned, but it cannot appreciably affect his volume of production or his continuance in business. The gain to the consumer from sporadic dumping, such as it is, is probably not wholly offset in the majority of cases by the injury to the domestic producer. To merchants who sell large quantities of imported goods and who make a specialty of finding bargains for their customers, the prevention of sporadic dumping may be a matter of considerable consequence.[1] The penalization or outright prohibition of the sporadic importation of goods sold at dumping prices is in any case not worth the administrative burden which it involves.

The chief menace of dumping from the point of view of the importing country arises out of intermittent or short-run dumping—dumping which is continued steadily and systematically for several months or years and then, its objective having been attained or having failed of realization, is terminated. Short-run dumping, whatever its objective, may result in serious injury to or even the total elimination of the domestic industry. The gain to the consumer from a short period of abnormally low prices may not be nearly great enough to offset the damage to the domestic industry, including the capital invested therein, the labor which it employs, and the managerial ability which directs it. The dumping will be especially likely to result in a net loss to the importing country if it serves to bring about later the establishment of abnormally high prices, either because it has facilitated the acquisition of monopoly control by the dumper or because the losses incurred by the domestic industry during the continuance of the dumping or the check to its expansion of productive facilities have lessened its ability to serve its market economically or its willingness to engage in active price-competition within its own ranks or with its foreign rivals. The disadvantages to the importing country of intermittent dumping have been well stated by William Smart in a passage which merits quotation in full:

If we knew that, for all time, some kind foreigner would send us our pig iron and steel sheets 50 per cent under our price, we should know what

[1] The Canadian department stores have been among the chief complainants against the manner of operation of the Canadian antidumping law. They claim that this law, which penalizes all types of dumping, makes it impossible for them to seek bargains or specially cheap merchandise in other countries and especially in the United States. The loss in the long run must of course be mainly to their Canadian patrons rather than to themselves (cf. U.S. Tariff Commission, *Information Concerning Dumping*, p. 30).

to expect, and no one in this country would make pig iron or sheet steel. But what we know is, that this dumped supply will be intermittent, and that it will remain cheap only so long as we continue making the same goods. Its uncertainty is its evil. When other countries are prosperous, little comes in, and our makers get a decent price; when these countries are depressed, in come the dumped goods, and wipe out the profits. I can scarcely believe that this intermittent underselling is a good thing for us. It is not a spur to invention and economy. I hesitate, indeed, to call it "unfair competition." But it is not competition that can be counted on and prepared for. No watching and economy of costs will meet it. At any moment, a manufacturer may be put on short time, because a good line is snatched from his fingers by a foreign firm which wishes to get rid of its surplus.

But as the dumping is intermittent, employers do not sacrifice their fixed capital and change their trade. They hang on, hoping that it will stop. They go on short time—which means waste of fixed capital, waste of organization, waste of labour. Similarly, workers do not change into other trades. They put up with the short time, hoping that it will be short. And short time is wasted time. Our manufacturers may deserve well of the community. They may have done all that men can do, kept profits low and prices low. It does not seem healthy that, for no fault of theirs, they should now and then be thrown idle. If there had been makers of manna among the Israelites, who had specialised and sunk their fortunes and energies in supplying their fellows with the morning bread, I think they would have had something of a grievance even against high Heaven that sent it for nothing.[1]

Complaints of injury from the importation of foreign products at dumping prices have been frequent in most of the countries which have important manufacturing industries, and especially in Great Britain, the United States, Canada, Switzerland, and Italy. There is sufficient reason to believe that in many cases there was adequate ground for complaint. The distress of the British sugar-refiners as a result of the European bounties, of the Italian and Swiss steel industries as a result of German dumping, of the American alcohol distillers as a result of the German official export bounties, are instances in point to which many others could be added. A somewhat different aspect of the problem is presented where the producers of one country are

[1] *The Return to Protection*, pp. 149–51.

injured by the dumping of another country in the markets of a third country. Such was the situation of the producers of cane sugar as the result of the dumping of beet sugar by Europe in the British and American markets. Nevertheless there has been a large element of exaggeration in the complaints of injury suffered through dumping. Domestic manufacturers are often insufficiently acquainted with the export and domestic prices of their foreign competitors to be in a position to determine with certainty whether the pressure of foreign competition is the consequence of dumping or of comparative advantages in production of the foreign producer. If they feel keenly the effects of foreign competition, manufacturers are all too prone to make sweeping charges of foreign dumping or foreign unfair methods of competition without being in a position to substantiate such charges by any evidence. They often exhibit a deplorable tendency to identify any manner of foreign competition with unfair competition. They often use alleged foreign dumping as a pretext for higher import duties where what they really seek is a greater measure of tariff protection against foreign competition in general. In many cases little would remain of the alleged injury from dumping if the complaints were sufficiently discounted for the elements of exaggeration, misrepresentation, inadequate analysis of facts, and even outright lying, which entered into them.

There occurred in England in 1903 in the course of a vigorous tariff controversy in which the supposed need of British manufacturers for protection against foreign dumping played a prominent rôle what was probably the fullest examination and discussion that has ever taken place of the effects of dumping under specific circumstances on the industries of the country dumped on. English steel manufacturers were at this time making vigorous complaints against German and American dumping, and some of them were claiming that they were suffering serious injury from this dumping. But these complaints lost most of their force when it was demonstrated that two of the most prominent complainants were the heads of steel-manufacturing concerns which had never before been as prosperous as at the very moment when they were allegedly in serious danger of being forced out of business by foreign dumping competition. Another steel manufacturer, who was concerned lest such complaints convert the British public to the policy of tariff protection, challenged the protectionists who were making use of the dumping argument to cite a single instance of an English steel concern which had been driven into liquidation by foreign dumping, and asserted that he knew of many which had been saved from serious financial difficulties by the availability at low prices of foreign dumped raw materials.[1] The valid conclusions to be drawn from this controversy apparently were to the effect that the injury to British producers of raw materials from the foreign dumping was more than offset by the gains to the producers of more highly manufactured steel products from the cheapness of their raw materials resulting from the dumping. The dumping served to hasten the process of shifting from the production of iron and steel to the production of finished commodities which had already been under way and which the changed conditions of the British steel industry demanded in any case.

This incident not only illustrates the need of exercising circumspection in considering complaints of domestic producers that they are suffering injury from foreign dumping but it emphasizes the wisdom of avoiding unqualified generalizations concerning the economic effects of dumping and of acknowledging the probability that any general rule which applies in the majority of cases may nevertheless be inapplicable in some specific instances. It has sometimes been maintained, for instance, that while in general intermittent dumping was harmful to the

[1] For this controversy, see letter of Joseph Brailsford to Joseph Chamberlain in the *Times*, London, November 30, 1903; William Smart, *The Return to Protection*, pp. 154 ff.; *Memorandum on the Export Policy of Trusts*, pp. 308 ff.; the *Spectator*, November 1, 1903.

domestic industry which must compete with the dumped commodities, an occasional spell of dumping might give needed stimulus to improvement and efficiency to the domestic industry if it had for a long time been in undisputed control of its domestic market.[1] The availability of dumped raw materials at abnormally low prices, on the other hand, might enable another industry to retain obsolete plant and inefficient methods and appliances, where the necessity of paying normal prices for its raw materials would force it to modernize its production methods.

FREE TRADE AND DUMPING

Free-trade economists have in general (there have been some notable exceptions) been more inclined than the relatively few protectionist economists to minimize the possibility both that dumping may be profitable to the dumping country and that it may be injurious to the country dumped on.   Many free traders, especially in England during the sugar-bounty controversy and the general tariff controversies of more recent years, have taken the position that restrictions on the free importation of dumped commodities are as undesirable as import restrictions of the ordinary protectionist kind.   Some supporters of antidumping legislation, on the other hand, have maintained that such legislation does no violence to the free-trade principles, since it does not interfere with the normal course of trade, but on the contrary places obstacles in the way of the departure of commerce from its normal and economically desirable channels.   The relative merits of these opposing claims depend in great degree on the particular form which it is assumed antidumping legislation must take.   But in general neither of these claims can be accepted without important reservations; both of them have a substantial degree of validity and the correct answer lies somewhere between.

[1] Cf. Great Britain, Board of Trade, *Report of the Committee on the Iron and Steel Trades after the War*, 1918 (Cd. 9071), p. 29.

The fanatic free trader, who can see no difference in principle between dumping and ordinary imports, goes farther than the fundamentals of the free-trade argument, properly interpreted, will carry him. The "orthodox" theory of international trade which the great body of economists regard as constituting under ordinary circumstances an irrefutable case for free trade has little immediate bearing on the question of dumping. It rests on long-run considerations and on assumptions which posit the indefinite continuance of existing competitive conditions, although these assumptions are often not made sufficiently explicit. There is, let it be fully and unreservedly conceded, a valid case against restrictions on cheap imports, regardless of the cause of the cheapness, even though an established domestic industry is threatened thereby, if there is reasonable ground to anticipate that the cheapness of the imported goods will be permanent or at least of long duration. There is no economic— as distinguished from military, or sentimental, or political, or sociological—argument which has as yet been presented by upholders of tariff protection which makes an adequate reply to the free-trade case against the restriction of *permanently cheap* imports.

If the cheapness of foreign commodities of a given kind is the result of superiority of productive conditions for the foreign producer, and if this superiority does not clearly arise from circumstances which are essentially temporary or artificial in character, the free-trade argument against import restrictions is fully applicable. But where there is good reason to believe that the cheapness of foreign commodities will prove to be of but temporary duration, the assumptions on which the free-trade argument rests are not in accordance with the actual situation, and the free-trade reasoning does not even establish a presumption against the desirability of interfering with the free importation of such commodities. Even the staunchest upholders of free trade, from Adam Smith on, have conceded that there is at least a theoretical case for restriction of import where there is a possibility that such restriction will permit a domestic industry to develop and to attain before long the strength to meet foreign competition on even terms. There is surely even a stronger case for the temporary protection of an established industry with a long record of successful survival of the test of foreign competition, if such industry is threatened by foreign competition of an abnormal and temporary character. But cheapness of foreign commodities resulting from their sale at dumping prices is predominantly a temporary cheapness. The fact that foreign producers' are exporting at dumping prices affords a strong presumption that these prices are temporarily and abnormally low.

Dumping, it is true, may conceivably be practiced by a given concern for an indefinitely long period; or the domestic price of a dumping concern may, under the shelter of a high protective tariff, be abnormally high and its export price, even though a dumping price, may be a normal price; there is the further problem of how to regard a dumping price which is lower than the average cost of production but which is nevertheless profitable even in the long run to the dumper. In general, however, the evidence strongly supports the conclusion that dumping is likely to be practiced only temporarily, or at least intermittently. A great deal of dumping results from the ability of producers to exact monopoly or quasi-monopoly prices in their domestic markets, but it is impossible to distinguish in particular instances between the dumping price which is an abnormally low price and the dumping price which provides a fair return on cost of production. But while the restriction without discrimination of all dumping would in numerous instances result in forcing production and commerce out of the channels which they would follow even if normal prices were always charged, the weight of evidence appears to my mind wholly to justify the conclusion that such restriction has as its net result a closer conformance of production

and trade to their normal and economically advantageous territorial distribution than would be operative in its absence. In
fact, if the free-trade doctrine be regarded as the positive doctrine
that commerce and industry should be kept in their natural
channels and not merely the negative doctrine that nothing be
done by legislatures to force them out of their natural channels,
it would not merely be invalid to cite the doctrine as opposed to
restrictions on dumping but it would be valid to argue that it calls
for such restrictions. Where the dumping is activated by
predatory motives, the suppression of such dumping is clearly and
unqualifiedly consistent with free-trade principles, just as the
suppression of unfair competition in domestic trade is wholly
reconcilable with the general argument for free and unhampered
competition in such trade.

There is a sound case, therefore, for the restriction of imports
of dumped commodities, not because such imports are cheap in
price, nor because their prices are lower than those prevailing in
their home markets, but because dumping prices are presumptive
evidence of abnormal and temporary cheapness. There is even a
stronger theoretical case for the restriction of imports sold at a
price less than their cost of production, whether or not this is
lower than their price in their home market, than for the restriction of dumped imports. The sale of goods at less than their cost
of production must necessarily be of limited duration, whereas
dumping may continue indefinitely. The greater attention
which has been given to dumping than to sales at prices below
cost of production has been due in part to a widespread assumption that the two are identical or at least that all instances of the
latter are also instances of the former, but it has also been due
to the fact that the determination of the existence of dumping is
not an insuperable administrative problem whereas the determination of foreign costs of production on a comprehensive scale
would be.

CHAPTER IX

ORDINARY PROTECTIVE TARIFFS AS SAFEGUARDS AGAINST DUMPING

ORDINARY IMPORT DUTIES AS BARRIERS AGAINST DUMPING

In the tariff controversies of the nineteenth century in this and other countries the need for tariff protection as a means of safeguarding domestic industries from dumping has been a constantly recurring argument. It was practically invariably taken for granted by both protectionists and free traders that a protective tariff, if high enough, was an effective barrier against dumping, and the only point at issue, in so far as this phase of the tariff question was concerned, was whether the danger from dumping was real enough or serious enough to warrant the adoption of a protectionist policy as a means of eliminating that 'danger. In recent years, however, some economists have questioned the effectiveness of ordinary import duties as a safeguard against dumping. This view has been most fully presented by Dietzel, a renowned German economist of the free-trade school.[1] Dietzel claims that in so far as "occasional, chance dumping" is concerned, a protective tariff, unless it is a "prohibitive" tariff, is not a defense against dumping. He makes clear that by a prohibitive tariff he means a tariff "such as those of the United States, Russia, and, to some extent, France—i.e., duties of 40, 50, 60, and more per cent *ad valorem*." Pigou, in a reply to Dietzel, goes even farther. He agrees that the exposure to

[1] H. Dietzel, "Free Trade and the Labour Market," *Economic Journal*, XV (1905), 1–3. Dietzel was not the first to take this position, unless he had presented his thesis before in some other publication, for Alfred Marshall, in a memorandum written in 1903, though not published until 1908, briefly discusses the reasoning upon which it rests ("Fiscal Policy of International Trade," Great Britain, *House of Commons Papers*, 321, p. 26).

148

sporadic dumping is the same for a protectionist as for a free-trade country if the duties are specific. But he claims that if the duties are ad valorem the protectionist country is *more* exposed than the free-trade country to the danger of dumping.[1]

These writers here take a position which is counter to the generally accepted theory, but their reasoning has seemed convincing to some later writers.[2] Upon close examination, however, their argument will be found to rest on assumptions which are either at direct variance with the facts or else have but a limited degree of applicability to probable situations. This can readily be demonstrated. The substance of Dietzel's argument is contained in the following paragraphs:

Suppose, for example, that England imposes a duty of 10 per cent on iron, then Belgium in future will produce and export less for England than hitherto; but if as a result of overproduction in Belgium there is a fall of prices in Belgium, then an extra quantity of goods will be sent to England, and, consequently, the English iron trade will be disturbed. A *moderate* system of protection affords no security that the floods due to overproduction in other countries will not wash over the tariff wall. . . . .

In the second place it is forgotten that a Free Trade country is protected against the danger of dumping by the fact that in it, under normal conditions, the prices of all home produced goods are *lower* than elsewhere. . . . .

Thus a Free Trade country is naturally protected against the danger of dumping. In Protectionist countries, it is true, the duty must be paid; but if the price of the protected goods is higher by the amount of the duty than in the Free Trade country, the danger of dumping will be exactly equal in the Protectionist and in the Free Trade country.[3]

[1] A. C. Pigou, "Professor Dietzel on Dumping and Retaliation," *Economic Journal*, XV (1905), 436 ff.

[2] Cf. T. E. G. Gregory, *Tariffs: a Study in Method*, p. 180: "Certain theoretical points here require examination. The first matter concerns the relative liability of a protectionist and a free trade country to exposure to 'dumping.' The first adequate analysis in this connection was made by Prof. Dietzel, whose position has been usefully criticised and supplemented by Prof. Pigou." Gregory, in presenting a "simplified" version of Pigou's argument, really departs from it in several important respects.

[3] *Op. cit.*, pp. 2, 3. Italics in original. Dietzel, in spite of his use of the term "dumping" is apparently considering the relative exposure of free trade and protectionist countries to the inrush of surplus goods at abnormally cheap rather than

Dietzel's denial that moderate protection is an obstacle to occasional inroads of abnormally cheap goods rests essentially on the theory that prices of a given commodity are normally higher in a protectionist country than in a free-trade country by the full amount of the duty. It may be provisionally conceded that a duty which merely equalizes the difference between the domestic cost—including the usual profit—and the full foreign price is not a protection against imports at dumping prices and that in order to secure protection against foreign dumping as well as against foreign competition at the full foreign prices a protectionist country must levy an import duty which exceeds the difference between the domestic cost and the full foreign price. If under normal competitive conditions the cost of the domestic product would be as low as the full foreign price, no protection would ordinarily be needed against foreign competition at the full foreign prices, but any import duty which was levied would serve to the full extent of the duty as a barrier to imports of foreign goods sold at dumping prices.

Suppose that England has a duty of $5 a ton on steel, and that the cost of production of steel in England is higher than the full Belgian price by the amount of the duty, e.g., that the price is $35 a ton in England and $30 in Belgium. The transportation costs between Belgium and England, small as they are, together with the $5 import duty, adequately protect England against the importation of Belgian steel at the full Belgian prices. England is not at all protected, however, against Belgian dumping,[1] but she can secure such protection to any extent she desires by raising her import duty so that it exceeds the difference between the English cost and the full Belgian price.

---

at specifically dumping prices. But this does not affect the issue. His denial that moderate protection is an obstacle to occasional inroads of abnormally cheap goods, whether the cheapness is confined to the export prices or applies also to the home prices in the exporting country, rests on reasoning which is equally valid or equally invalid in either case.

[1] See, however, p. 156, *infra*.

Suppose on the other hand that England has no import duties, that steel can be produced in both countries to sell profitably at $30 a ton, and that there are small transportation costs. England needs no tariff protection against imports of Belgian steel at the full Belgian price of $30. But suppose that the Belgians cut their export price. The imposition of a duty will, to the extent of the duty, protect the English market against Belgian dumping. If the duty is $5 a ton, the Belgians will have to cut their export price by more than $5 to sell any steel in England, whereas in the absence of a duty *any* reduction in the Belgian price would enable them to obtain English orders.

In the first case a moderate increase in an existing import duty and in the second case the enactment anew of a moderate import duty serve to the extent of the duty as barriers to dumping. Dietzel would probably reply to this criticism of his reasoning: (1) that his argument was based on the assumption that Belgium had been regularly exporting steel to England at her full prices in spite of the English duty and that the English price must, therefore, have exceeded the full Belgian price by the amount of the duty; and (2) that he had conceded that "prohibitive" duties were an effective barrier against sporadic dumping. If, however, the issue is as to the relative effectiveness of protective duties *in their normal manner of operation* and free trade, respectively, as safeguards against dumping, the first point evades the issue, and the second point is a mere quibble about terminology. If the English duty were an effective protective duty, Belgium would not have been able under ordinary conditions regularly to export steel to England at the full Belgian price. A duty operates as a protective duty only as it restricts imports, and under usual conditions and disregarding transportation costs a duty can restrict imports of commodities which are also produced at home only if it exceeds the difference between the domestic price and the foreign price. If such a duty is a prohibitive duty then, with some exceptions to be noted later, all effective protective duties are prohibitive duties whether they be high or low.

It is true, of course, that there are circumstances under which an import duty which merely equals the difference between the domestic price and the foreign price, transportation costs being negligible, provides some protection to domestic industry and at the same time permits some imports regularly to continue. .In the case of products produced under conditions of increasing cost per unit as output is increased, if the domestic demand calls for a greater output than can be produced at home at compara- atively low costs, low import duties will not altogether cut off imports but they will increase the share of the domestic consump- tion which the domestic industry can supply profitably to itself. This is clearly the way in which the American import duty on raw sugar operates.   The domestic price of sugar is higher than the foreign price by the amount of the duty, but the duty never- theless affords some protection to the domestic sugar-growing industry and enables it profitably to extend its operations. Such conditions are practically confined, however, to the products of the extractive industries, which have not figured prominently in international dumping.   Even in the case of manufactured commodities, it may be the temporary situation that the control of the domestic market is being gradually won by the domestic industry and that the existence of an import duty may hasten the extension of domestic producing capacity so as to absorb all of the domestic demand, although until this has been finally achieved foreign sales may continue to some extent and domestic prices may exceed foreign prices by the full amount of the duty. Where manufactured commodities are not absolutely identical, so that they do not compete wholly on a price-basis, an import duty may increase the extent to which the domestic commodities supply the domestic demand without altogether shutting off imports.   Where the internal costs of transportation in the domestic market are high a moderate import duty may give domestic producers complete control over part of the domestic market but may leave foreign producers in control of another part and may result in the sharing of still another part between domestic and foreign producers.   But these while not exceptional are not the most common situations, and it may be accepted that normally and in the long run identical or even substantially similar manufactured commodities are not at the same time both produced at home and imported from abroad in large quantities. As dumping is largely confined to such products, it is invalid, therefore, to assume as does Dietzel that where protective import duties are imposed prices are normally higher in the duty-levying country than in foreign countries by the full amount of the duty. In so far as revenue duties are concerned, however, Dietzel's reasoning is sound; the duties do not present any obstacle to dumping.   But there are few instances where a country would be concerned about the importation at dumping prices of articles upon which it levies import duties which operate, and are intended to operate, as revenue duties.

Pigou accepts the substance of Dietzel's argument.   He repeats in even more categorical terms Dietzel's assumption that prices in the duty-levying country are higher than elsewhere by the full amount of the duty.[1]   And he attempts to demonstrate that if the duty is ad valorem, the danger that dumping will occur is not equal but is greater for the duty-levying country than for the free-trade country:

Dietzel's proposition was to the effect that the distribution of the foreign surplus as between England and other countries would not be affected by the presence of an import duty at the ports of one of them—or, in other words, that the danger of surplus dumping is the same for a Protectionist as

[1] *Economic Journal*, XV, 437: "The price in the country with a 10 per cent. duty will be normally 10 per cent. higher than elsewhere." Cf. also, by the same author, *Protective and Preferential Import Duties*, p. 75: "A country with a surplus tries to spread that surplus over a wide area.   Since the normal price in Protectionist tends to exceed that in Free Trade countries by the amount of the duty, it has no inducement to send more to the latter than to the former group."

for a Free Trade country. This, however, is not the case, except on the hypothesis, not contemplated by Professor Dietzel, that the duty is *specific*. If the duty is *ad valorem*, the danger is not the same, but is greater for the Protectionist than for the Free Trade country. For suppose that the duty is 10 per cent, and that the foreigner in normal times exports some of the commodity in question to both countries. Then the normal price in the Protectionist country will, apart from cost of carriage, exceed that in the other by 10 per cent. Consequently, by reducing the price that he actually receives from sales in the Protectionist country by 5 per cent, the foreigner causes the amount of the tax he has to pay to fall, and so can reduce his selling price there by more than 5 per cent. In the Free Trade country, on the other hand, his selling price can only be reduced by the same amount as his receipts price. Hence, for a like sacrifice of receipts price, he can reduce selling price more in the Protectionist than in the Free Trade country, and so, other things equal, can dispose of a larger part of his surplus there.[1]

If, as appears to be the case, Pigou is comparing the percentage reductions in price which result to the importer in the duty-levying and the free-trade country respectively from a given reduction in export price, and not the absolute reductions, it can readily be demonstrated that Pigou falls into error both in his concession to Dietzel and in his modification of Dietzel's conclusions. The discussion will be confined here to the cases in which the assumption of both writers that prices will be higher in the duty-levying than in the free-trade country by the full amount of the duty holds true. Pigou also assumes that an ad valorem duty is assessed on the export price and not on the domestic price in the exporting country. This assumption will also be followed here, for the time being. The question at issue is fundamentally one of simple arithmetic: given a stated reduction in the export price, how will the percentage reductions in price which result therefrom in the importing countries after importation compare as between the country with no duty, the country with a specific duty, and the country with an ad valorem duty? It is assumed that the stimulus to sales from the reduction in export price will vary as between the countries according

[1] *Economic Journal*, XV, 439.

to the percentage reduction in the price to the importer which results from the given reduction in export price.

Suppose that the domestic price in the exporting country is $1.00, and that, of the importing countries, A has no duty, B has a specific duty of 50 cents, and C has an ad valorem duty of 50 per cent assessed on the export price. Disregarding transportation and other costs of importation, the price in A will be $1.00, in B $1.50, and in C, also $1.50. Suppose now that the export price is reduced to 80 cents. The price in A will now be 80 cents, a reduction from the previous price of 20 per cent; in B the new price will be $1.30, a reduction of $13\frac{1}{3}$ per cent; in C the new price will be $1.20, a reduction of 20 per cent. In other words, if the percentage reduction in price which results to the importer from resort to dumping by the foreign exporter is the measure of exposure to dumping, both Dietzel and Pigou were mistaken in their position that the country with the specific duty was not better safeguarded against dumping than the free-trade country, even if the price in the duty country were higher than elsewhere by the full amount of the duty; Pigou was mistaken in his claim that the free-trade country was better safeguarded against dumping than the country with an ad valorem duty assessed on the export price.

If, on the other hand, Pigou is, in spite of indications to the contrary, thinking of the absolute and not the percentage reductions in price to the importer in the different countries resulting from the exporter's resort to dumping, and if it be again assumed that prices in the duty-levying country are higher than elsewhere by the amount of the duty, there is a limited measure of soundness in his argument. Resort to dumping will result in a greater absolute reduction in price to the importer in the country levying an ad valorem duty assessed on the export price than in the free trade or specific duty[1] country. In fact, the higher the ad valorem duty the greater will be the

[1] If the specific duty is equivalent to the original ad valorem duty.

amount whereby the reduction in price to the importer in the ad valorem duty country will exceed the reduction in price in the free trade and specific duty countries. Moreover, where there is competition between domestic and imported commodities it is conceivable that the stimulus to sales of a reduction in the price of the imported commodity may depend more on the absolute than on the percentage amount of reduction.

As a matter of fact, however, few tariff laws provide for the assessment of duties on the basis of the export price of foreign commodities, especially if the export price is lower than the foreign market value. In most countries which make use of ad valorem duties they are levied in theory at least on the foreign market value, or else on an officially determined value which is more or less independent of the export price.[1] Where this is the case, ad valorem duties operate with reference to dumping precisely as do specific duties and nothing remains of Pigou's argument that the country with the ad valorem duty is less well protected against dumping than the specific duty or the free trade country even if it be assumed that it is the amount of absolute and not of percentage reduction in price to the importer which is important in measuring the stimulus to sales of the reduction. If it be assumed that the amount of percentage reduction in price to the importer is what is important, then both the specific duty country and the country levying an ad valorem duty which is not assessed on the export price are both better protected against dumping than the free-trade country even if the prices in the duty-levying countries are higher than elsewhere by the amounts of the duties.[2]

[1] Cf. T. E. G. Gregory, *Tariffs: a Study in Method*, pp. 302 ff. Pigou shows elsewhere that he is aware of this (*Protective and Preferential Import Duties*, p. 75).

[2] It is interesting to compare Alfred Marshall's treatment of the problem with that of the two writers considered in the text: "The statement that a trust or cartel can more easily sell surplus goods in England than in any other market *in which it habitually sells* seems only in part true. It may be conceded that if the tax remains fixed in amount, then a given fall in the price of the goods in bond will make a less proportionate fall in their price duty paid than it would in their price where

IMPORT DUTIES AS A CAUSE OF DUMPING

Import duties which exceed the difference between the domestic and the full foreign prices, and also (though to a much smaller extent and with the exception of ad valorem duties assessed on export prices) import duties which do not exceed this difference, make it more difficult, therefore, for dumping to take place. Such import duties may nevertheless not only fail to prevent dumping but they may be responsible for the occurrence of dumping which would not have taken place in their absence. Many dumping concerns have explained their resort to dumping as due to the import duties which foreign countries levy on their products. They have claimed that they could sell to foreign purchasers at their full home prices were it not for the import duties, but that a reduction in their export prices was necessary if they were to be able to sell in protected markets in competition with domestic producers. In some cases exporters sell at lower prices to high duty than to low duty or free-trade countries in order to overcome the tariff barriers.[1] This is not, however, a

---

there was no duty, and, therefore, might not stimulate sales so much. . . . . (This argument would of course be inverted if the practice were to lower the tax on dumped goods in proportion to the special reduction of price made for the occasion. If that practice prevailed, it would render dumping slightly easier into protected markets in which it habitually sells, than into free markets.) "—*The Fiscal Policy of International Trade*, p. 26. Italics in the original.

Marshall was careful, by repetition of and italicization of the qualifying phrase "in which it habitually sells" to avoid giving the impression that the reasoning was applicable to cases where the protective duty was high enough to prevent importation in the absence of dumping. He assumed that it was the percentage, not the absolute, reduction in price to the importer which counted. He saw that even if the duty were not high enough to stop importation in the absence of dumping it would still if it were a fixed duty be somewhat of a hindrance to dumping. But he fell into the same error as did Pigou when he claimed that the country with an ad valorem duty assessed on the export price was more exposed to dumping than the free trade country. (It appears, in fact, that Marshall led Pigou into this error. Cf. *Economic Journal*, XV, 439, n.)

[1] Cf., for example, *Selling Foreign Manufactures in the United States*, Part I, p. 63; Part III, p. 8; *Report of U.S. Industrial Commission*, XIII, 727.

belated acceptance of Dietzel's reasoning. The obstacles to dumping are greater in the protected than in the open market, but the necessity of dumping if sales are to be made is generally also greater.

An import duty is a protection against dumping to the extent, and with the qualifications which have been discussed above *only* to the extent, that the duty exceeds the difference between the domestic price and the full foreign price. But the higher the duty, the more likely it will be that the foreign producer will be obliged to resort to dumping if he is to make any sales in the protected market. Suppose that the domestic price in the United States is the same as the full foreign price, and that the United States levies a duty on imports. The higher the American duty, the greater will be the reduction in his export price which the foreigner will find it necessary to make if he is determined to obtain some orders in the United States.

In such a case the import duty may be regarded as the cause of the dumping. It does not follow, however, that the exposure of the United States to dumping increases if it imposes a duty and increases with every increase in this duty. Adhering to the hypothesis that the foreign producer cuts his export price only as the American duties force him to, he is no better off in so far as the volume of his American sales is concerned after each added cut in his export prices, and he is much worse off in so far as the profitability of his export trade is concerned. The imposition of a duty by the United States will tend, therefore, to restrict the volume of his export sales although it may increase the extent to which he resorts to dumping in order to make these sales. If the foreign producer meets the imposition of a duty in the United States by reducing his export price, and meets every increase in the American duty by a corresponding reduction in his export price, the American producer is in the same position at every stage, in so far as his ability to compete is concerned, as if there were no duty. The only advantage to him of the duty under these circumstances is that the ability of the foreign producer to reduce his export prices is not unlimited and at some point he will give up the attempt to surmount the tariff barrier.

To the extent, also, that the foreign producer meets every addition in the American duty by a corresponding reduction in his export price, the American consumer is not affected in either direction by the combination of increasing import duties and decreasing foreign export prices. The price to him remains the same. To the American Treasury, on the other hand, there is a clear gain of the entire amount of the duties collected on the dumped imports. To the extent, therefore, that import duties are countered by foreign dumping, the imposition of the duties does not alter the situation of the domestic producer and the domestic consumer, but it yields to the Treasury a revenue whose burden falls wholly on the foreign producer.

ORDINARY IMPORT DUTIES AN UNSATISFACTORY ANTIDUMPING DEVICE

Though ordinary import duties operate to check dumping and if high enough will wholly eliminate it, it does not follow that if it is sought to prevent dumping the enactment of a protective tariff or the increase of an existing tariff is the best method of attaining that objective. General import duties will operate to check importation regardless of whether or not the imported goods have been sold at dumping prices. The history of the use to which the infant industry argument has been put in tariff controversy and of the applications which have been made thereof shows that to place in the hands of a legislature the power to levy general duties on imports with the intent that this power shall be exercised only when dumping is being practiced or threatened is to invite abuse of this power. John Stuart Mill, who first gave the rising industry argument for protection prominence, was led to modify his support of the argument by the misuse of it to bring about the adoption of a general protectionist policy and by the general tendency for import duties which had ostensibly been imposed temporarily and experimentally to become as permanent as any other duties, regardless of the degree of success or of failure of the protected industry in achieving independence of tariff subsidies.[1]   The many attempts which have been made, some of them successful, to secure the permanent adoption or increase of ordinary tariff protection on the ground that it was needed as a temporary safeguard against foreign dumping likewise justify the free trader in suspecting the sincerity of the dumping argument for protection and of refusing to accept it even though he concedes its theoretical validity.[2] In any case the disadvantages and the dangers of dumping to an importing country are not serious enough to warrant the adoption of a protective tariff or the increase of an already existing tariff merely as a safeguard against dumping.[3]

If the authorization to the government to impose ordinary import duties applicable to all imports at times when dumping was taking place were the only available means of protection

[1] Cf. *Principles of Political Economy*, Book V, chap. x., §I; *Letters of John Stuart Mill*, London, 1910, pp. 27 ff., 57 ff., 154 ff.

[2] An episode in Belgian tariff history forcibly illustrates the lack of sincerity with which protectionists often use the dumping argument.   In the Belgian protectionist reaction of 1895, the Agrarians succeeded in obtaining the passage of a law imposing what was for Belgium a high duty on flour.   The ostensible object of the duty was to countervail the French indirect export bounty which resulted from the French system of transferable drawbacks of import duties on grain.   But the duty was applied to flour coming from any country and irrespective of whether or not it had received a bounty.   Moreover there had been since 1892 a law on the statute books which authorized the Belgian government to impose on any import which had received an export bounty in its country of origin a countervailing duty equal to the amount of the bounty.   In other words, the need of protection against bounty-fed imports was made the pretext for the enactment of a general protective duty, though there was already available a law which if enforced would effectively suppress the importation of bounty-fed goods.   (Cf. M.N. Cosoiu, *Die Belgische Handelspolitik der Letzten 40 Jahre*, Stuttgart, 1914, pp. 28 ff.)

[3] Cf. William Smart, *The Return to Protection*, p. 167: "If, however, Protection is the only remedy for Dumping, we may well hesitate.   A man may be suffering from a slight cold, but may object to take a medicine that will throw him into fits."

against dumping, the virtual impossibility of restricting the application of such duties to occasions when dumping was actually taking place and the necessity of applying them when invoked at all to all imports regardless of whether they were dumped or not would make it preferable to reconcile oneself to the continuance of dumping. But the development of specialized types of import duties which provide adequate safeguards against the menace of dumping without involving an extra measure of protection against normal foreign competition makes the case for such protection, other things being equal, much stronger than the case for the protection of infant industries. It is moreover a task within the administrative capacity of the ordinary government to determine with approximate accuracy whether or not in particular instances foreign competition is resting on a temporary and abnormal price basis, whereas the same cannot be said with respect to the determination of whether or not an infant industry is likely to attain a maturity sufficiently healthy and vigorous to repay the cost of artificially nurturing it through its period of infancy.

ANTIDUMPING LEGISLATION BY PROTECTIONIST COUNTRIES

The free trader can make a valid case against antidumping legislation where imports are already subject to ordinary protective duties. The latter being (normally) indefensible on free-trade principles as a restraint against foreign competition at the full foreign prices, the domestic producer should be able to withstand foreign dumping competition if he receives a substantial measure of tariff protection. This reasoning will certainly make no appeal to those who defend ordinary tariff protection on its own merits, and will appear to involve a failure to distinguish between two separate problems, the problem of normal foreign competition and the problem of foreign competition under abnormal or artificial conditions. But even if the protectionist reasoning be accepted, there is still a case against additional dumping duties if the rates of duty in the ordinary tariff were deliberately made high enough to afford domestic producers the amount of protection judged by the legislators to be sufficient to enable them to meet both normal and abnormal foreign competition. The administrative provisions of many tariff laws, and especially of the American and Canadian laws, show that the legislators fully anticipated the possibility that importers would occasionally buy foreign goods at prices lower than those current in the foreign producers' domestic markets. The legislative debates on tariffs frequently reveal that the ordinary import duties were intended to afford ample protection against foreign competition in all its forms.[1] This would not hold true, of course, of tariffs carefully arranged to "equalize foreign and domestic costs," but there have been no such tariffs, and there is no prospect that there ever will be. It would not hold true, also, of tariffs which though protective in intent were limited to moderate rates of duty. But where the ordinary tariff duties have been made sufficiently high to afford generous protection against both normal and abnormal foreign competition, it would be reasonable to demand—and overoptimistic to expect— that when additional duties are enacted, to be applied in case of dumping, the rates of duty in the general tariff shall be correspondingly reduced.

[1] Cf. *Brief of the Merchants' Association of New York*, in *Hearings on General Tariff Revision before the Committee on Ways and Means, House of Representatives*, 1921, pp. 4232, 4233.

CHAPTER X

COUNTERVAILING MEASURES AGAINST OFFICIAL EXPORT BOUNTIES

THE EXPORT-BOUNTY SYSTEM

The development of dumping on private initiative and on a systematic and substantial scale necessarily waited, as has been shown, upon the development of large-scale production under monopolistic or quasi-monopolistic control. Dumping may be systematically practiced, however, even by small-scale and highly competitive producers if official bounties, direct or indirect,[1] are granted upon export. The export bounties which had been a prominent feature of the mercantilistic systems of the seventeenth and eighteenth centuries had largely disappeared by the early part of the nineteenth century. They were succeeded after a time, however, by a new system of indirect export bounties, which, unlike those of the mercantilistic period, were not open and easily ascertainable, but were more or less concealed in complex legislation. These bounties took three main forms: (a) refunds, upon the export of commodities which had been subjected to internal excise taxation, of amounts in excess of the taxes which had actually been collected upon them; (b) refunds, upon the export of goods manufactured from imported materials upon which import duties had been imposed, of drawbacks of duty in excess of the amounts of import duties which had actually been collected upon the materials from which they were made; and (c) grants of drawbacks upon the export of

---

[1] In connection with official export bounties, the term direct is generally applied to open and acknowledged bounties and the term indirect to bounties which result from excessive refunds of excise taxes or excessive drawbacks upon import duties which had been collected on the exported commodities or the materials from which they were made.

goods made from materials of a kind subject to duty upon importation, even though the materials actually used in their manufacture or production were of domestic origin and not imported. In the case of export bounties of this last class, which were most systematically developed by France and Germany, the grant of the drawback was generally made conditional upon the presentation of a certificate of import of materials, in the case of France, identical in kind, in the case of Germany, identical or similar in kind, with those used in the manufacture or production of the exports. These certificates were transferable and had a market value, and there were various possibilities of manipulation according to the particular drawback system in effect. It was, for example, possible for a French miller to obtain a drawback upon the export of flour milled from French wheat by presenting a certificate of importation of foreign wheat which he had milled into flour for the domestic market. French exporters of flour milled from French wheat could secure certificates of importation of wheat which would entitle them to export drawbacks by purchase from other millers who had imported foreign wheat to be milled into flour for the French market. These certificates of importation of wheat were commonly sold by grain importers in the deficiency regions of France to flour exporters in the surplus regions of France. In Germany a drawback could be obtained upon the export of wheat flour milled from German wheat by presentation of a certificate of importation of foreign rye or barley!

These indirect bounties were not granted on all commodities and were important only for the flour-milling, sugar, and spirits industries of Europe. There were many minor variations of form within the three main classes outlined above, and the whole system was usually involved in such complexities and intricacies of legislation and technology that it was extremely difficult for outsiders to detect the existence and to ascertain the amount of a bounty. It was sometimes even a matter of controversy between those most immediately affected whether or not an export bounty was being paid. A given drawback provision, for instance, might operate as a subsidy measure to the export trade at some period or for some exporters but might provide for an inadequate refund of taxes actually collected at some other period or for some other exporters. In Germany a drawback of import duties on wheat was granted upon the export of flour on the basis of an official and arbitrary ratio between a given quantity of flour and the amount of wheat necessary for milling that quantity of flour, and an export bounty resulted for the millers of coarse flour, i.e., flour in whose milling a large percentage of the grain was used, but not for the millers of fine flour. The governments employing these devices were often unwilling to admit that they resulted in bounties on exports, even when to customs officials in other countries the evidence appeared conclusive. In some cases, it is true, the bounties were unintentional. In the case of sugar, especially, it was almost impossible to maintain without frequent amendments a system of drawbacks on import duties or of refunds of internal taxes upon exports which would neither impose upon government and industry intolerable administrative burdens, nor, if less strictly administered, result at least occasionally or for some producers in excessive refunds.[1] It still seems to be true that if a country wishes to maintain the drawback system, it must either guard it with such intricate and expensive regulations as to deny its privileges to all but the largest producers, or make the drawback only a moderate fraction of the original duties collected, or redraft the drawback provision at frequent

---

[1] That the bounties were sometimes unintentional is made evident by the fact that both the British and the American drawbacks on exported refined sugar were at times and for certain grades in excess of the amounts of duty collected upon the imported raw sugar, though neither of these countries had any intention of granting bounties. Cf. United States, *Foreign Relations*, 1888, p. 690, and United States Treasury Department, *Annual Report*, 1887, p. xviii; Great Britain, *Miscellaneous Papers*, No. 5, 1902, p. 33.

intervals to make adjustment to changed technological conditions, or else frankly accept the possibility that the drawbacks will in some instances embody export bounties. But however innocent may have been the motives of European governments when they established drawback systems which either immediately or later operated as subsidies to exports, as long as the importing countries did not offset them by countervailing duties many of these countries on mercantilistic grounds tolerated and even facilitated their incidental use for this purpose. In some cases the attempt at concealment was frankly abandoned.

ANTI-BOUNTY CLAUSES IN BILATERAL TREATIES

Many importing countries, however, regarded these export bounties as injurious and unfair to their domestic industries, and attempted to secure their abolition. The earliest method used was to endeavor to secure the insertion in commercial treaties of clauses pledging that no refunds or drawbacks of excise or import duties would be granted upon exported commodities in excess of the amount of such taxes as had actually been collected upon these commodities or the materials from which they were manufactured. This feature of the commercial-treaty practice of modern times has received no notice in the literature in English on commercial policy, but it has historical interest as the antecedent of present-day bounty-countervailing and antidumping legislation. Pledges not to grant export bounties were a common feature of the commercial treaties negotiated by Continental European countries in the latter half of the nineteenth century, and there have been several instances of such pledges in treaties signed after 1900.[1]

[1] I have found twenty-nine treaties containing a pledge against bounties, of which seven were signed after 1900. France, Austria, Italy, Switzerland, and Germany, in the order named, entered most frequently into treaty arrangements containing the anti-bounty pledge. Russia, Great Britain, and the United States do not appear ever to have given a pledge in a bilateral treaty not to grant export bounties. The only instances of such a pledge having been given by a non-European country were by Canada in 1910 and again in 1922 in treaties with France.

The treaty of 1862 between France and the German Zollverein appears to have been the first treaty to contain an anti-
bounty clause. In this treaty, however, the pledge was unilat-
eral, being given only by France, and it applied only to excessive
refunds of excise taxes. France pledged herself in this treaty
not to grant refunds of excise taxes upon exports in excess of the
amounts of such taxes which had been levied upon the exported
commodities or the materials from which they were manufactured.[1] In the treaty of 1865 between Austria and the
Zollverein the pledge was made reciprocal and applicable to
open or direct export bounties and to excessive drawbacks of
import duties as well as to excessive refunds of excise taxes.[2]
Later treaties containing the anti-bounty clause have generally
followed this model, although with minor variations. Some of
the clauses refer only to indirect bounties, probably because of the
rarity in modern times of direct official export bounties, which
might make it appear an excess of caution to demand pledges
against their establishment. The Austria-Servia treaty of 1881
contained the somewhat paradoxically worded provision that
"Goods which have not been subjected to an import duty shall
not receive a drawback of duty upon exportation."[3] The Italy-
Switzerland treaty of 1904 pledged each party not to grant export

---

[1] *British and Foreign State Papers*, LV, 301.

[2] L. Neumann and A. de Plason, *Recueil des Traités et Conventions conclus par
L' Autriche* (N.S.), IV (1877), 18: "Art. 5 (2). In jedem der vertragenden Staaten
sollen die bei der Ausfuhr gewisser Erzeugnisse bewilligten Ausfuhrvergütungen
nur die Zölle oder inneren Steuern ersetzen, welche von den gedachten Erzeugnissen
oder von den Stoffen, aus denen sie verfertigt worden, erhoben sind. Eine darüber
hinausgehende Ausfuhrprämie sollen sie nicht enthalten."

[3] Wilhelm Feld, "Anti-Dumping, Prämienklausel, und Ausgleichzölle," *Archiv
für Sozialwissenschaft*, XLIV, p. 474: "Für Waren, welche in den freien Verkehr
übergegangen sind, darf eine Zollrückerstattung bei der Ausfuhr nicht stattfinden."
Feld interprets this provision as a pledge against ordinary drawbacks, with the
purpose of checking abuse of the bounty clause through evasion of its provisions.
It can be more reasonably interpreted to mean that an export bounty shall not be
granted in the guise of a drawback where no import duties had been levied.

bounties in any form on any commodities without the consent
of the other party.[1]

These treaty pledges were wholly ineffective in suppressing
the practices against which they were directed. France, Germany, and Austria, countries which frequently pledged themselves not to grant export bounties, were during the life of the
treaties containing these pledges the outstanding examples of
countries granting export bounties. None of the treaties contained any provision for the enforcement by penalty duties or
otherwise of the pledge against bounties. The good faith of the
signatories, and the possibility of retaliatory action by the other
parties to the pledges upon their violation, were the sole guaranties of the execution of the pledges, and they proved inadequate.
In many cases the countries granting bounties were unwilling to
acknowledge that they were doing so, and there was no higher
authority to convict them of the practice. There is no recorded
instance, prior to the Brussels Sugar Convention of 1902, of a
country abolishing an export bounty in order to carry out its
treaty obligations, though it is possible that some countries
refrained from instituting them because of their treaty pledges.

BOUNTY-COUNTERVAILING DUTIES

The failure of the treaty pledges to bring to an end the system
of export bounties led to the enactment by many countries of
statutory provisions for the imposition of countervailing duties
on imports of commodities which had received direct or indirect
official export bounties. The first measure of this kind was the
provision in the United States Tariff Act of 1890 for the imposition on all sugar above number sixteen Dutch standard in color,
i.e., all refined sugar, of a duty of one-tenth of one cent per pound

---

[1] *Recueil International des Traités du XXe Siècle*, 1904, p. 272, Art. 8: "Cha-
cune des Parties Contractantes s'engage par contre, à ne pas accorder des primes
d'exportation, pour aucun article et sous quelque titre ou quelque forme que ce soit,
sauf consentement de l'autre Partie."

in addition to the ordinary duty, when exported from any country which paid, directly or indirectly, a higher bounty on the exportation of such sugar than on raw sugars of a lower saccharine content.[1]   In 1892 Belgium enacted the first general bounty-countervailing provision, which authorized the government to impose on any import which had received an export bounty in the country of export an additional duty equal to the amount of the bounty.[2]   In the United States Tariff Act of 1894 there was substituted for the countervailing duty on sugar in the Act of 1890 a provision for the application of an additional duty of one-tenth of one cent a pound on *all* imports of sugar from countries which granted direct or indirect bounties thereon.   It contained a clause not reproduced in later American legislation of a similar character which authorized the Secretary of the Treasury to relieve an importer from the additional duty even if the sugar came from a country granting export bounties if he produced a certificate from the government of that country affirming that no direct or indirect bounty had been paid upon that particular shipment.[3]   The United States Tariff Act of 1897 contained a broader bounty-countervailing provision, which imposed on all imports subject to ordinary duty in the United States and coming from countries which granted direct or indirect bounties upon their export, additional duties equal to the amount of the bounty as determined by the Secretary of the Treasury. This provision was retained without any alteration in the Tariff Acts of 1909 and 1913.   In the Tariff Act of 1922 the provision was extended so as to make the additional duties applicable to imports of commodities coming from a country in which an official bounty was granted on their manufacture or production and also to imports which had received unofficial production or

[1] Act of October 1, 1890, Sec. 237.

[2] Mihail N. Cosoiu, *Die Belgische Handelspolitik der letzten 40 Jahre*, Stuttgart, 1914, p. 29. See p. 160, n., *supra*.

[3] Act of August 28, 1894, Par. 182.

export bounties.[1]   The extension of the countervailing duties to
goods coming from countries in which they receive production
bounties is a reasonable one.   The significance for the importing country of production bounties and of export bounties in
the country of export is essentially the same; both types of
bounty tend to result in the artificial cheapening of foreign goods,
and thus to give them an artificial advantage in their competition
with domestic goods.

In the meantime other countries had been inserting similar
provisions in their tariff laws.   In 1899 the government of
India adopted a general bounty-countervailing provision practically identical with and modeled on the provision in the United
States Tariff Act of 1897, but with this difference, that the application of the Indian countervailing duties, instead of being
mandatory upon the customs authorities in the case of imports
of bounty-fed articles, was made subject to the discretion of the
Governor General in Council.[2]   In 1902, India adopted a further
measure, modeled after the "surtax" provision of the Brussels
Sugar Convention of 1902,[3] providing for a special duty on
imports of sugar from a country in which the duty on imported
sugar exceeded the tax on domestic sugar by more than 6 francs
per 100 kilograms for refined sugar and 5.50 francs per 100
kilograms for other sugars, the amount of the duty not to exceed
half the amount of this excess.[4]   In 1903 the British South
Africa Customs Union enacted as part of the Customs Union

---

[1] Act of July 24, 1897, Sec. 5; Act of August 5, 1909, Sec. 6; Act of October 3,
1913, Par. E, Sec. IV; Act of September 21, 1922, Sec. 303.   For the text of the
provision as it appeared in the Acts of 1897, 1909, and 1913, and as amended in
the Act of 1922, and for a further discussion of the changes made in 1922, see
pp. 268 ff., *infra*.

[2] For the text of this provision and a discussion of its operation, see Wilhelm
Kaufmann, *Welt-Zuckerindustrie und Internationales und Koloniales Recht*, Berlin,
1904, pp. 125 ff.

[3] See pp. 182 ff., *infra*.

[4] Great Britain, Board of Trade, *Colonial Import Duties*, 1906, p. 560.

Convention a provision for the imposition on sugar imported from any country not a party to the Brussels Sugar Convention of an additional duty equal to any bounty which sugar had received.[1] Switzerland in 1902 enacted a measure which gave the government authority, in case the measures adopted by foreign governments were of such a nature as to hinder Swiss commerce, and in case the operation of Swiss import duties was neutralized ("paralysé") by foreign export bounties or similar favors to foreign commodities, to take such action as seemed to it to be appropriate to the situation.[2] Servia in 1904, Spain in 1906, France and Japan in 1910, Portugal in 1921, enacted bounty-countervailing laws similar to the Belgian measure of 1892. British South Africa in 1914 and New Zealand in 1921 incorporated discretionary bounty-countervailing duties in their general antidumping laws. In both cases these countervailing duties were applicable to imports which had received in the country of exportation official bounties of any kind, whether direct or indirect, or whether on production or on export.[3] Most of these foreign provisions differed from the American provision as it appeared in the Tariff Acts of 1897, 1909, and 1913 in two respects: the additional duties were made applicable to all imports which had received official export bounties and not only to imports dutiable under the ordinary tariff; the application of the countervailing duties was made subject to the discretion of the government or of some high official instead of being, as in the American legislation, mandatory upon the customs officials.

[1] Wilhelm Kaufmann, *op. cit.*, p. 129.

[2] Swiss Tariff Act of October 10, 1902, Art. 4:

"D'une manière générale, le Conseil fédéral est autorisé, dans les cas où des mesures arrêtées par l'étranger sont de nature à entraver le commerce suisse, et dans ceux où l'effet des droits de douane suisses est paralysé par des primes d'exportation ou faveurs analogues, à prendre des dispositions qui lui paraîtront appropriées aux circonstances" (France, Ministère des Finances, *Bulletin de Statistique et de Législation Comparée*, LIII, 724).

[3] See pp. 211, 232, *infra*.

This last-named difference proved important in practice.   The American countervailing duties were frequently applied, were applied on imports from many countries, and were applied on imports of many kinds of commodities.[1]   With the exception of the Indian duties of 1899 and 1902 and the British South African duties of 1903, there does not appear to have been a single instance of the application of a non-mandatory provision.   The Indian duties under the 1899 law were applied in a number of instances to sugar which had received an export bounty in the country of exportation and there were also several instances of the application of the 1902 provision to imports of sugar from countries in which the import duties on sugar exceeded the internal tax on domestic sugar by more than the amounts specified in the law.[2]   The British South African provision of 1903, which was applicable only to imports of bounty-fed sugar, was also frequently applied.[3]   But in both cases, the special situation in the sugar industry was an important factor both in bringing about the enactment of the bounty-countervailing provisions and in stimulating their vigorous enforcement against imports of bountied sugar.   There does not appear to have been a single instance in any country of the application of a non-mandatory bounty-countervailing duty to the import of any commodity other than sugar.   It might be argued, of course, that the countervailing duties were not applied because there was no occasion for their application, and even that the existence of the duties was responsible for the rarity of export bounties. But export bounties, at least in the indirect form, still exist. The French Minister of Commerce recently declared, however,

[1] For the commodities which have been subjected to bounty-countervailing duties in the United States, and the countries from which these were imported, see U.S. Treasury Department: *Digest of Customs Decisions*, 1908–1915, pp. 376 ff., and *Compilation of Customs Laws and Digest of Decisions Thereunder 1916*, II, 1532 ff.

[2] Great Britain, Board of Trade, *Colonial Import Duties*, 1902, p. 423; 1906, p. 560.

[3] *Ibid.*, 1906, p. 560.

that in a number of instances it had been necessary only to bring to the attention of foreign governments the bounty-countervailing provision in the French Tariff Act of 1910 to secure the suspension or abolition of export bounties.[1]

The American countervailing duties were strictly, perhaps even harshly, enforced. For example, in the case of refined sugar imported from a country which did not grant export bounties but not accompanied by a certificate of origin of the raw sugar from which it was produced, a countervailing duty was imposed equal to the highest export bounty which *any* country paid.[2] A countervailing duty was imposed for a time on *all* sugar imported from Denmark, though only one grade of refined sugar actually received an export bounty from the Danish government.[3]

Court decisions in the United States have made legally possible in this country the extension of the countervailing duties to imports which had not received in the exporting country any export or other bounties in the generally accepted meaning of the word "bounty." In 1901 a New York federal court held that the remission of internal excise taxes on exports by Holland was *under the existent circumstances* a bounty on exportation, and as such made the goods subject to additional duties under the bounty-countervailing clause in the Tariff Act of 1897.[4] The United States Supreme Court in 1903, in the famous Russian sugar bounty case, held that when a country grants its exporters drawbacks of import duties or refunds of excise taxes which had actually been collected on the exported commodities or the materials from which they were manufactured, it is granting export bounties, even though these refunds do not exceed the

[1] *La Journée Industrielle*, March 31, 1923.

[2] United States Treasury Department, *Treasury Decisions*, 19108.

[3] Cf. Great Britain, *Correspondence relating to Sugar Bounties*, 1898 (C. 8780), p. 19; U.S. Department of State, *Foreign Relations*, 1895, pp. 206, 207.

[4] *Hills* v. *United States*, 99 Fed. Rep. 425; 107 Fed. Rep. 107.

amounts of tax which had actually been collected on these commodities.

The details of this elaborate procedure for the production, sale, taxation and exportation of Russian sugar are of much less importance than the two facts which appear clearly through this maze of regulations, viz.: that no sugar is permitted to be sold in Russia that does not pay an excise tax of R. 1.75 per pood, and that sugar exported pays no tax at all. . . . . When a tax is imposed upon all sugar produced, but is remitted upon all sugar exported, then, by whatever process, or in whatever manner, or under whatever name it is disguised, it is a bounty upon exportation.[1]

In 1919, in *Nicholas & Co.* v. *United States*, the Supreme Court held not only that a special British allowance to exporters of spirits to compensate them for the greater cost of manufacture resulting from the excise regulations constituted a bounty, but that the British remission of the excise tax on exported spirits was a bounty even if no additional allowance was made.[2]

These decisions are clearly inconsistent with the general body of economic doctrine on these matters and with the universal practice of customs authorities where the application of countervailing duties is in question. Congress has shown time and again that it does not regard the American drawbacks on exports or remissions of excise on exports as bounties, and the specific provision in the antidumping section of the Emergency Tariff Act of 1921 which makes allowance for foreign drawbacks and remissions or refunds of excise taxes is further evidence that Congress does not regard imports as bounty-fed if they receive in the exporting country merely a refund or remission of domestic commodity taxes.[3]   The court based its decisions in the main on the reasoning in previous decisions whereby American courts had uniformly held that the special remission from excise taxation of one producer or his product was a bounty (or "grant"). Fundamentally, however, the two situations are quite dissimilar. If one do-

---

[1] *Downs* v. *United States*, 187 U.S. 515. For an even more emphatic declaration that drawbacks and refunds of excises are bounties, cf. 187 U.S. 502.

[2] 249 U.S. 34.   [3] See p. 261, *infra*.

mestic producer for the domestic market receives an exemption for his product from taxes to which the products of all his domestic competitors are subject, he is clearly receiving a bounty. The remission of taxation in his case gives him a special and artificial advantage in his competition with other producers. But if a commodity is subjected to excise taxation in a foreign country and the tax is remitted upon the export of such commodity, the exporter receives no special favor or advantage either in his domestic or in his export trade. His production for sale in the domestic market is subject to excise taxation alike with the products of all his competitors. His production for export receives no special advantage, in its competition with the export products of other domestic producers or with the products of producers in other countries, from the remission of the excise tax. The sole significance of the remission of domestic taxation upon exported commodities is that the exporter is thereby freed from a special artificial handicap in his competition in foreign markets with foreign producers, and is by so much placed in a position of equality with them.

In *Downs* v. *United States*, the court cited as support for its position the provision in the Brussels Sugar Convention for the penalization of bounty-fed imports. But there is no confirmation in the Convention itself or in the manner of its execution for the court's definition of a bounty. The Convention treated as bounties, in so far as the present issue is concerned, only refunds of taxes in excess of the amount of tax actually collected. In the case of drawbacks the Convention specifically states that drawbacks are of concern to it only when they are "exaggerated."[1] Moreover, the Brussels Convention is a poor authority as to the proper definition of the word "bounty," since it includes as bounties import duties in excess of internal taxes by more than a very moderate amount, a definition which virtually identifies protective duties with export bounties.

[1] Brussels Sugar Convention, 1902, Art. I (*e*).

If the bounty-countervailing provisions in American tariff legislation were administered by the Treasury in strict accordance with these decisions of the Supreme Court, these provisions would acquire a much greater significance than they now have. With the wide prevalence in foreign tariffs of import duties on raw materials for which drawbacks are later given upon the re-export of the materials in a more advanced stage of manufacture and with the great extension in foreign countries since 1914 of internal taxes on commodities which are refunded or remitted on exports, a considerable fraction of American imports would be subjected, in addition to the sufficiently high ordinary duties, to the additional duties provided for under the countervailing clause. As a matter of fact, the Treasury did not seek in either of the cases which reached the Supreme Court as wide a field of application for the countervailing duties as was given to them by the court. In each case the question whether bounties were being granted by the exporting countries was subject to reasonable doubt because of unusual circumstances surrounding the case. In the Russian bounty case, the elaborate and complicated Russian system made recourse to the courts necessary in order to find out, not whether the remission on exports of internal taxes was a bounty, but whether the Russian treatment of export sugar went beyond the mere remission of internal taxes. In the British spirits case, the question raised was not whether the British remission of the excise on export spirits was a bounty, but whether the additional British allowance to compensate manufacturers for export for the greater costs of manufacture resulting from the excise regulations was a bounty. In both cases the Supreme Court not only answered these questions in the affirmative, but went farther and held that even if the answers had been in the negative, Russian sugar and British spirits would be subject to the countervailing duties because of the remission on exports in both these countries of the internal taxes. In each case the Treasury followed as much of the court decision as authorized it to apply countervailing duties equal in amount to the amount whereby the mere remission of excise taxes of exports was exceeded by the foreign country, and disregarded the remainder of the decision.[1] The Treasury has never attempted to apply the countervailing duties to imports which had received in the exporting country a remission or refund of taxes not in excess of the amount of tax which had actually been levied upon them and which had not received any additional favor constituting a bounty. The Treasury derives its legal authority to disregard those portions of the Supreme Court decisions which depart from its own and the generally accepted definition of a bounty from the wording of the countervailing provision in the tariff law, which states that "The net amount of all such bounties or grants shall be from time to time ascertained, determined, and declared by the Secretary of the Treasury, who shall make all needful regulations for the identification of such articles and merchandise and for the assessment and collection of such additional duties." But until Congress provides to the contrary, it will be possible for any Secretary of the Treasury with protectionist leanings to make of the countervailing provision an instrument for the establishment of a substantial measure of additional protection applying to a wide range of commodities coming from many countries. It is highly desirable, therefore, that Congress should guard against this possibility by amending the bounty-countervailing provision so as to exempt from the additional

[1] Cf. *Treasury Decisions*, 31659, 33182, etc., and *Decisions of Board of General Appraisers*, 3577. Even the *Treasury Decision* issued to guide customs officials in the application of the finding in *Downs v. United States* did not wholly follow the court decision. Instead of advising the officials that any remission or refund of an excise tax was to be treated as a bounty, it instructed them to treat the Russian remissions of excise taxes as export bounties *if* they were accompanied by the grant to exporters of certificates of exportation carrying with them the privilege of further exemption from taxation, which certificates were transferable and had a market value, i.e., only if the exporters received both a refund or remission of excise taxes and something in addition having cash value (*Treasury Decisions*, 24355).

duties imports which had received in the exporting country remissions of internal taxes not in excess of the amount of taxes actually levied thereon.

THE BRUSSELS SUGAR CONVENTION

By far the most important phase of the export bounty problem in modern times was the ruinous competition of the important European sugar-growing countries which took the form of high subsidies for their sugar-raising and sugar-refining industries through production and export bounties, direct and indirect, concealed and open and avowed. The stimulative effect on the industries which might have been expected to result from the bounties was largely offset by the generality of the bounties in the beet-sugar raising countries,[1] and by the necessity in some countries of meeting the heavy drain of the bounties on the national treasuries by heavy consumption taxes on sugar which greatly checked the domestic consumption thereof. It was quite generally perceived early in the history of the sugar bounties that their general suppression would be in the common interest of the sugar-raising countries, but no one country was willing to take the initiative and thus to leave its own industry seriously handicapped in its competition both in the domestic and in the export markets with the subsidized sugar of those countries which did not follow its example in suppressing the bounties. There had developed under the bounty system powerful vested interests which exerted all their influence to assure the continuance of the bounties. Joint action by all the important sugar-producing countries was essential if the bounty system was to be abolished, and the exertion of pressure from outside the bounty-granting countries themselves was necessary if joint action was to be secured.

[1] Even the United States succumbed to the bounty craze, and from 1890 to 1894 granted a bounty on the production of sugar.

External pressure could come only from the sugar-importing countries which were the important markets for the surplus supplies of bountied sugar. By far the most important of the sugar-importing countries, so far as the beet-sugar producing countries of the Continent were concerned, was Great Britain, and it was by this country, motivated by the desire to reduce her sugar duties but reluctant to leave her important refining indus- try subject to the subsidized competition of European sugar, that the first move toward the suppression of the bounties was taken.[1] In 1864 Great Britain, France, Holland and Belgium entered into a Sugar Convention, negotiated upon the initiative of Great Britain, whereby each of the parties to the agreement agreed to base their drawbacks of import duty and refunds of excises on the normal yields of refined from raw sugar as deter- mined experimentally on behalf of the Convention and thus to eliminate bounties through excessive drawbacks or refunds of excises. Each of the members of the Convention was to be free to apply surtaxes to refined sugar imported from countries granting bounties on its export.[2] This Convention remained in effect until 1875, but technical difficulties in the determination of the normal yield of refined from raw sugar and the failure of France to carry out her part of the agreement made it inoper- ative.[3] Repeated conferences failed to produce a solution. In the early eighties there began to be seriously considered in Great

[1] The question of the sugar bounties has been exhaustively investigated and the bibliography is voluminous. A condensed account will, therefore, adequately serve the present purpose. The best and most comprehensive history of the sugar-bounty question prior to 1903 is in Wilhelm Kaufmann, *Welt-Zuckerindustrie und Internationales und Koloniales Recht*, which also contains an extensive bibli- ography.

[2] Sir Edward Hertslet (editor), *Commercial Treaties. Treaties and Conventions between Great Britain and Foreign Powers*, XII, 199.

[3] C. J. Fuchs, *The Trade Policy of Great Britain and Her Colonies since 1860*, London, 1905 (translated from the German edition of 1893), p. 95. The commis- sion established by the Convention to determine the exact scale of equivalents

Britain the desirability of imposing countervailing duties on imports of bountied sugar, and in 1887 the British Government threatened to establish such duties unless the bounties were suppressed. The threat, however, was not carried out, largely because of the opposition of British free traders to countervailing duties.[1]

There continued to be held at irregular intervals international conferences with a view to reaching a satisfactory solution, but they all failed of result. The establishment of countervailing duties by the United States in 1890 and by India in 1899, the indication in 1899 by the British House of Commons, in its refusal to disallow the Indian countervailing duty, that it would not raise objections to British penalizing measures on the ground of their supposed conflict with free-trade principles, and the increasing drain of the bounties on the finances of the bounty-granting countries, were all factors, however, which were operating to overcome the opposition to the suppression of the bounties. Great Britain, the United States, and the British Dominions and Colonies were the important export markets for bountied sugar. If special restrictions were imposed in these countries on the importation of bountied sugar the advantage given by the bounties to the beet-sugar industries of Europe over the non-bountied cane sugar of the tropics would be largely or wholly destroyed in so far as the export trade was concerned. In some of the bounty-granting countries heavy consumption taxes on sugar levied to help finance the export bounties largely offset the stimulus to production resulting from the latter. With the wide prevalence of export bounties in the sugar-producing

---

between refined sugar and the various grades of raw sugar used average data in establishing the scale, with results which were unsatisfactory to French and other refiners who commonly used special, and not average, grades of raw sugar. (Cf. J. L. Laughlin and H. P. Willis, *Reciprocity*, New York, 1903, p. 170.)

[1] For the attitude toward countervailing duties taken by British free traders, see C. J. Fuchs, *op. cit.*, chap. ii.

countries the bounties were losing their effectiveness even as a stimulus to exports. With the growing insistence of Great Britain, now acting less in the interest of her declining sugar-refining industry than of the cane-sugar producers in her colonies, that the bounties should be suppressed, it finally became possible to secure the adherence of most of the important beet-sugar producing countries to an international agreement providing for the suppression of bounties in countries entering the agreement and for the penalization of bounty-fed imports from other countries. In 1902 Great Britain and all the important beet-sugar producing countries except Russia signed the Brussels Sugar Convention whereby they agreed to abolish the bounty-system within their own territories and to penalize or prohibit the importation of bounty-fed sugar from other countries. Russia refused to enter the Convention on the pretext that it was too limited in its scope and that she would be willing to co-operate in international action to suppress unfair methods of competition in international trade if such action was devised to cover the whole range of the problem, including the export policies of trusts and any other method of artificially lowering prices in world markets.[1]

The signatories to the Convention agreed therein not to grant direct or indirect bounties on production or export; in the case of sugar-producing countries, to limit the "surtax," i.e., the difference between the rate of taxation on foreign and on domestic sugar, to a maximum of 6 francs per 100 kilograms on refined sugar and 5.50 francs on other sugar; to impose special duties on import of sugar from countries which granted bounties either on production or on export, these special duties not to be less than the amount of the bounty and to be replaceable at the discretion of the signatory countries by absolute prohibitions of im-

[1] The text of the Russian memorandum explaining her refusal to enter the Convention is given in Great Britain, *Commercial No. 1*, 1903, p. 6. Russia adhered to the Convention, with reservations, in 1907.

port of bountied sugar. In determining the amounts of bounty half of the amount by which the "surtax,' or the excess of the tax on foreign over domestic sugar, exceeded 6 francs per 100 kilograms on refined sugar and 5.50 francs on other sugars was to be considered a bounty. The Convention provided for the establishment of a permanent commission to exercise surveillance over the execution of its provisions, to determine the existence and the amount of bounties, and to issue advice on litigious questions. The decisions of the commission with respect to the existence and the amount of bounties were made binding on the members of the Convention. Each of the members of the Convention was given a representation of one in the Commission, and its decisions were to be established by majority vote.[1]

The extension of the prohibition of bounties to production as well as to export bounties was a logical step to take, as it is a matter of equal concern to an importing country, if its industries are injured by artificially cheap imports, whether the cheapness is due to export or to production bounties. In fact, a bounty of a given amount per unit is likely to operate as a greater stimulus to production and is therefore likely to bring about a greater reduction in the export price if it is not confined to exports but is granted to all units produced. The provisions limiting the amount of "surtax" which any of the participating countries could maintain and requiring half of the surtax in excess of these amounts to be treated as if they were bounties were intended as restraints on dumping of sugar by monopolistic combinations, and were based on the theory that high tariff protection in the domestic market facilitates export dumping even in the absence of official export bounties, "especially in cases where the public

---

[1] The text of the Convention is given in Great Britain, *Miscellaneous Papers No. 4*, 1902 (Cd. 1003). The provision for international control by a Commission in which all the members are equally represented and in which decisions are established by a simple majority vote has few parallels in the history of international organization.

authorities impose, provoke, or encourage coalitions among producers of sugar."[1]

In Great Britain there was considerable opposition to British adherence to the Convention, mainly on the ground that countervailing duties were inconsistent with the principle of free trade, but also because the British consumer and British industries using sugar as a raw material had greatly profited from the artificial cheapness of sugar resulting from the bounty system. Great Britain entered into the Convention during the Salisbury (Conservative) Ministry, which was less decided in its opposition to protectionist measures than had been the preceding Liberal governments. It was nevertheless on British recommendation that the Convention was drafted so as to leave the member countries free to substitute prohibitions of import for countervailing duties, the former being regarded by the British Government as less of a concession to, and less of an entering wedge for, tariff protectionism. Great Britain, in carrying out the terms of the Convention, uniformly used the prohibition of import method instead of countervailing duties. When in 1908 the Convention was either to be renewed or to be allowed to terminate, Great Britain, again under a Liberal ministry, consented to participate in an extension of the Convention only upon the condition that she be relieved of the obligation of imposing either countervailing duties or prohibitions of import on bounty-fed sugar, but she agreed to prohibit the re-export to any member country of products made of bounty-fed sugar.[2]

---

[1] As explained in the text of the unratified Convention of 1898, from which the surtax provision in the 1902 Convention was taken. Cf. Great Britain, *Miscellaneous Papers No. 5*, 1902 (Cd. 1013) p. 19. Cf. also, C. S. Griffin, "The Sugar Industry and Legislation in Europe," *Quarterly Journal of Economics*, XVII, 24.

[2] U.S. Tariff Commission, *Colonial Tariff Policies*, p. 815, n. Great Britain's pledge not to permit the re-exportation to member countries of products made from bounty-fed sugar is an interesting anticipation of the provision in Article III of the International Opium Convention of 1912, which required the contracting countries to prevent the export of raw opium to countries prohibiting its import and to control

The Liberal Party had pledged itself, if successful at the polls, to withdraw from the Convention on the ground that it was inconsistent with free-trade principles. It was only because of the urgent appeals of the sugar-growing colonies that this pledge was not fully carried out.[1]

In 1912 the revised Convention was to terminate, and this time, because of free-trade opposition and because the Convention was held responsible for the rise in the price of sugar which had occurred in Great Britain and which was felt to be injurious to the interests of the British sugar consumers and sugar-using industries, Great Britain withdrew from all obligations under the Convention, but agreed not to depart from its fundamental provisions without previously giving six months' notice.[2]   In 1918 Great Britain withdrew absolutely from all obligations with respect to her fiscal treatment of sugar, but this time not because of its supposed inconsistency with her free-trade policy.   Great Britain had pledged herself under the Convention not to grant preferential treatment to imports of colonial sugar, and the Coalition Government, which had formally adopted the policy of Imperial preference, wished to be free from this restraint upon the execution of their policy.   In the same year France also withdrew in order to be free to grant a greater measure of tariff protection to her domestic sugar producers.   Italy had withdrawn for the same reason in 1915.   Holland withdrew in 1920.

---

the export to countries which limited its import.   Of this provision in the Opium Convention Mr. Hamilton Wright, the chairman of the American delegation, remarked: "Upon the ratification [of Article III] it will become an accepted principle of international commercial law that where a country has prohibited the importation of a drug or commodity, it is the business of the producing country to prevent the exportation of such products unless the exporter conforms to the importation regulations of a regulating country." (62d Cong. 2d Sess., *Sen. Doc. 733*, p. 18.)   The extension of this principle to alcoholic liquors would be very convenient for the United States at the present moment!

[1] United States Tariff Commission, *Colonial Tariff Policies*, p. 815 n.

[2] *Ibid*. and Great Britain, *Commercial No. 1*, 1912, pp. 1, 6.

With the unsettled political conditions in Russia, the changes which have resulted from the war in the sovereignty over some of the important sugar-growing regions, and the apparent expulsion of Germany from the Convention by the terms of the Treaty of Versailles,[1] the Brussels Sugar Convention ceased to be effective. It had been completely successful in attaining its objectives, and was a distinct achievement in the difficult task of establishing international control of an economic problem essentially international in character. But the increase in prices in recent years has made the limitation to 6 francs per kilogram of the permissible amount of protection to domestic producers against foreign competition seem unreasonably low and the intensification of protectionist sentiment together with the forgetfulness on the part of a new generation of the evils of the bounty system have made any surrender of full national control over tariff policy appear to be an excessive price to pay for safety against the re-establishment of bounties.

Many writers and statesmen who believed that high protective tariffs were in the main responsible for dumping in the case of commodities other than sugar and who were impressed by the success of the Brussels Sugar Convention have urged, as the only effective means of suppressing the practice of dumping, the extension to other commodities than sugar, and even to all commodities, of international agreements modeled after the Sugar Convention and reproducing in particular its surtax   provision.[1] There is no doubt that an international agreement containing

---

[1] Cf. Part X, Sec. II, Arts. 282, 283, 292.

[1] Cf. Geoffrey Drage, *The Imperial Organization of Trade*, pp. 138 ff; Georg Gothein, "La Réglementation Internationale des Droits de Douane sur les Fers, *Revue Économique Internationale*, August, 1904; Wilhelm Feld, "Anti-Dumping, Prämienklausel, und Ausgleichzölle," *Archiv für Sozialwissenschaft*, XLIV, 476 ff.; C. Colson, *Cours d'Économie Politique*, Paris, 1903, II, 678; W. S. Notz and R. S. Harvey, *American Foreign Trade*, pp. 383 ff.; W. F. Notz, "New Phases of Unfair Competition," *Yale Law Journal*, XXX (1921), 384 ff., "International Private Agreements in the form of Cartels, Syndicates, and Other Combinations," *Journal of Political Economy*, XXVIII (1920), 658 ff.

a surtax provision modeled after the provision in the Brussels Sugar Convention and not more liberal with respect to the amount of surtax permitted without penalization if signed by all the important exporting and importing countries and vigorously enforced would act as a check to, if it would not altogether suppress, all such dumping as results from the maintenance of abnormally high prices in the domestic market behind the shelter of tariff protection. This would, however, leave untouched such dumping as is not dependent upon high tariff protection in the domestic market of the dumper. Moreover, it would be a somewhat circuitous method of reaching dumping and its penalties would fall on the products of tariff-protected industries regardless of whether or not the tariff legislation had as its object or its consequence the facilitation of export dumping. There have been no instances other than the Sugar Convention of such agreements and there are not likely to be until the world is converted to free trade or at least to a close approximation to it. The peculiarly acute circumstances which were characteristic of the sugar industry at the time that the Convention, after fifty years of almost continuous controversy, was finally negotiated and ratified, are not likely to be duplicated in the same degree in any other industry, especially if there is no recrudescence of the bounty system. There are not many countries which would voluntarily surrender a large measure of their tariff autonomy merely in order to promote the removal of an objectionable practice in international competition. It is significant that even the Brussels Sugar Convention finally succumbed to the adverse pressure of protectionist policies. If an international solution of the problem of bounties and of dumping is to be found it must be sought in other forms than the surtax provision of the Sugar Convention.

RECENT DEVELOPMENTS IN BOUNTY-COUNTERVAILING LEGISLATION

In recently enacted antidumping laws there has been evident a tendency to broaden the scope of the penalizing duties so as to apply not only to dumping proper but to bounties and subsidies, official and unofficial, and of whatever character. Thus the New Zealand and the Australian antidumping laws of 1921, which are discussed elsewhere in this study, make subject to the dumping duties imports which have received freight or shipping subsidies or concessions.[1] The United States Tariff Act of 1922, (the Fordney-McCumber Act) contains a somewhat obscurely worded provision which apparently authorizes the president, when he finds: that any foreign country discriminates in its taxation against American commerce and that benefits accrue from this discrimination to the industry of *another* foreign country; that retaliatory duties against foreign discriminations elsewhere provided for in the act do not effectively remove such discrimination; and that the public interest will be served thereby, to proclaim such additional duties on the products of a foreign industry benefiting from such discrimination as will offset such benefits, but not to exceed 50 per cent ad valorem. Imports of such products are to be subject to these additional duties on and after thirty days after the date of the President's proclamation.[2]

[1] See pp. 229 and 232, *infra.*

[2] Sec. 317 (*e*): "Whenever the President shall find as a fact that any foreign country imposes any unequal imposition or discrimination as aforesaid upon the commerce of the United States, or that any benefits accrue or are likely to accrue to *any industry in any foreign country by reason of any such imposition or discrimination imposed by any foreign country other than the foreign country in which such industry is located,* and whenever the President shall determine that any new or additional rate or rates of duty or any prohibition hereinbefore provided for do not effectively remove such imposition or discrimination and that any benefits from any such imposition or discrimination accrue or are likely to accrue *to any industry in any foreign country,* he shall, when he finds that the public interest will be served thereby, by proclamation specify and declare such new or additional rate or rates

This provision was written by the Tariff Commission and handed to the Senate Finance Committee, which incorporated it in the tariff bill without much study and apparently with little understanding of its intent or significance.[1]   It received but scant attention in the Senate and none at all in the House debates. To discover its purpose it is necessary, therefore, to refer to its sponsors.   The Tariff Commission explains the provision as being in principle similar to that of countervailing duties to offset foreign official bounties.   As an illustration of the circumstances under which it might be applied, there is cited the situation which arises under a system of preferential export duties: "For instance, if the existence of a differential export duty puts American industries at a disadvantage in compelling them to pay a higher price for their raw materials, then such industries may receive special protection against *any third country* in whose favor the differential duties operate."[2]   Other evidence in the Sixth Annual Report of the Tariff Commission indicates that preferential (or differential)

------

of duty upon the articles wholly or in part the growth or product of any such industry as he shall determine will offset such benefits, not to exceed 50 per centum ad valorem or its equivalent, upon importation from any foreign country into the United States of such articles and on and after thirty days after the date of any such proclamation such new or additional rate or rates of duty so specified and declared in such proclamation shall be levied, collected, and paid upon such articles." The italics are mine.   The second italicized portion is either unnecessary repetition or else it makes doubtful whether the benefits from the foreign discrimination may accrue to an industry in *any* foreign country or must accrue to an industry in a foreign country other than the discriminating country in order that the products of such industry shall become subject to the additional duties.   There is nothing in the Congressional committee reports or in the Congressional Debates to throw light on this point.)

[1] Cf. *Congressional Record*, August 11, 1922, pp. 12278–83.   This applies, with minor qualifications, to all of Section 317.

[2] U.S. Tariff Commission, *Sixth Annual Report*, p. 6.   (Italics mine.   The portion in italics makes it appear that the Tariff Commission interprets the provision as applicable only to imports from a country other than that which discriminates.)

export duties are the only type of discrimination against which this provision is intended to operate.[1]

Preferential export duties undoubtedly operate under normal circumstances as an official bounty by the government of the exporting country to the consuming interests of the favored importing country. This provision may be regarded, therefore, as a countervailing provision against a special form of official bounty not covered by the ordinary type of countervailing clause. Usually, if not invariably, preferential export duties are confined to colonies, and apply only to exports to some other portion of the colonial empire. They are an integral part of the colonial tariff policy of Portugal, and they are also to be found in isolated instances in the export tariffs of Spanish, French, and Italian colonies. But most important for the United States have been the British preferential export duties, in the Federated Malay States, on tin ore, in force, with modifications, since 1903, and in British India on hides and skins, in force since 1919. Both of these preferential export duties have operated to place at a disadvantage American industries using these products as raw materials in their competition with producers in the British Empire, and the enactment of Section 317 (e) was undoubtedly influenced by the opinion of the Tariff Commission that preferential export duties in the colonial empires were a growing menace to American industry.[2] Vice-Chairman W. C. Culbertson,

[1] The statement that "The presence of subsection (e) should set at rest any doubt as to the meaning of subsection (i), since discriminatory export duties are found almost exclusively in colonies" (ibid.) clearly implies that subsection (e) is directed only against discriminatory export duties, since there are conceivable other types of discrimination, such as discriminatory internal taxes or privileges and discriminatory import duties, which may confer differential advantages on industries of the discriminating country or of other favored countries to the detriment of American commerce.

[2] For details as to preferential export duties and for the position of the Tariff Commission with respect to them, see its report on *Colonial Tariff Policies* ("Export Duties" in Index, p. 846); also its *Fifth Annual Report*, 1921, p. 54, and its *Sixth Annual Report*, 1922, p. 6.

of the Tariff Commission, has thrown further light on the purpose of this provision by his statement that the United States
is hardly in a position to penalize the colonial preferences of
other nations as long as it does not maintain the "open door"
in its own colonies, and that Congress probably contemplated
when it enacted this and related provisions in the Fordney-
McCumber Act, not "an indiscriminate use of penalty duties
against colonial preferences" but a starting-point for serious
diplomatic negotiations.[1]

The only parallel in earlier legislation to this provision in the
Fordney-McCumber Tariff Act, and this a somewhat distant one,
was the bounty which the Canadian government in 1903 granted
to Canadian manufacturers of binder twine from manila fiber
produced in the Philippines and extended in 1907 to manufacturers of cordage, equal in each case to the amount of export

---

[1] "The Making of Tariffs," *Yale Review* XII (1923), 273. There is not much
evidence that Congress did any contemplating on this subject. The Tariff Commission should know best what was intended by the legislation drafted by itself. If
there should be occasion for judicial determination of the meaning of the provision
and the court should not find the text of the provision sufficiently clear to disclose its
meaning the interpretation given to it by the Tariff Commission as its drafters
would in conformity with a well-established legal principle have great weight. On
the theory that the entire section 317 was intended to apply only in instances of
foreign discrimination against American trade which were not in keeping with most-
favored-nation treatment—more specifically which were not the outcome of reciprocity arrangements consistent with the conditional interpretation of the most-
favored-nation pledge—and on the theory that the word "differences" connoted both
differences in treatment of American trade which were and differences which were not
in violation of most-favored-nation treatment whereas the word "discriminations"
included only the latter, the Senate substituted "discriminations" for "differences"
throughout the provision wherever the latter word appeared in the original draft.
Intra-imperial preferences have been universally regarded as consistent with most-
favored-nation obligations, and on this interpretation would not be subject, therefore, to the application of Section 317 (*e*). It is clear, however, that the Tariff
Commission intended no such limitation, and it is extremely doubtful, moreover,
whether there is any such established divergence of meaning between differential
treatment and discriminatory treatment as the Senate supposed. If the Senate
interpretation should hold, Section 317 (*e*) would become meaningless.

tax which had been levied on the manila fiber in the Philippines and intended to offset the virtual bounty which American manufacturers received through the remission on exports of manila fiber to the United States of the Philippine export tax.[1] With the abolition of the Philippine export duties by the United States Tariff Act of 1913 the Canadian bounty provisions ceased to be effective.[2]

[1] Canada, 3 Edward VII, chap. 5, and 6–7 Edward VII, chap. 5.

[2] For an account of the Philippine preferential export duties, see U.S. Tariff Commission, *Colonial Tariff Policies*, pp. 592 ff.

CHAPTER XI

FOREIGN ANTIDUMPING LEGISLATION. I

Canada in 1904 enacted the first general measure applicable to dumping in any of its common forms. Its example was soon followed by several other countries, all of them, like Canada, British self-governing dominions, but it was not until 1921 that any of the more important countries adopted antidumping measures. In this one year, four countries, including Great Britain, the United States, and two British dominions, enacted new and comprehensive antidumping laws and two other countries extended by amendment the scope of their existing antidumping legislation. Legislative enactments against dumping other than in the form of countervailing duties on bountied imports are therefore a comparatively recent phenomenon. At the present time antidumping laws are in effect in Great Britain, in each of her five self-governing dominions, and in the United States, and a measure which can readily be made to operate as an antidumping law is in force in Japan. The model of the original Canadian law has been closely followed in most of this legislation, but some of the antidumping laws vary substantially in form and in manner of operation from that of Canada. In this and the two following chapters, a detailed description is given of each of the laws which deal with dumping. In the chapter then following, these laws are compared and analyzed with a view to discovering the principles which should govern the drafting of the detailed provisions of antidumping legislation.

THE CANADIAN ANTIDUMPING LAW

The antidumping measure enacted by Canada in 1904 was introduced by the Liberal government then in power largely in order to neutralize the aggressive campaign of Canadian manu-

facturers for higher import duties on the plea that they were
necessary to protect Canadian industry from dumping.[1] The
Liberal Party was in theory a free trade party, but it had failed
to redeem its pledges substantially to reduce the level of the
tariff, and was by this time already beginning to hear complaints
on this ground from many of its followers, and especially from
the farmers—complaints which later were to give rise to the
"agrarian revolt" and to the creation and rapid growth of an
independent farmers' party. The manufacturers, on the other
hand, were an important source of campaign funds for both
parties, and were generally able in recent years to exercise considerable control over the trend of tariff legislation.   Faced with
this dilemma, the government found an ingenious escape in the
enactment of the antidumping law, which gave the manufacturers
the specific type of protection which they claimed they needed
without antagonizing the farmers by an increase in the rates of
duty of the ordinary tariff. The Minister of Finance, W. S.
Fielding, in introducing the measure claimed that it was unscien-
tific to meet special and temporary cases of dumping by a general
and permanent raising of the tariff wall and that the proper
method was the one which he now proposed, namely, to impose
special duties upon dumped goods.[2]

The antidumping clause was redrafted in 1907, but with only
a few substantial changes from the original measure.   In its
amended form it was as follows:

6. In the case of articles exported to Canada of a class or kind made or
produced in Canada, if the export or actual selling price to an importer in
Canada is less than the fair market value of the same article when sold for
home consumption in the usual and ordinary course in the country whence
exported to Canada at the time of its exportation to Canada, there shall,
in addition to the duties otherwise established, be levied, collected, and paid
on such article, on its importation into Canada, a special duty (or dumping

[1] Cf. Edward Porritt, *Sixty Years of Protection in Canada*, p. 406.
[2] Canada: *House of Commons Debates*, June 7, 1904, col. 4365.

duty) equal to the difference between the said selling price of the article for export and the said fair market value thereof for home consumption; and such special duty (or dumping duty) shall be levied, collected, and paid on such article, although it is not otherwise dutiable.

Provided that the said special duty shall not exceed 15 per cent ad valorem in any case;

Provided also that the following goods shall be exempt from such special duty, viz:

(a) Goods whereon the duties otherwise established are equal to 50 per cent ad valorem;

(b) Goods of a class subject to excise duty in Canada;

(c) Sugar refined in the United Kingdom;

(d) Binder twine or twine for harvest binders manufactured from New Zealand hemp, istle, or tampico fiber, sisal grass, or sunn, or a mixture of any two or more of them, of single ply and measuring not exceeding 600 feet to the pound.

Provided further that excise duties shall be disregarded in estimating the market value of goods for the purposes of special duty when the goods are entitled to entry under the British Preferential Tariff.

2. "Export price" or "selling price" in this section shall be held to mean and include the exporter's price for the goods, exclusive of all charges thereon after their shipment from the place whence exported directly to Canada.

3. If at any time it appears to the satisfaction of the Governor in Council, on a report from the Minister of Customs, that the payment of the special duty by this section provided for is being evaded by the shipment of goods on consignment without sale prior to such shipment, the Governor in Council may in any case or class of cases authorize such action as is deemed necessary to collect on such goods or any of them the same special duty as if the goods had been sold to an importer in Canada prior to their shipment to Canada.

4. If the full amount of any special duty of Customs is not paid on goods imported, the Customs entry thereof shall be amended and the deficiency paid upon the demand of the collector of customs.

5. The Minister of Customs may make such regulations as are deemed necessary for carrying out the provisions of this section and for the enforcement thereof.

6. Such regulations may provide for the temporary exemption from special duty of any article or class of articles when it is established to the satisfaction of the Minister of Customs that such articles are not made or

sold in Canada in substantial quantities and offered for sale to all purchasers on equal terms under like conditions, having regard to the custom and usage of trade.

7. Such regulations may also provide for the exemption from special duty of any article when the difference between the fair market value and the selling price thereof to the importer as aforesaid amounts only to a small percentage of its fair market value.[1]

In the 1904 measure the application of the dumping-duty was limited, with the one exception of wire rods,[2] to commodities which were dutiable under the ordinary tariff, but the dumping-duty was now made applicable to all imports, whether dutiable or free under the ordinary tariff, if they were of a kind or class produced in Canada. In the original law the maximum dumping-duty which could be applied was: for a few specified commodities, 15 per cent ad valorem; for all other commodities, one-half of the duty to which they were subject under the ordinary tariff, which, in practice, generally meant a maximum duty of 15 per cent ad valorem or less. The maximum dumping-duty was now made 15 per cent ad valorem for all commodities. The exemption from the dumping-duty of goods which under the ordinary tariff were subject to duties equal to 50 per cent ad valorem was now made mandatory, whereas in the original measure it was subject to the discretion of the Minister of Customs. This provision was, however, of little importance, since there have been in Canadian tariff legislation no instances of ad valorem duties equaling 50 per cent and only a few instances of specific duties so heavy that they might conceivably under normal conditions be the equivalent of an ad valorem duty of 50 per cent or higher. The provisions for the exemption from the dumping-duty of binder twine and of sugar refined in the United Kingdom and for disregarding excise duties in estimating the market

[1] *Statutes of Canada*, 1907, 6–7 Edward VII, Vol. I–II, p. 134.

[2] Complaints of injury from American dumping had been especially numerous and vigorous on the part of Canadian producers of wire rods. This explains their special treatment in the antidumping law. Cf. Edward Porritt, *op. cit.*, p. 406.

values of goods entitled to entry under the British preferential
tariff were wholly new.   What other changes were made were
mainly of a merely verbal character.

The limitation of the maximum dumping-duty to 15 per cent
ad valorem was explained by Mr. Fielding, the Minister of
Finance, as conforming to the estimate that the difference
between the export price and the fair market value in the exporting country of goods dumped in Canada amounted on the average
to 15 per cent.[1]   The limitation could have been defended on
more logical grounds.   To the Canadian producer who faced
dumping competition what was a matter of concern was not
the average reduction from the foreign market price at which
dumped goods were exported to Canada but the actual reduction
at which the goods which competed in the Canadian market
with his own products were exported.   The provision authorizing the temporary exemption from the dumping-duty of articles
not produced in Canada on a substantial scale and not sold to
all purchasers on equal terms was explained as intended to protect
Canadian consumers against exploitation by a Canadian monopoly and against emergency shortages such as might arise
from a strike in Canada.[2]

Binder twine was exempted from the dumping-duty in order
not to jeopardize the continued free admission of Canadian
binder twine into the United States under a provision in the
American Tariff Act of 1897 which admitted this commodity
free of duty only when imported from a country which admitted

---

[1] Canada: *House of Commons Debates*, 1904, col. 4367.

[2] *Ibid.*, cols. 5737-38. This provision was applied in 1909. Tin plate was
being manufactured in Canada, but on a small scale, altogether inadequate to
meet Canadian needs. The United States Steel Corporation was dumping tin
plate in Canada, which was its chief export market, and in 1908 the dumping-duty
was applied to its tin plate. This caused such complaint from Canadian users of
tin plate that in 1909 the dumping-duty was withheld from it by customs regulation
issued under authority of this provision. See W. J. A. Donald, *The Canadian Iron
and Steel Industry*, p. 185: *Hearings before (H.R.) Committee on Investigation of
United States Steel Corporation*, 1912, pp. 23-24; D. E. Dunbar, *The Tin Plate
Industry*, pp. 112 ff.

American binder twine free of duty.   The Canadian authorities took it for granted—probably mistakenly, in the light of later developments—that the dumping-duty would be held to be a duty in the meaning of the American tariff law.[1]   The two items of preferential treatment to the British products were no doubt embodied in the law as concessions to the principle that what has been defined in this study as spurious dumping should not be penalized where it could readily be distinguished from genuine dumping.   In the case of sugar refined in Great Britain, the raw sugar was subject to an import duty in Great Britain which was refunded as a drawback upon export of the refined product. There was little cause for fear that Great Britain would make use of the drawback system to conceal an export bounty.[2] There were no commodities subject to excise taxation in Great Britain which were not also subject to excise taxation in Canada, and therefore exempt in any case from the Canadian dumping-duty.   But the provision that excise taxes should be disregarded in estimating the market value of goods entitled to entry under the preferential tariff may have had some degree of significance for other portions of the British Empire which levied excises on commodities not subject to excise in Canada.   Here also it was reasonably safe for Canada to assume that British countries would not use refunds of excise taxes as a means of concealing the payment of export bounties.

The law specifically made the comparison of foreign market values and actual export prices *as of the date of exportation* the basis for the determination of the existence of dumping, but a customs regulation of 1904 nevertheless provided that in the case of goods purchased abroad for future shipment an increase in the home value of the exported products between the date of purchase and the date of exportation should not be made the basis for the application of the dumping-duty.[3]

[1] Canada: *House of Commons Debates*, 1906-7, col. 1207.

[2] Cf., however, p. 165 n., *supra*.

[3] J. W. Root, *Colonial Tariffs*, Liverpool, 1906, p. 225.

In order to eliminate disputes between importers and the customs authorities about alleged differences between foreign domestic and export prices where the differences, if they existed at all, were trifling in amount, a customs regulation was issued providing that the dumping-duty shall not be applied to commodities dutiable under the ordinary tariff "except as otherwise decided in specified cases" unless the difference between the foreign domestic and the foreign export price exceeds 5 per cent of the former. If, however, the difference exceeds 5 per cent, the whole amount of the difference is taken into account in applying the dumping-duty.[1] A later regulation provides that foreign excise duties are not to be taken into account in determining for the purposes of the antidumping provision the foreign market value of imported goods, thus extending to imports from foreign countries a concession which had already been granted by statute to imports entitled to entry under the preferential tariff.[2]

The "fair market value" in the exporting country for home consumption is estimated on the usual *credit* basis, but a bona fide discount of $2\frac{1}{2}$ per cent for cash is allowed on export prices if deducted on the invoice. If goods are usually sold at home on thirty days' terms but a discount of 10 per cent is allowed to domestic purchasers for cash, the sale to Canadian purchasers for cash at a price less than the home credit price by 10 per cent would make the goods subject to the dumping-duty.

In 1921, by amendment to the Customs Act, a change was made in the method to be used in determining the "fair market value" in the exporting country for purposes of assessment of the ad valorem duties of the ordinary tariff which also became applicable for the purpose of assessment of the dumping-duty.

[1] Canada, Department of Customs: *Customs Memorandum* No. 1293 B, August 10, 1904.

[2] *Ibid., Customs Memorandum* No. 2307 B, April 15, 1919. It is to be presumed that imports from British countries not entitled to entry under the preferential tariff, for which no specific provision is made, are not in practice excluded from the benefit of this concession.

This amendment provides that the definition of "fair market value" in the customs act is to be changed by the addition of the following:

"Such value in no case to be lower than the wholesale price thereof at such time or place.

(2) Provided that the value for duty of new or unused goods shall in no case be less than the actual cost of production of similar goods at date of shipment direct to Canada, plus a reasonable profit thereon, and the Minister of Customs and Inland Revenue shall be the sole judge of what constitutes a reasonable profit under the circumstances.[1]

The purpose of this amendment, as explained by the Canadian Minister of Finance when introducing it, was that "goods ought to be valued for customs purposes, not at forced-sale prices, justified by temporary quotations in the foreign market, but having regard to the regular standard value in that market and to cost of production and a reasonable profit thereon."[2] The first provision, to the effect that the "fair market value" to be used as a basis for the assessment of duty shall in no case be lower than the wholesale price at such time or place, i.e., the date of exportation and the country of direct exportation, is apparently merely explanatory of the original provision and will not alter its effect under usual conditions. The second provision, to the effect that the "fair market value" for customs purposes must not be less than the actual cost of production *at date of shipment* apparently invalidates the customs regulation of 1904, which prescribed that an increase in value between date of purchase and date of shipment should not be made the basis for the assessment of the dumping duty, to the extent that such increase in value is accompanied by an increase in cost of production. But administrative regulations have a wider latitude and are less strictly bound by statutory provisions in Canada than in the United States. The second provision also

[1] Revised Statutes of Canada, 1906, Sec. 40, chap. 48, as amended June 4, 1921.

[2] Canada: *House of Commons Debates*, May 9, 1921.

makes subject to the dumping-duty goods imported at prices lower than cost of production even if the prices to home purchasers are equally low. The difficulty of determining foreign costs of production may be expected, however, to make this provision inoperative except in extreme cases, although it may conceivably become important because of the greater latitude which it gives to the customs authorities in deciding whether·dumping is being practiced in particular instances.

With the sole exceptions that no allowance is made for drawbacks of import duties in determining the home market value in the country of export, that only a limited allowance is made for possible differences between export and home prices due to differences in credit terms, and that by the amendment of 1921 export sales below cost of production are made subject to the dumping-duty even though the domestic sales are made at prices equally low, the Canadian antidumping law, if read together with the customs regulations issued to govern its administration, answers satisfactorily the requirements for technically correct antidumping legislation. It reaches by definition all cases of genuine dumping, whether open or concealed, and with the exceptions noted, it applies only to instances of genuine dumping.

The Canadian law does not impose on the Canadian customs authorities a very onerous administrative burden, unless, under the latest amendment, they feel themselves obliged to discover foreign costs of production. Substantially all the information which is required for the administration of the dumping-duty is also required for the administration of the ad valorem duties in the ordinary tariff. In the case of goods subject under the ordinary tariff to specific duties and goods admitted free of duty there does result from the dumping-duty the necessity of determining the "fair market value" in the exporting country and of checking the export prices quoted in the invoices. But there are few specific duties in the Canadian tariff and most of the products which are produced in Canada on a substantial scale and which therefore come under the protection of the dumping clause are either dutiable ad valorem or, if not subject to duty, are not commonly imported. The Canadian Customs Department maintains a few officials abroad, chiefly in the United States, to aid in determining the foreign market values of imported goods, but such officials are necessary to secure the efficient administration of ad valorem customs duties assessed as are the Canadian duties on the basis of foreign market values and have been employed by the United States for such a purpose even when no attempt was made to penalize dumping. Where it is difficult to check from current sources of information the accuracy of the prices certified to in the invoices by both exporters and importers (the invoices are required to give in parallel columns both the actual export price and the fair market value for home consumption in the country of export) these customs officers visit the exporter and request permission to examine his books. If he refuses, as he rarely does, the dumping-duty is immediately applied to his products.[1] Hearings are usually granted by the commissioner of customs to Canadian importers who are dissatisfied with customs decisions.

The Canadian antidumping law has on the whole worked smoothly and without much friction and has generally been credited with having been effective in accomplishing its purpose of checking dumping on the Canadian market.[2] When the United States Steel Corporation was commonly selling rails abroad at much below its domestic price of $28 a ton, it sold to Canada at $26.60 a ton, thus taking full advantage of the

---

[1] Cf. U.S. Tariff Commission, *Information Concerning Dumping and Unfair Competition*, pp. 28, 29. It is often said that if an exporter refuses access to his books to a Canadian customs official his products are refused admission into Canada, but this is not the case.

[2] Cf. *ibid.*, pp. 29, 30, and Adam Shortt, "The Anti-Dumping Feature of the Canadian Tariff," *Quarterly Journal of Economics*, XX (1906), 257, who says that the law "attains its object with remarkable efficiency."

5 per cent dumping margin permitted under the Canadian regulation, but not exceeding it as it did elsewhere.[1]

Canada has been in an especially favorable position for the effective administration of antidumping legislation. The great bulk of Canada's imports, and particularly of its imports of manufactured commodities of a kind produced in Canada, comes from only two countries, the United States and Great Britain. As long as Great Britain remained on virtually a free trade basis, there was little danger of British dumping, and similarity of language and of business methods, and proximity and familiarity with American conditions make it comparatively easy for the Canadian customs officials to discover the prices current for home consumption in the American market. It is not so certain that the Canadian customs authorities have as yet succeeded in putting a stop to dumping in Canada by Continental or Japanese exporters, or that they could do so without a disproportionate expenditure of money and effort in investigating home prices in these countries. But the imports into Canada from these countries are small in amount and are generally of a kind not closely competitive with Canadian products.

The dumping-duty has produced a small amount of revenue, averaging from 1907 to 1918 about $75,000 per annum or less than one-tenth of 1 per cent of the total duties collected,[2] but it was never intended that the antidumping provision should be a revenue producer, and the small amount of revenue collected, in spite of the vigorous effort made to enforce the provision, is evidence of the effectiveness of the law in checking dumping.

[1] *Hearings before the (H.R.) Committee on Investigation of United States Steel Corporation*, 1912, p. 2729. Mr. Farrell, president of the Steel Corporation, explained the smaller differential between the American and Canadian prices than between the American and other export prices as due to the fact that "the customs law in Canada makes it impossible to sell American materials in Canada at less than 5 per cent below the domestic price."

[2] U.S. Tariff Commission, *Information concerning Dumping and Unfair Competition*, p. 29.

Some of the revenue undoubtedly comes from penalties on imports purchased by Canadians in ignorance of the fact that they would be liable to the dumping-duty.   It is probable that there are few instances in which foreign exporters find it profitable continuously to sell to Canada under conditions which will subject their products to the dumping-duty.

There is no doubt that there is in Canada general satisfactior. with the working of the dumping-duty and that it now meets with no important opposition from any quarter.   Occasional criticisms of the law and of its administration are, however, encountered.   The Canadian Manufacturers' Association at first opposed it because its introduction deprived them of their most effective argument for higher protection, but they later became reconciled to it, especially as it became apparent that there was growing opposition on the part of the farmers against any further increase in the tariff.   Some Canadian industries, however, and especially the railroads and producers of specialized steel products, complained that the dumping-duties deprived them of access to low-price American materials.[1]   After the law had been in operation for a year or two, the president of the Toronto Board of Trade, on which importing interests are largely represented, asked for its repeal on the ground that it was impossible of equitable administration, that it encouraged fraud, that it was therefore an injustice to the honest importer, and that it was an unwarranted restriction upon the freedom of purchase at the best prices obtainable.[2]   Large importers, and especially department stores, complain that it deprives the Canadian consumers of the benefits of foreign bargains.[3]   Complaint has also been made of harsh and inequitable administration

[1] Cf. Edward Porritt, *Sixty Years of Protection in Canada*, p. 409; W. J. A. Donald, *The Canadian Iron and Steel Industry*, p. 185.

[2] *Canadian Annual Review*, 1906, p. 584.

[3] U.S. Tariff Commission, *Information concerning Dumping and Unfair Competition*, p. 30.

of the law by the customs authorities. It has been charged that the customs officials use as the basis of determination of foreign market values price lists which are often inaccurate or obsolete, and that Canadian importers are occasionally subjected to the dumping penalty although they demonstrate by affidavits from the foreign manufacturers and letters from dealers in the export market that the invoice price was the fair market value in the country of export and that the price fixed by the customs authorities was too high because based on obsolete price lists or on inadequate allowance for trade discounts from the listed prices.[1]

NEW ZEALAND ANTIDUMPING MEASURE OF 1905

In 1905 New Zealand, in response to complaints from domestic and British manufacturers of agricultural implements that an American harvester trust was attempting to monopolize the New Zealand market by systematic price-cutting to New Zealand purchasers, enacted the Agricultural Implement Manufacture, Importation, and Sale Act. This act established an administrative board consisting mainly of non-official members, to whom the commissioner of customs, upon receipt of complaint from manufacturers in New Zealand or in Great Britain that the New Zealand price of foreign implements had been materially reduced and that competition on unfair lines was being carried on by importers of foreign implements, was to refer such complaint for investigation and report. Upon recommendation by the board to that effect, the commissioner of customs was authorized to grant the manufacturers of agricultural implements in New Zealand or in Great Britain such bonus, not exceeding 33 per cent, as he deemed necessary to enable such manufacturers to compete with the importers of foreign implements.[2] If the New Zealand or British manufacturers agreed to reduce their

---

[1] Cf. *Toronto Globe*, "Why Houses Are Dear," May 23, 1919.

[2] The text of the Act is given in New Zealand, *Consolidated Statutes*, 1908, IV, 283–85.

prices on certain implements by at least 20 per cent the board could recommend in lieu of the bonus and the commissioner of customs could impose upon such recommendation, a special countervailing duty on the imports of foreign implements sold under unfair conditions. The Act was to be in force for only one year, but by subsequent legislation it was continued in effect until December 31, 1915.

This Act was an ingenious compromise between conflicting policies. There were no import duties on agricultural implements in the New Zealand tariff, and the farmers were determined that there should not be. But the New Zealanders, including the farmers, were not willing to stand by while a foreign trust destroyed a domestic industry and thereby gained full control over New Zealand prices. The bonus method enabled the government to protect the domestic manufacturers against foreign unfair competition without causing thereby an increase in the price of the foreign or New Zealand implements to New Zealand purchasers.[1]

No bonus was ever granted nor countervailing duty imposed under this Act. The board met only once, in 1908, to consider a complaint against an American concern. The board reported that the complaint was not justified since the price-cutting against which complaint was lodged was intended to clear old stock acquired through purchase of a minor company and not to injure competitors, and recommended that no bonus should be granted.[2]

The extension to British manufacturers of the same privileges as to the bonus and as to appeal for investigation as were given to domestic manufacturers was in keeping with the general policy of preferential treatment to British trade which had

[1] G. H. Scholefield, *New Zealand in Evolution*, pp. 326 ff.; *Das Handels-Museum* (Vienna), XXI (1906), 149.

[2] G. H. Scholefield, *op. cit.*, p. 327, and U.S. Department of Commerce, Bureau of Corporations, *Trust Laws and Unfair Competition*, 1916, p. 551 n.

recently been adopted in New Zealand with the almost unanimous support of public opinion in the Dominion.[1] To extend to outside manufacturers the privilege of drawing upon the New Zealand treasury, under certain circumstances, for a substantial subsidy to aid them in resisting the unfair competition of a foreign trust was to perform an act of generous sentiment probably without parallel in the history of tariffs and not to be unduly minimized because no occasion arose for putting it into practical operation. It is of some significance, however, that the same privilege was not extended to Canada, whose manufacturers of agricultural implements were the principal competitors of the American trust in the trade with New Zealand. There was something very closely resembling a harvester trust in Canada also, which, it was suspected, was not wholly independent of the American trust, and which commonly practiced dumping in its export trade.

AUSTRALIAN ANTIDUMPING LEGISLATION OF 1906

Australia in 1906 enacted a law which was aimed chiefly at the suppression of monopolies, but which also contained provisions dealing with dumping.[2] The dumping section of the law was extremely unusual in a number of respects, including its terminology and its provisions for the administration of the penalties which it provided. The dumping section is long and complicated, and as there does not appear to have been a single instance of its application, it will suffice if a concise summary of its provisions is presented.

The provisions dealing with what the act defines as dumping are a part of an act which is concerned primarily with the general

[1] Cf. U.S. Tariff Commission, *Colonial Tariff Policies*, p. 768.

[2] The Australian Industries Preservation Act, 1906–10. The text of the section dealing with dumping is given in U.S. Tariff Commission, *Information concerning Dumping and Unfair Competition*, pp. 39 ff. Cf. also, U.S. Department of Commerce, Bureau of Corporations, *Trust Laws and Unfair Competition*, pp. 243 ff., 551 ff., for an analysis of the law. It was amended several times but is still in effect.

problems of monopoly control of industry and of unfair competition, and the dumping section was intended to deal with unfair competition in connection with imports as other sections deal with unfair competition in internal trade and in export trade. The act as a whole transcends the field of tariff and customs legislation, and the dumping section is not primarily a tariff provision. For the purposes of the dumping section, competition is to be regarded as "unfair," unless the contrary is proved, if (a) it would ordinarily lead to competing Australian goods being no longer produced or being sold at a loss unless produced at an inadequate remuneration for labor; or (b) the means adopted by the person importing or selling the imported goods are in the opinion of the comptroller-general of customs or a justice of the High Court "unfair in the circumstances"; or (c) the competition results or probably would result in an inadequate remuneration for labor in the Australian industry; or (d) the competition results or probably would result in substantial disorganization of Australian industry or unemployment of Australian labor; or (e) the imported goods were purchased abroad from the manufacturer at prices greatly below their ordinary cost of production where produced or market price where purchased; or (f) the goods were imported into Australia by the manufacturer thereof or on his account and were sold in Australia at a price which is insufficient to give the importer a fair profit upon their fair foreign market value together with all charges including customs duty.

This definition of unfair competition in connection with imports thus not only covers dumping proper and selling below cost of production, but it also applies to ordinary keen competition if it embarrasses Australian industry. When the measure was introduced in the Australian Parliament critics pointed out that under so comprehensive a definition of unfair competition the penalties could be applied to almost any imports on the ground that they would lead to a diminution or cessation of Australian production of similar goods, or to Australian goods being sold at a loss unless produced at a lower remuneration for labor.[1] But many commentators on the dumping section have failed to give adequate consideration to a number of other provisions in the section which greatly modify the comprehensiveness of this definition. It is provided, for instance, that competition from foreign goods is not to be regarded as unfair competition if the Australian industries which are affected thereby give inadequate remuneration to the majority of their employees or otherwise subject them to unfair terms or conditions of labor or employment. In determining whether the competition is "unfair" there must also be taken into consideration whether the preservation of the Australian industry is advantageous to the Commonwealth, and whether the Australian industry is reasonably efficient and "up-do-date" in its management, processes, plant, and machinery. Moreover, before any steps can be instituted against imports which are in unfair competition, so explained, with Australian industry, the comptroller-general must have reason to believe that some person is importing the goods *with intent to destroy or injure an Australian industry by their sale or disposal within the Commonwealth,* i.e., there must be both unfair competition as defined in the law and unfair intent on the part of an importer *in* Australia before proceedings can be instituted. The peculiar and unreasonably extreme definition of unfair competition is thus deprived by later provisions of almost all of its significance.

A complicated procedure is stipulated for the enforcement of the provisions relating to dumping.[2] The comptroller-general of customs, upon receipt of a written complaint, and after giving a hearing to the importer, *may,* if he has reason to believe that "unfair competition" and unfair intent on the part of an Australian importer are present, report accordingly to the Minister of Customs. The latter *may* refer the matter for

[1] Cf. Commonwealth of Australia, *Parliamentary Debates,* June 19, 1906, p. 346.
[2] Cf. *Trust Laws and Unfair Competition,* p. 555.

investigation and action to a justice of the High Court, and issue a notice to that effect in the official gazette. From the date of such notice until the publication of the decision of the justice, the import of the goods subject to investigation is prohibited unless accompanied by such bonds as are required by the minister. The justice may, as he thinks fit, issue the decision himself, or he may refer the question or some phase of it to Full Court. The court proceedings are to be informal and not subject to the rules of general jurisprudence or of the laws of evidence, and the decisions of the justice of the Full Court are to be conclusive and without appeal. If the decision is that the goods are imported with unfair intent, the import of the goods in question is to be prohibited or restricted in such manner as the justice sees fit. The decision must be laid immediately before both Houses of Parliament in all cases of prohibition of import. The obstacles which so complicated and drawn-out a procedure must place in the way of the application of the penalty are undoubtedly so serious that they are an ample explanation of the complete ineffectiveness of the measure as evidenced by the absence of a single instance of even the beginning of proceedings under this section.

THE UNION OF SOUTH AFRICA AND THE NEWFOUNDLAND ANTIDUMPING LAWS

Two other antidumping measures, enacted respectively by the Union of South Africa and Newfoundland, follow so closely the Canadian act that it is not necessary to consider them in detail. The South African law, enacted in 1914, is as follows:[1]

SEC. 8. Anything to the contrary notwithstanding in this act contained, the following provisions shall be in force in respect of the charging, levying, collection, and payment of customs duty:

(1) In the case of goods imported into the Union of a class or kind made or produced in the Union, if the export or actual selling price to an importer in the Union be less than the true current value (as defined in

[1] Union of South Africa, *Statutes*, 1914, Act No. 26, Sec. 8.

this act) of the same goods when sold for home consumption in the usual and ordinary course in the country from which they were exported to the Union at the time of their exportation thereto, there may, in addition to the duties otherwise prescribed, be charged, levied, collected, and paid on those goods on importation into the Union a special customs duty (or dumping duty) equal to the difference between the said selling price of the goods for export and the true current value thereof for home consumption as defined in this act: *Provided*, That the special customs duty (or dumping duty) shall not in any case exceed 15 per cent *ad valorem*.

(2) When a bounty is granted in the country of origin on any goods of a class or kind made or produced in the Union an additional customs duty equal to the amount of such bounty may be charged, levied, and collected upon the importation of those goods into the Union.

(3) The goods in respect of which there may be charged, levied, and collected any special (or dumping) customs duty under subsection (1) or any additional customs duty under subsection (2) shall be from time to time determined by the governor general and notified by him by proclamation in the Gazette, together with the date as from which such his determination shall take effect: *Provided*, That such date shall not be less than six weeks after the publication of the proclamation.

The text of paragraph (1) is almost identical with the main provision of the Canadian antidumping law.[1]   The substitution of the term "true current value" for "fair market value" in the definition of the foreign price which is to be taken as the basis for the determination of the existence of dumping conforms to a difference in the established terminological practice in the tariff legislation of the two countries and probably makes no change in meaning. A more important variation from the Canadian model is the substitution of the word "may" in the South African act for "shall" as in the Canadian act, with the effect of making the application of the dumping-duty in South Africa subject to the discretion of the governor-general, which in practice means the Cabinet, instead of being mandatory upon the customs authorities as in Canada. Moreover, paragraph (3) requires that six weeks' notice be given by proclamation of the governor-general before the dumping-duty can be applied. This must in practice remove instances of casual or sporadic

[1]See p. 193, *supra*.

dumping from the operation of the antidumping provision, since the time which must elapse between the discovery that dumping is taking place and the coming into effect of the dumping-duty will normally be sufficient to permit the completion of a campaign of sporadic dumping.

The South African law does not contain the various qualifying provisions which moderate the severity of the Canadian measure, with the single exception that the maximum dumping-duty is limited in both laws to 15 per cent ad valorem. But the complete measure of discretion which is allowed to the governor-general in applying the South African law permits of an even more liberal administration than is effective in Canada. It is to be noted that the South African law contains a discretionary bounty-countervailing provision. There is no indication in the law as to whether this provision is applicable to private as well as to official bounties, and to indirect as well as to direct bounties. It is also not made clear whether the same imports may be subjected to both the dumping- and the bounty-countervailing duties.[1]

In 1922 South Africa strengthened its antidumping legislation by the enactment of a provision that where imported goods were sold in the union at less than the wholesale price in the country of manufacture plus the cost of packing, free on board charges and freight to the port of entry, and by reason of such sale a Union industry was threatened, there could be levied in addition to the ordinary duty a special duty equal to the difference between this price and the actual price of sale.[2] The effect of this additional provision would be to authorize the application of penalty duties to goods which were sold nominally at the full foreign price f.o.b., but which were delivered to the importer without added charges sufficient to cover all the costs of shipment from the country of export to South Africa, or to goods which

---

[1] The regulations issued to govern the administration of the antidumping law are given in the *Union Government Gazette*, March 12, 1920.

[2] *Board of Trade Journal*, July 13, 1922, p. 51; July 27, 1922, p. 107.

were shipped to South Africa on consignment or for sale by an agent of the exporter and there sold at prices which, after deduction of costs of shipment and other charges, returned to the exporter less than the current market value in the country of export.

There appears to have been only one instance of the application of the South African antidumping law. In 1921, the requisite six weeks' notice was issued of intent to apply the dumping-duties to imports of Australian flour.[1]

Newfoundland enacted in 1921 an antidumping law which is almost an exact duplicate of the Canadian law of 1907.[2] There are three variations from the Canadian model: (1) the Newfoundland act omits the Canadian exemptions from dumping-duty of (a) goods subject to ordinary duty equal to 50 per cent ad valorem, (b) goods of a class subject to excise duty in Canada, (c) sugar refined in the United Kingdom, and (d) binder twine; (2) the statutory provision for disregarding excise duties in the exporting country in determining the fair market value for the purpose of assessing the dumping-duty extends to all imported goods in the Newfoundland act, whereas in the Canadian act it applies only to goods entitled to entry under the preferential tariff and has been extended to foreign goods by administrative regulation; (3) in the Newfoundland measure the maximum dumping-duty is set at 25 per cent ad valorem, instead of 15 per cent as in the Canadian law.

THE PROPOSED FRENCH ANTIDUMPING MEASURE OF 1908

In 1908 the committee of the French Chamber of Deputies charged with the duty of recommending changes in the existing tariff legislation proposed the insertion in the tariff law of an antidumping measure which it regarded as essentially similar to

---

[1] Union of South Africa, *Proclamation 83*, 1921.

[2] Act of August 12, 1921, Clause 6. The text of the law is given in the *Board of Trade Journal*, September 15, 1921, pp 284, 285.

the Canadian law, but which differed from it in some important particulars. The proposal was not received with favor and was withdrawn, but its original features and the wide significance for antidumping legislation of the objections raised against it, justify its examination here. The proposed measure, freely translated, was as follows:[1]

The rates of duty (in the ordinary tariff) shall be increased by the amount of the bounties, direct or indirect, which are granted to exporters in the country of origin or of manufacture of products imported into France, if these bounties or privileges, whatever their nature, have the effect of changing the normal course of prices and of establishing in the French market prices lower than the average prices current, for the same articles, in the country of origin at the time of their exportation.

A decree of the President of the Republic, given out in the Cabinet, and published in the official journal, shall determine, in each case, the amount of the additional duties, and their collection shall thereupon be directed and their payment be immediately required.

In outward appearance the proposed measure closely resembles the ordinary bounty-countervailing provision, but unlike provisions of this type it was intended to apply to imports which had received private bounties as well as to those which had received official bounties. Moreover, the ordinary bounty-countervailing duty penalizes bounty-fed imports on the assumption that the grant of an export bounty necessarily results in

[1] France: Chambre des Députés, Commission des Douanes: *Rapport Général*, 1908, p. 100:

"Les droits inscrits au tableau A annexé à la loi du 11 janvier 1892 et modifié par la présente loi seront majorés du montant des primes directes ou indirectes accordées aux exportateurs, dans les pays d'origine ou de fabrication des produits importés en France, lorsque ces primes ou avantages, de quelque nature qu'ils soient, auront pour effet de fausser les cours normaux et de déterminer sur le marché français des prix inférieurs aux prix moyens pratiqués, pour les mêmes marchandises, dans les pays de provenance au moment de leur expédition.

Un décret du Président de la République, rendu en Conseil des Ministres et inséré au Journal officiel, fixera, pour chaque cas, le taux de ces majorations exceptionnelles de droits d'entrée dont la perception sera prescrite et dont le payement deviendra immédiatement exigible."

dumping, whereas this measure would be applicable only in those cases in which there resulted, from the grant of an export bounty, dumping to an extent sufficient to make the prices *in the importing country* lower than the average prices in the exporting country. It resembled the Canadian law in the fundamental particular that the additional duty was to be applied only to imports sold at prices lower than those current in the exporting country. It differed, however, from the Canadian law in that it was to apply only to instances of dumping resulting from the grant of export bounties, that the amount of the bounty instead of the amount of difference between the domestic price in the exporting country and the export price was to be the measure of the additional duty, and that the application of the additional duty was not mandatory upon the customs officials but was subject in each case to the discretion of the president and the Cabinet.

The chairman of the committee, M. Jean Morel, who was the originator of the proposal, tried to forestal the objection of "timorous souls" ("les esprits timorés") that the measure would prove in operation to be a drastic protectionist device by pointing out that the requirement that the additional duties should not be enforced in any instance except upon the authority of the Cabinet and after the issuance of a formal proclamation by the president of the Republic was a sufficient guaranty that caution and wisdom would govern the administration of the measure.[1] The government, however, declared the proposed measure inexpedient. It would require the determination of the normal values of imported merchandise in the exporting countries at the time of exportation. Under the existing customs regulations it was necessary to determine values only for imports subject to ad valorem duties, which were exceptional in the French tariff. Even under the ad valorem duties the values to be determined were the values at the place and time of entrance for customs and

[1] *Ibid.*, p. 101.

not the values at the place and time of exportation. The administration of the proposed measure would therefore require the complete revision of the French customs system. It would be difficult, moreover, to determine normal values in the country of exportation and to discover the existence of indirect bounties.

The government advised on these grounds against the acceptance of the proposed measure, and the committee thereupon withdrew it without its being submitted to a vote. It recommended, however, as a substitute measure, that there be inserted in all commercial treaties negotiated by France a reciprocal pledge against export bounties such as the one in the French-Swiss Treaty of 1906.[1] In the revised tariff law as finally enacted in 1910, there was inserted instead a bounty-countervailing duty of the ordinary kind.[2]

[1] *Ibid., 2e Rapport Général Supplémentaire*, 1909, pp. 11–13.

[2] The enactment of a general antidumping measure is now under consideration in France (cf. *La Journée Industrielle*, March 31, 1923).

CHAPTER XII

FOREIGN ANTIDUMPING LEGISLATION. II,

The wartime discussion of the menace of German dumping, the fear. that Germany during the war and the post-armistice period was storing up her energies for a campaign of predatory competition with the industries of the Allied countries, above all the marked increase of protectionist sentiment since 1914—all of these factors contributed to the development of what was apparently a strong and widespread feeling in Great Britain that there should be enacted in some form or other protective legislation which would safeguard British industries against injury by foreign dumping or abnormally keen competition. It was the British delegation at the Paris Conference of the Allies in 1916 which drafted and proposed the resolution, which was adopted, calling for joint action to be taken after the war by the Allies to protect their interests against German "economic aggression resulting from dumping or any other mode of unfair competition."[1] The Committee on Commercial and Industrial Policy after the war recommended the enactment of antidumping legislation which should in most respects follow the lines of the Canadian law but which should provide for a different and especially a less arbitrary administrative procedure. The committee urged that the antidumping law should establish a strong and competent board, which should have charge of the examination of all applications from British producers for the imposition of the dumping-duties and of any other duties which should be enacted, and which should be independent of any government department, should have no administrative duties, and should

---

[1] *Parliamentary Debates, Commons*, August 2, 1916, col. 340.

reports its findings and its recommendations directly to Parliament. It recommended that the final authority to decree the imposition of the dumping-duties in specific cases should be retained by Parliament and should not be delegated to any government bureau or official.[1] Other wartime investigating committees made similar recommendations.[2]

In 1919 the Coalition Cabinet pledged itself in Parliament and in its election manifesto to introduce antidumping legislation, and on November 19, 1919, after its re-election to office, the Lloyd George government introduced a bill in the House of Commons which contained, among other tariff proposals, provisions dealing with dumping.[3]

By the terms of this bill the antidumping provisions were to apply in cases where goods were being imported into the United Kingdom in substantial quantities and systematically, or were being offered for sale, or threatened to be sold, at prices which were lower than the prices at which the same goods were being sold in similar quantities in the country of production, after deducting any excise or other internal taxes levied in that country, provided that the production of similar goods in the United Kingdom was, or was likely to be, adversely affected thereby. In such cases the Board of Trade was empowered to issue orders that the goods should not be imported without (a) declarations as to values and prices by importers and foreign exporters closely resembling those required in the United States in connection with the administration of ad valorem customs duties, and (b) the

---

[1] *Final Report*, 1918 (Cd. 9035), p. 45.

[2] Cf. Great Britain Board of Trade, *Departmental Committee Reports*, all issued in 1918: *On the Electrical Trades* (Cd. 9092), p. 12; *On the Engineering Trades* (Cd. 9073), pp. 27, 39; *On the Iron and Steel Trades* (Cd. 9071), p. 28; *On Shipping and Shipbuilding Industries* (Cd. 9092), p. 39; *On the Textile Trades* (Cd. 9070), p. 124. Cf. also, Great Britain, Ministry of Reconstruction, Advisory Council, Section II, *Final Report on Anti-Dumping Legislation*, 1919 (Cmd. 455).

[3] The text of the bill, the "Imports and Exports Regulation Bill," is given in the *Board of Trade Journal*, December 27, 1919, pp. 640 ff.

payment of "such sum as in the opinion of the commissioners [of customs and excise] is equal to the amount by which the foreign value of the goods exceeds the import price thereof." To safeguard against evasion of these provisions by shipment on consignment, the bill provided for an elaborate procedure of investigation and declaration in the case of consigned goods. Except in the case of provisional orders, which were to be issued only in emergency cases and which were to continue in operation for twenty-one days only, the Board of Trade was to be required to submit its orders before their publication to an advisory committee, the Trade Regulation Committee, to be composed of ten members of the House of Commons, nominated by the House, two Board of Trade officials and a representative of the Treasury. This committee might approve the draft order, modify it, or reject it, as it saw fit.

The bill met with general opposition and was clearly unpopular. The excessive amount of administrative red tape, the difficulties which would result for the import trade from the enforcement of its requirements with respect to the certification of invoices, etc., the strong feeling in England against the delegation by Parliament to bureau officials of the power to impose taxes, were all factors operating to make the bill unpopular. In view of this general opposition in Parliament and from the public, and apparently also of divided counsel in the Cabinet itself, the government withdrew the bill without forcing a division on it in the House.

In March, 1920, Lord Balfour of Burleigh, who had been chairman of the Committee on Commercial and Industrial Policy, introduced in the House of Lords a Protection of Special Industries Bill, which contained an antidumping section purporting to follow the lines recommended in the Final Report of this committee. This bill proposed to give to the Board of Trade the power to prohibit the importation of goods if the prices of such goods to the English purchaser were "habitually" lower than the prices at which goods of the same kind or class were sold in the ordinary course of business in the country of origin.[1] This bill was rejected on its second reading in the House of Lords.

In 1921 there was finally enacted into law after a stormy passage in both Houses of Parliament the Safeguarding of Industries Act which in addition to provisions for the application of import duties on the products of "key industries" and on products coming from countries with depreciated currencies contains elaborate antidumping provisions.[2] The Act provides that if, on complaint being made to the Board of Trade to that effect, it appears to the Board that foreign manufactured goods of any class or description other than articles of food or drink are being sold or offered for sale in the United Kingdom at prices below the cost of production thereof as defined in the Act, and that by reason thereof employment in any industry in the United Kingdom is being or is likely to be seriously affected, the Board may refer the matter for inquiry to a committee constituted for the purposes of this part of the Act. Cost of production is defined as the current sterling equivalent of 95 per cent of the wholesale price charged at the factory to purchasers for domestic consumption less the amount of any excise or other internal tax included in the domestic price. If no such goods are sold at wholesale for domestic consumption, cost of production is to be taken to mean "the price at the works (subject to like deduction) which would have been reasonable if goods had been so sold, and in determining what price would have been reasonable regard should be had to the wholesale prices charged for goods as near as may be similar." The Board, in referring to a committee any case of the supposed import at dumping prices

[1] Cf. T. E. G. Gregory, *Tariffs: A Study in Method*, p. 225.

[2] 11 and 12 George V, chap. 47. The provisions dealing with "exchange dumping" and with dumping proper are contained in Part II of the Act. There is provided a common method of administration of the exchange-dumping and the genuine dumping provisions. The text of the Act is given in the *Law Reports*, 1921, Part II, pp. 260 ff.

of goods of a given kind from à specified country must also report on the effect which the imposition of a dumping-duty on such goods coming from such country would have on secondary industries, i.e., on industries using such goods as material for further manufacture. A committee consists of five persons selected by the president of the Board of Trade from a permanent panel of persons appointed by him who are to be mainly persons of commercial or industrial experience.

If the committee reports that conditions with respect to the importation of goods of a given kind from a specified country are as found by the Board of Trade, and if it also reports to the Board that in its opinion production in the industry manufacturing similar goods in the United Kingdom is being carried on with reasonable efficiency and economy, the Board of Trade *may*, after consideration of the effect of such action on secondary industries, issue an order applying the dumping-duties to goods of this class manufactured in the country of origin of the dumped goods. It is further provided, however, that no such order shall be issued if it would be in conflict with any existing treaty obligations with any foreign state, and, further, that if at the time when it is proposed to issue any such orders the House of Commons is in session or will be in session within one month, the drafts of the proposed orders must first be laid before that House, and the orders must not be issued unless and until that House passes a resolution approving of the drafts with or without modification. Upon such approval being given, the Board *may* then issue the orders in the form in which they have been approved. If the House is not in session the Board may issue its orders without waiting for the sanction of the House, but such orders must be submitted to the House as soon as possible after its next meeting, and will not continue in force for more than a month, unless the House by resolution declares that they shall continue in force. Modifications may be made by the House in such orders, but such modifications are not to invalidate anything which had been previously done under these orders. Orders continue in effect for three years or such lesser period as may be specified; they may be revoked, however, and are to be renewable from time to time subject to all the requirements described above relating to original orders.

Goods of a class specified in an order and manufactured in any of the countries specified therein are to pay upon importation into the United Kingdom in addition to any other customs duties to which they are liable a special duty equal to one-third of their value, defined as the price in bond at the point of importation which an importer would give for the goods. But if any person from whom such a duty is demanded proves to the satisfaction of the commissioners of customs and excise that the goods in question have already been sold in the United Kingdom at a price which is not less than the cost of production as defined in the Act, the payment of the duty is to be remitted. And if any person who had already paid such a duty proves to the satisfaction of the commissioners of customs and excise that the goods in question were at the first sale thereof in the United Kingdom sold at a price which was not less than the cost of production, or if he shows "that there has been a change in the market conditions of the country of manufacture, not less than the amount which would on the date of sale have been the cost of production in that country of similar goods," he is entitled to the repayment of the duty so paid. No such remission of the duty is to be made, however, unless the consignor makes a declaration, certified by the British consular or other officer at the point of manufacture, stating the cost of production at the date of declaration. Such declaration, unless proved to have been obtained by fraud, must be accepted as conclusive evidence of the cost of production. Where goods which have been charged with the dumping-duty are used in the United Kingdom by the importer without sale, the sale price for the purpose of this section is to be taken to be an amount equal to the price at which the goods were purchased from the exporter plus freight, insurance, and the amount of any other customs duty which had been paid on such goods.

An order issued under this part of the Act is not to be applicable to goods which left the place from which they were consigned to Great Britain within fourteen days after the date of such order. The Lord Chancellor appoints a referee to settle disputes as to the value of goods or the applicability to any particular goods of an order issued under this Act. Such referee must not be an official of any government department, and his decision is to be final and conclusive.

The antidumping provisions are in form provisions for the application of penalty duties on imports sold below cost of production. In reality, however, the Act has nothing to do with cost of production and is directed against imports sold in the United Kingdom at prices below the foreign market price by more than 5 per cent, regardless of whether these prices are below the cost of production. The strange and illogical use of the term "cost of production" in the Act can be explained only as arising out of the desire of the government to attain at least a verbal redemption of its pre-election pledge to introduce legislation penalizing imports sold at prices below cost of production and its reluctance to commit itself to measures which would actually necessitate for their execution the determination of that elusive quantity, cost of production. The Act was criticized while in the resolutions and bill stage on the ground that cost of production was so defined as to have no relation to cost of production.[1] These critics, who were generally hostile to antidumping legislation in any form thereof, failed to see that a provision which was genuinely directed against imports sold at a price below cost of production would penalize some imports which would escape a duty applied only to instances of dumping proper.[2] The pro-

---

[1] Cf. *Parliamentary Debates, Commons,* May 9, 1921, cols. 1606, 1751. Cf. also, Mr. Asquith, in the *Liberal Magazine,* July, 1921, p. 493.

[2] I.e., goods sold below cost of production both to domestic purchasers and for export.

vision that cost of production is to be taken as equal to 95 per cent of the wholesale price in the country of manufacture was substituted by the government for an original provision making it equal 100 per cent partly in order to meet such criticism, on the assumption, not necessarily valid in specific cases, that a deduction for producer's profit from foreign wholesale price would make it more nearly approximate cost of production.

The measure is a genuine antidumping measure, but it is so hedged with restrictions and qualifications as to give no promise of having any practical significance. Aside from the elaborate procedure which is prescribed before the dumping-duties can be imposed, and the unlimited discretion which is given at almost every step in this procedure to the particular official or body concerned to check the imposition of the duties, there are important mandatory qualifications in the Act, not all of which are apparent at first glance, which must in practice exclude many genuine instances of dumping from the scope of the Act. There must be a complaint from someone before proceedings can be instituted and in practice the only persons likely to be complainants, the domestic producers of commodities similar to those being dumped from abroad, are rarely possessed of the information necessary to demonstrate even the probability that dumping is taking place.[1] Articles of food and drink and all non-manufactured articles are by specific provision exempt from dumping-duty. The Board of Trade must be convinced that the dumping is seriously affecting (or is likely seriously to affect) employment in a British industry before it can proceed in any specific case, and, judging from the experience of other countries with tariff legislation limited in its application by such a pro-

[1] The government may have been influenced in introducing this provision by the statement of the Committee on Commercial and Industrial Policy after the war that the Canadian customs authorities rely largely on information as to suspected dumping in Canada given to them by Canadian manufacturers. (*Final Report*, 1918 [Cd. 9035], p. 45.) The available evidence indicates that the Canadian Customs are almost wholly dependent on their own machinery for the discovery of the existence of dumping.

vision, such conviction is difficult of honest attainment. Sporadic dumping is virtually assured of freedom from interference by the provision exempting from the dumping-duty goods shipped from the point of manufacture within fourteen days after the issue of an antidumping order. Before the Board of Trade may issue an order applying the dumping-duties to goods of a specified kind coming from a specified country, the committee must report that in its opinion the British industry which is affected by such imports is operated with reasonable efficiency and economy.

Even where dumping occurs and all of these conditions necessary to the application of the dumping-duties are fulfilled, there still remain important limitations. The difference between the domestic price in the exporting country and the export price to British purchasers must be substantial before shipments at dumping prices can be made subject to an antidumping order. In the first place, there is the 5 per cent of the foreign wholesale price which is to be deducted in determining "cost of production." More important in most instances is the fact that for the purposes of this Act dumping consists not in the sale for export at prices lower than for the domestic market, but the sale *in the United Kingdom*, after the expenses of freight, insurance, importer's profit, and ordinary customs duties have been incurred, at prices lower by more than 5 per cent than the foreign wholesale prices. For bulky products, for products coming from distant countries, and for products subject in Great Britain to ordinary customs duties, it is scarcely conceivable that there should be many instances where the dumping-duties could be applied.

Once an order should be issued, however, the antidumping provision with its high flat-rate duty of $33\frac{1}{3}$ per cent ad valorem on all imports of goods of the kind specified in the order manufactured in any country specified in the order would operate with great severity, were it not for additional limitations. If one concern in a foreign country were dumping to an extent sufficient to result in the issue of an antidumping order, the dumping-duty would apply, even though it should cease its dumping, to all imports of its products of the kind specified until the order was revoked. Moreover imports of the class of goods and from the country specified in the order would be subject to the dumping-duty, even though sold at the full foreign prices and even though manufactured by firms other than the dumping concern. But the provisions requiring the refund or remission of the dumping-duties in cases where the importer can demonstrate that there was no dumping as defined in the Act make the severity of this phase of the Act more apparent than real.

The procedure prescribed for the administration of the dumping-duties is remarkably elaborate, and if it were seriously attempted to apply the dumping-duties on a comprehensive scale, it would appear to be necessary to assign a large fraction of the governmental service to its administration. To summarize this procedure: in cases where the dumping-duties are finally ordered, there must ordinarily be (1) a complaint to the Board of Trade, (2) an investigation by the Board, (3) a reference to a committee, (4) a report by the committee, (5) the drafting of an order by the Board, (6) its submission to the House of Commons, (7) the passage of a resolution by the House, (8) the issue of the order by the Board, (9) the administration of the order by the commissioners of customs and excise. There may result disputes with importers regarding the values of, or the applicability of orders to, specific shipments, and such disputes must be referred to a referee appointed by the Lord Chancellor. The commissioners of customs and excise must handle appeals for remission or refund of duties, and here also the prescribed procedure is complicated.

It is abundantly clear that there was no enthusiasm on the part of the government for this portion of the Act, that it was intentionally made restricted in its scope, and that its main object was to achieve a formal redemption of election pledges. The free-trade wing of the coalition government obtained from Lloyd George a pledge that the committees appointed under the Act would consist mainly of consumers.[1]   Official assurance was also given that the Act would not be made to apply against sporadic dumping.   In the resolutions stage of the bill one Minister assured the House of Commons that the measure would be directed only against "sales, as part of a deliberate policy, made by the producers of one country in order to ruin or destroy an industry in another country," i.e., against predatory dumping,[2] but there was nothing in the bill as finally presented or as enacted which confined its application to such cases.   That the government did not take this portion of the Act very seriously is indicated by the announcement of the government, in reply to a question, that it did not intend to denounce any treaties sections of which were in conflict with the Safeguarding of Industries Act, but that, if in connection with the imposition of duties on imports from countries with depreciated currencies under the "exchange-dumping" provisions of the Act there should arise conflicts with treaty obligations, denunciation would be considered.[3]   Up to November 25, 1922, committees of inquiry under the genuine antidumping provisions of the Act had been set up in only two instances, glass bottles from Holland and vulcanized fiber from the United States, and in both instances the complainants failed to establish an adequate case.[4]   How difficult it will be for any case to survive through the elaborate administrative barricade is indicated by the experience of complainants under the exchange-dumping provisions, which are subject to the same pro-cedure as in the case of the dumping-proper provisions.   Of 123

[1] Wedgwood Benn, "The Safeguarding of Industries Act: Orders under Part II," *Economic Journal*, XXIII (September, 1922), 409. Cf. also, *Manchester Guardian*, May 7, 1921.

[2] Sir Alfred Mond, Minister of Health in the Coalition Cabinet, in *Parliamentary Debates, Commons*, May 9, 1921, col. 1598.

[3] *Parliamentary Debates, Commons*, July 6, 1921, col. 395.

[4] *The Economist* (London), XCV (November 25, 1922), 967.

applications for the imposition of duties up to July 31, 1922, only four passed through the Board of Trade and reached the House of Commons.[1] By the end of 1922 there had been only two cases of the issue of orders under the exchange-dumping provisions. As it stands today the antidumping section of the Safeguarding of Industries Act is of little significance. But the recent change in the political situation in Great Britain, whereby an outright Conservative and protectionist government has been substituted for a coalition government including free-trade elements, may result in the revision of these provisions so as to increase their severity and to remove some of the administrative barriers to their application.

AUSTRALIAN ANTIDUMPING LAW OF 1921

Australia enacted in 1921 a comprehensive antidumping law which apparently does not repeal the earlier antidumping provisions in the 1906 law discussed in the previous chapter but is supplementary thereto.[2] The Tariff Board Act of 1921 established a Tariff Board of three members, independent of the customs department, with the general duties of studying the effects of tariff legislation on Australian industries and of recommending such tariff changes as it found desirable. The administration of the "industries preservation" or antidumping law is largely intrusted to this board. Section 4 of the Industries Preservation Act provides that if the Minister of Customs is satisfied, after inquiry and report by the Tariff Board, that foreign goods of a kind produced in Australia had been or are being sold to Australian importers at an export price which is less than the fair market value of the goods in the country of export at the time of shipment and that detriment may thereby

---

[1] Wedgwood Benn, *op. cit.*, p. 408, citing Mr. Asquith.

[2] Customs Tariff (Industries Preservation) Act, December 16, 1921. The text of the act is given in the *Board of Trade Journal*, February 16, 1922, pp. 189–91.

result to an Australian industry, the Minister may publish a notice in the official gazette specifying such goods. Upon the publication of this notice there is to be collected on these goods a "dumping-duty" equal in each case to the difference between the fair market value at the time of shipment and the export price. There are, however, several qualifying provisions. For the purpose of this Act excise duties are not to be included in the foreign fair market value. If goods have been purchased abroad within six months prior to shipment and their foreign market price has risen in the interval, the fair market value to be taken for the purpose of this section is to be the fair market value at the date of purchase.[1]   The law also authorizes the issue of regulations exempting from the operation of this section of: (a) goods not made in Australia in substantial quantities and offered for sale on equal terms to all purchasers; (b) goods for which the difference between the fair market value and the export price does not exceed 5 per cent; or, if the Minister of Customs is satisfied, after report by the Tariff Board, that the exemption would not be detrimental to Australian industries, goods for which such difference does not exceed 10 per cent; (c) samples.

Section 5 provides that if goods are being sold to Australian importers at an export price less than a "reasonable price," defined as "a price which represents the cost of production of the goods, plus five per cent plus free on board charges" there may be imposed on such goods after a procedure identical with that prescribed for the "dumping-duty," a "dumping below cost duty" to be equal in each case to the difference between the reasonable price at the time of shipment and the export price. In the absence of satisfactory evidence as to cost of production, the Minister of Customs is given full discretion to fix such cost for the purposes of this section after report by the Tariff Board.

---

[1] "This proviso was inserted to meet cases where importers are not immediately able to obtain space on vessels for goods purchased for shipment to Australia." (Australia, Tariff Board: *Memorandum on Anti-Dumping Provisions, 1922*, reprinted in *Board of Trade Journal*, September 14, 1922, p. 299.)

Section 6 is intended to guard against evasion of the preceding sections by resort to sales on consignment. Where goods are shipped to Australia on consignment and are being sold in Australia by the consignees at less than a "reasonable selling price" the Minister is authorized, after procedure such as is required in the case of the "dumping-duty," to assess against such goods a "dumping consignment duty" equal in each case to the difference between the wholesale selling price in Australia of the consigned goods and a reasonable selling price. A reasonable selling price is defined as (a) either the fair market value, or in lieu of the fair market value, the cost of production plus 5 per cent of such cost, plus (b) the freight, insurance, landing, and other charges, ordinary duty and 5 per cent on the aggregate of all these items.

Section 7 authorizes the imposition, after the usual procedure, of a "dumping freight duty" of 5 per cent of the fair market value on goods shipped to Australia of a class or kind produced in Australia at rates of freight lower than those prevailing at the date of shipment, whether these lower rates are due to shipment as ballast, to shipping rebates, or to other special allowances. The circumstances under which this duty might be applied have been explained by the Tariff Board as follows:

. . . . If any country granted an indirect subsidy to shipping, for example, granted an extraordinarily high poundage rate for mail matter conveyed by ships, it is probable that the section would be put into operation.

An instance came under our notice where goods were carried on the local railways at a reduced rate of inland freight because the goods were to be shipped in a vessel belonging to that country, whereas goods to be shipped in vessels of other nationalities were charged higher rates of inland freight. In the former instance the dumping duty under section 7 could be applied.[1]

Sections 8 to 11 contain elaborate provisions which have no direct relation to dumping proper but provide for the application of "exchange-dumping duties" to imports from countries with

[1] *Ibid.*

depreciated currencies. Section 12 provides that the duties
under sections 4 to 11 inclusive must not exceed in any case either
severally or collectively 15 per cent of the value of the goods for
ordinary duty.[1]   Sections 13 to 17 contain the provisions governing the administration of the dumping-duties, of which the most
important are the provisions charging the governor-general—
which in practice means the Cabinet—with the duty of making
necessary administrative regulations and giving full discretion to
the Minister of Customs, in issuing the notices required before the
dumping-duties can be imposed, to specify the goods which are
to be subject to these duties in each specific case in such manner
as he sees fit.   He may, for instance, specify goods of any particular class or kind, or any particular shipment of goods, or goods
exported by any particular exporter.   He may confine the application of his notice to goods entered for consumption after the
date of the notice or he may make it retroactive, applying to
goods already entered.

   With the exception of the provisions of the Act which are
concerned with exchange dumping, which in Canada is dealt with
by legislation independent of the antidumping law, the Australian
law closely resembles in its intent, although not in its form and
phraseology, the Canadian antidumping legislation as it stands
today.   The definition of dumping, the method prescribed for
the determination of the amount of the dumping-duties, the
limitation of the dumping-duties to a maximum of 15 per cent,
the provisions for the exclusion of foreign excises from fair market
value for the purpose of the antidumping law, and for the use of
values at date of shipment instead of at date of purchase except
under specified circumstances, the extension of the dumping-
duties to imports of goods sold at a price less than cost of production, the special treatment of goods sold on consignment, all of

   [1] In Australian customs procedure, 10 per cent is added to the fair market
value in the country of export to obtain the value for the purpose of assessment
of the ordinary ad valorem tariff duties.

these closely parallel the corresponding provisions in the Canadian law. Aside from the special feature of the "dumping freight duty" which has no counterpart in Canadian legislation, the only important departures from the Canadian model are: the methods prescribed for the administration of the dumping-duties, and especially the distribution of the administrative duties among several agencies of the government; the requirement that notice be issued before imports may be subjected to the dumping-duties; and the discretion allowed to the officials administering the law to decide whether or not the duties shall be applied in particular cases.[1]

THE NEW ZEALAND ANTIDUMPING LAW OF 1921

New Zealand enacted in 1921 as part of a general revision of its tariff legislation an antidumping measure which to some extent follows closely the Canadian legislation but in other respects introduces novel features into antidumping legislation.[2] The law makes subject to dumping-duty three classes of imports: goods imported into New Zealand of a class or kind produced in New Zealand, if the f.o.b. selling price to the importer is less than the current domestic value in the country of export; (b) goods imported into New Zealand at a price which in the opinion of the Minister of Customs is less than the cost of production, including a reasonable profit, in the country of origin or the country of exportation at the time of exportation; (c) goods imported into New Zealand of a class or kind produced in New Zealand, or goods imported into New Zealand from a non-British country of a class or kind produced in some other part of the British

---

[1] A notice was issued in 1922 under Section 4 specifying rubber tires of a special type and in millimeter sizes exported to Australia by an American concern. These tires were of a type whose manufacture had been discontinued. In the United States tires of this type were commonly sold only in inch sizes, and a special discount of 15 per cent was granted only on export orders and only on the millimeter sizes.

[2] The Customs Amendment Act, December 22, 1921, Sec. 11. The text of the Act is given in the *Board of Trade Journal*, February 9, 1922, Supplement.

Empire, if the Minister of Customs is satisfied that any special concession, whether by way of railway or shipping freight, subsidy, special bounty, rebate, or otherwise, is given to such goods and that there results from such concession injury to a New Zealand or other British industry. In all of these cases the imposition of the dumping-duty is mandatory "save where the Minister may otherwise specially direct on the ground that the imposition of such duty is not required in the public interest."

The first two of these provisions closely follow the Canadian law as it now stands. The third provision, which has no parallel in Canadian legislation, combines the bounty-countervailing duty of the South African and the freight dumping-duty of the Australian antidumping laws. But in authorizing the penalization of bounty-fed imports from any foreign (i.e., non-British) country even though they are of a kind not produced in New Zealand if the grant of a bounty to such goods has an injurious effect on any industry in any part of the British Empire, New Zealand displays a striking degree of solicitude for the economic welfare of the remainder of the Empire. The extension to the industries of the remainder of the Empire of the protection of this countervailing duty presumably rests on the theory either (a) that this duty will operate to equalize conditions in the export trade to New Zealand as between a subsidized non-British exporter and a non-subsidized British exporter, or, (b) that if the British industry which is injured by the bounty does not export to New Zealand, the special penalty placed on the products of the subsidized non-British industry will operate to bring about an abandonment of the bounty. It is to be noted that, unlike the two preceding provisions, the bounty-countervailing provision specifies that the duty is not to be applied unless "an effect prejudicial or injurious" results from the bounty to an industry in New Zealand or some other part of the British Empire.

In all instances of sale for export to New Zealand below the domestic price, or sale below cost of production, or sale of subsidized goods, there is left to the final determination of the Minister of Customs: (1) the amount by which the foreign domestic exceeds the foreign export price, or the amount by which the foreign cost of production exceeds the foreign export price, or the amount of the subsidy, as the case may be; and also (2) the rate of penalty duty to be imposed in each case, provided, however, that such duty must not exceed the difference between foreign domestic and export price, or between foreign cost of production and export price, or the amount of the subsidy or bounty. The authority to make the necessary regulations for the administration of these provisions is given to the governor-general, which in practice means the Cabinet.

Where for any reason it is difficult to determine the value of goods for customs purposes or where it appears that goods are shipped on consignment or in any way other than on sale in order to evade the dumping-duty the Minister of Customs is authorized, as in the Canadian law, to determine the foreign market value, the export price, or the cost of production for the purpose of assessment of duty in such manner as he sees fit and to assess the duty accordingly.[1] The act authorizes the issue of regulations exempting from the dumping-duties goods of a class or kind (a) not made in substantial quantities, or (b) not offered for sale to all purchasers on equal terms under like conditions, in New Zealand *or in some other part of the British Empire*. The object of the second part of this provision is obviously to protect consumers in New Zealand and in other portions of the British Empire from exploitation by a monopoly or from an abnormal shortage of goods, in so far as this can be achieved by removing restrictions on the importation of dumped goods into New Zealand. It is not apparent, however, how the removal of restrictions on import into New Zealand can benefit consumers of monopolized or abnormally scarce goods in other parts of the British Empire; if it had any effect at all

[1] Sec. 11 (5) and Sec. 23.

on consumers outside of New Zealand, it might be expected on the contrary to make the supply of the particular commodity more, instead of less, scarce outside of New Zealand.

The same act amends the Customs Act of 1913 so as to require the deduction from current domestic value in the exporting country of excise taxes and drawbacks in determining the current domestic value for purpose of assessment both of ordinary ad valorem duties and of dumping-duties.[1]

The New Zealand customs department has announced that as far as practicable three months' notice would be given before the dumping-duties would be applied to any particular class of imports. Where industries in other parts of the British Empire are affected by dumping into New Zealand, the customs officials are instructed not to levy the dumping-duties without such notice without special reference to the Minister of Customs and only important cases are to be referred to him. Where New Zealand industries are affected by dumping into New Zealand, no dumping-duties are to be levied without such notice "unless the importations are of such a character that they are likely immediately and for some time to affect local industries, e.g. (a) the importation of 10,000 casks of cement to be landed by reason of dumping at a cost below that at which locally made cement can be sold; (b) the importation of £10,000 worth of tweeds under similar conditions."[2] In the few instances in which notice of intention to apply the dumping-duties has to date been issued it was made clear that the duties would not be applied unless the dumped imports promised "by their magnitude or otherwise" to injure an established industry in New Zealand.[3]

[1] Sec. 114 (3) of Customs Act, 1913, as amended by Customs Amendment Act, 1921.

[2] New Zealand, Customs Department, *Customs Notice*, July 6, 1922.

[3] Cf. *Board of Trade Journal*, October 12, 1922, p. 415.

FLEXIBLE TARIFF PROVISIONS

There has been evident in recent tariff legislation a tendency to give to customs or other administrative officials a wide measure of discretion in fixing the rates of duty to be imposed on imports where temporary or abnormal conditions either at home or in the foreign exporting countries change the competitive status of domestic industries in relation to foreign products. Such measures are not properly speaking antidumping provisions and usually require that any increase of duties decreed under their authority shall be imposed on all imports of the kind specified in the order without respect to whether or not these goods have been sold by their exporters abroad at dumping prices, but they may readily be invoked in cases where dumping is being practiced or is suspected of being practiced.   Even where there is a genuine antidumping law on the statute books, the flexible tariff provision may be used in preference to the antidumping measure as a remedy against dumped imports because of the greater speed and elasticity with which it can perhaps be applied in emergency situations. So-called "exchange-dumping" measures which provide for the imposition of special duties on imports from countries with greatly depreciated currencies—generally on the theory that exporters in such countries can afford to sell at prices which when converted into foreign non-depreciated currencies are abnormally low—have been enacted in the last few years by many countries and to a considerable degree they fall in the class of what are here termed flexible tariff provisions. They are excluded, however, from consideration in this study, partly because they are so varied and elaborate in their provisions, so recent in their origin, and so far-spreading in the ramifications of the problems to which they give rise, that they could not be given adequate consideration within the limits of a study which is concerned only with dumping proper and with measures directed primarily against dumping proper.   There follows a summarized description of several foreign measures which without special reference to the cause of the abnormal cheapness of foreign goods grant to administrative officials broad powers to change the statutory rates of import duty in order to protect domestic industries against the temporary inflow of foreign goods at abnormally low prices.

Japan in 1920, by an amendment to its general tariff law, authorized the government to impose special duties, in addition to the ordinary duties but not to exceed the value of the imported articles, on imports designated by the government after investigation as being imported at unreasonably cheap prices, provided that the staple industries of Japan were threatened thereby.[1] The purpose of the law, it was explained, was to provide against the possibility of dumping and especially to protect the Japanese industries which were developed during the war. A measure of this sort would obviously provide a more elastic device against dumping than a conventional antidumping measure which required in each case the establishment of the existence of dumping and placed narrow restrictions on the rates of additional duty which could be applied. In some countries constitutional restrictions and in other countries the reluctance to intrust to administrative authorities such wide powers would operate to prevent the adoption of a measure of this sort in preference to an antidumping measure of the more common type.

[1] "Art. V.: When the staple industries of Japan are threatened by the importation of unreasonably cheap goods, or by the sale of imports at an unreasonably cheap price, the Government by Imperial ordinance, after investigation by a board of inquiry, is authorized to designate those commodities for which during a certain period special import duties, in addition to the regular schedule, shall be paid, not to exceed, however, the value of the commodity itself.

"Regarding commodities which have thus been designated, which have already been imported, and which are owned or possessed by a merchant or his representative, the Government is authorized to levy superduties for such commodities from the seller or his representative, in accordance with the preceding paragraph. The superduties provided in the preceding paragraph shall be collected after the manner of collecting national taxes" (U.S. Department of Commerce, *Commerce Reports*, April 26, 1920, and the *Journal of Conational Law*, II [1921], 21).

New Zealand incorporated in its tariff legislation in 1921 a provision authorizing the governor-general by Order in Council to remove, reduce, or increase the rate of duty in special cases on any class of goods whenever he is satisfied that the existing duty or exemption from duty operates against the interest of the public in general or of a particular industry, trade, or occupation, or whenever trade concessions, in the form of bounties, rebates, freight concessions, or otherwise, are being granted on imports into New Zealand.[1] The New Zealand tariff legislation of 1921 thus provided the government with two alternative devices for meeting the problems both of dumped imports and of bounty-fed imports. It is to be presumed that this more elastic measure will be invoked, in so far as dumping is concerned, only where the more formal and restricted antidumping and bounty-countervailing provisions fail to meet an emergency situation rapidly or effectively enough, or where their stipulations are being technically evaded.

Canada in 1922 amended its Customs Act so as to empower the governor-general-in-council, on a report from the Minister of Customs that natural products of a kind produced in Canada are being imported into Canada under such conditions as prejudicially to affect the interests of Canadian producers, to author-

[1] New Zealand Customs Amendment Act, 1921, Sec. 12 (1):

"If and whenever the Governor-General is satisfied—

"(a) That the existence of a duty of Customs, or the rate of any such duty, or the exemption of any goods from duty, operates or is likely to operate in an injurious, unfair, or anomalous manner in respect either generally to the public interest or particularly to any industry, trade, business, or occupation; or

"(b) That trade concessions (whether by way of railway or shipping freight, special bounty, rebate, or otherwise) are being allowed, taken, or granted on goods imported into New Zealand; or

"(c) That the duties payable in any country on the importation of goods from New Zealand are excessive—he may, by Order in Council, suspend the existing Tariff in whole or in part, and by the same or a subsequent Order in Council may, in lieu thereof, impose on any goods such duties of Customs, or create such exemptions from duty, as appear to him just" (*Board of Trade Journal*, February 9, 1922, Supplement.)

ize the Minister of Customs to value such goods for customs without regard to other provisions of the Customs Act.[1]   The purpose of this provision is to permit a higher value to be placed on goods entered for customs than the actual current domestic value in the country of export and thus to make legally possible the collection of higher ordinary duties, and of dumping-duties,[2] on imports of natural products even though the prices to Canadian purchasers are not lower than the foreign domestic prices and are not below cost of production.

[1] Act to Amend the Customs Act, 12–13 George V, chap. 18:

"If at any time it appears to the satisfaction of the Governor in Council on a report from the Minister of Customs and Excise, that natural products of a class or kind produced in Canada are being imported into Canada, either on sale or consignment, under such conditions as prejudicially or injuriously to affect the interests of Canadian producers, the Governor in Council may, in any case or class of cases, authorize the Minister to value such goods for duty, notwithstanding any other provisions of this Act, and the value so determined shall be held to be the fair market value thereof" (*Statutes of Canada*, 1922, I–II, 75, 76).

[2] Because if a higher value is attributed to the imported goods than their actual foreign domestic price the imputed value for purposes of customs will ordinarily be higher than the export price and thus will make the goods subject to dumping-duty.

CHAPTER XIII
AMERICAN ANTIDUMPING LEGISLATION

There have been enacted in the United States a number of measures which provide remedies against dumping. Of these measures, the countervailing duties against official bounties have already been discussed; the remaining measures fall into two classes: (*a*) those which treat special types of dumping as a manifestation of unfair competition and apply judicial or quasi-judicial remedies, and (*b*) those which treat dumping as a special phase of the general problem of foreign competition with American industries and apply administrative remedies in the form of additional import duties. It will be convenient to follow the topical treatment in discussing these two classes of measures, especially as this will involve only minor departures from the chronological treatment.

DUMPING AND UNFAIR COMPETITION

The Sherman Antitrust Act, 1890.—Congress in 1890 passed the Sherman Antitrust Act, prohibiting, under severe penalties, every contract or combination in restraint of interstate or foreign commerce, and every monopolization or attempt to monopolize such commerce. The courts have in a number of instances held the use of unfair methods of competition to be evidence of an intent to establish monopoly or to restrain commerce, and as such to be in violation of this Act. Of special importance for our present purpose, the courts have enjoined under this Act cutting prices below the current rate, and especially below the cost of production, for the purpose of injuring competitors.[1] In several cases "local price-cutting," or the sale or offer for sale of a commodity in one part of the United States at prices

[1] *Trust Laws and Unfair Competition*, pp. 478 ff.

which were lower, after allowance for differences in cost of transportation, grade, quality, or quantity sold, than the prices charged in other parts of the United States, with the intent of thereby establishing a monopoly or destroying or injuring the trade or business of another or preventing another from engaging in the same business, was restrained as in violation of the Sherman Act.[1] Local price-cutting with such intent is, of course, the parallel in domestic commerce of predatory dumping in foreign commerce and if the Sherman Act were applicable to unfair acts done by foreigners abroad, it would serve as a remedy against predatory dumping by foreigners in the American market with the intent of injuring American competitors or establishing a monopoly of the American market. A Supreme Court decision, however, denied the jurisdiction of the United States under this Act over acts done in foreign countries, even if done by citizens of the United States, and even if there were conspiracy in the United States to perform these acts elsewhere, provided that these acts were not in violation of the law of the country where they were committed. The Court refused to validate the extraterritorial application of the law in the absence of an express provision in the law for such application.[2] But if a foreign exporter or his agent were to sell *in the United States* to American purchasers at dumping prices with intent to injure American producers or to monopolize the American market, i.e., if the sale contracts were made in this country and not in the exporting country, such practice might perhaps come under the prohibition of the Sherman Act consistently with this decision.

Section 73, Tariff Act of 1894.—The Wilson Tariff Act of 1894, by a provision which is still in effect, attempted to extend

---

[1] *Ibid.*, p. 479.

[2] *American Banana Co.* v. *United Fruit Co.*, 213 U.S. 347: "A conspiracy in this country to do acts in another jurisdiction does not draw to itself those acts and make them unlawful if they are permitted by the local law."

to the import trade into the United States a special protection against endeavors to monopolize the trade. Section 73 of this Act makes unlawful every conspiracy, combination, etc., of persons or corporations when any of them is engaged in importing articles into the United States and when such conspiracy or combination is intended to operate in restraint of lawful trade or to increase the market price in the United States of any imported article or of any manufacture of such article. Severe penalties, in the form of fines or imprisonment or both, are provided. It would undoubtedly be unlawful under this Act for an importer acting as agent or principal to enter into an agreement in the United States with a foreign exporter or with other American importers to import foreign goods at dumping prices with the intent of eliminating American competitors of the foreign producers or of establishing, even as against other foreign producers, a monopoly of the American market for some foreign producer. If the agreement were entered into in a foreign country, or if a foreign producer were dumping in the United States with predatory intent but without involving an American agent or importer in such unlawful intent, the decision of the Supreme Court in the United Fruit Co. case would indicate that the Wilson Act would not provide a remedy.[1] Except.for the unimportant difference in the penalties provided, it does not appear, therefore, that Section 73 of the Wilson Act added anything to the Sherman Act. In any case it has proved to be without practical significance. Proceedings against an importer have been instituted under it in only one instance, and in this instance, the Brazilian coffee valorization case, the abandonment of the allegedly unlawful act resulted in a dismissal of the proceed-

[1] This case was decided after the passage of the Wilson Act, but the Supreme Court decision made no reference to its provisions. It would appear to the layman that the alleged conspiracy of the United Fruit Company was unlawful under this Act, regardless of where the specific acts which executed the conspiracy were performed, if the conspiracy itself occurred in the United States.

ings.[1] Under ordinary circumstances the importer of goods sold with predatory intent at dumping prices or even the American agent of the foreign exporter would rarely be a participant in the predatory intent necessary to make the act of importation unlawful under this Act, and the predatory intent would be connected only with the exportation from the foreign country. Even if there should be conspiracy between importer and foreign exporter it would be difficult for the government to establish its existence with the certainty necessary under a criminal statute.

Sections 800–801, Revenue Act, 1916.—After the outbreak of the war the disclosure of the unfair methods of competition, and above all the practice of predatory dumping, which has supposedly been widely prevalent in the export trade of foreign countries—and especially Germany—led to a widespread demand in the United States for more effective protection to American industries against such unfair foreign competition. This demand was in some quarters made a pretext for insisting upon a general increase in the ordinary import duties; in other quarters the enactment of antidumping legislation of the Canadian type was urged upon Congress. The Wilson administration, while showing itself wholly sympathetic with the desire for adequate protection against unfair foreign competition, was determined that it should not be employed to build up sentiment for an upward revision of the existing tariff act. It therefore recommended that any measure adopted to meet the problem should be divorced from customs legislation and should take the form of a further extension to those engaged in the import trade of the

[1]This was a case not of predatory dumping but of the association of American bankers and importers, in co-operation with the state of Saõ Paulo, to control the importation of Brazilian coffee and to finance the withholding of surplus stocks thereof from the market, with the object of raising its price in the American market. Cf. Attorney General of the United States, *Annual Report*, 1912, pp. 19 ff.; "Valorization of Coffee," 63d Cong., 1st Sess., *Sen. Doc.* 36.

restraints against unfair competition which had been imposed on domestic commerce.[1]

Congress followed the recommendations of the administration. The Revenue Bill of 1916, as it passed the House, contained provisions making it unlawful for any importer commonly and systematically to sell imported articles in the United States at a price substantially less than the actual market value of such articles at the time of exportation to the United States in the principal markets of the country of production or of other foreign countries to which they were commonly exported after adding to such foreign market value the various costs incidental to importation, provided that such act or acts were done with intent to injure or destroy or prevent the establishment of an industry in the United States, or of restraining competition in such articles in the United States. Violation of these provisions was made subject to a fine not exceeding $5,000 or imprisonment not exceeding one year, or both, and any person injured by such violation was given the right to sue for and to recover threefold the damages sustained. The Senate amended the House bill so as to penalize importation as well as sale by an importer at dumping prices with intent to injure an American industry or to restrain competition in the United States,[2] and the bill was

[1] Cf. the recommendations of Mr. Redfield, Secretary of Commerce, in *Report of the Department of Commerce*, 1915, p. 43; *Report of Committee on Ways and Means on Revenue Bill of 1916*, 64th Cong., 1st Sess. *House Rept.* 922, p. 9. Cf. also, Samuel J. Graham, Assistant Attorney General, Department of Justice, in letter to *New York Times*, July 4, 1916: "Any anti-dumping provision is not a matter of taxation, or, strictly speaking, tariff. It is a power exercised under the commerce clause of the constitution and not under the taxing clause. Its purpose should be to prevent unfair competition. Just as we have said to our own people by the Clayton Act that they should not indulge in unfair competition, so we propose to say the same to the foreigner."

[2] *Congressional Record*, September 5, 1916, p. 13, 789. The bill was also amended by the addition of a provision penalizing by double duties the practice of "full line forcing" in the import trade, i.e. the importation of articles under an agreement that the importer should not use, buy, or deal in the similar products of any other concern.

enacted as so amended. This provision of the Revenue Act of 1916 has not been repealed, and therefore continues in effect.

This antidumping provision, beyond the fact that it makes the participation of the importer both as to act and intent in predatory dumping specifically unlawful and not merely unlawful by construction as a practice by which competition can be restrained or monopoly established, adds nothing to the Sherman Act. Beyond the fact that it makes unnecessary the proof of conspiracy between the importer and others, it adds nothing to the Wilson Act of 1894. It is not even clear that it adds anything but its penalties to Section 5 of the Federal Trade Commission Act of 1914, which, in the part pertinent here, merely declares unlawful "unfair methods of competition in commerce," since "commerce" covers both interstate and foreign commerce, and analogous price-practices in domestic commerce have been declared by the courts to be "unfair." Like Section 73 of the Wilson Act of 1894, this provision has proved to be wholly ineffective; there has not been a single instance of even the institution of proceedings under it.[1] It imposes no special duties in connection with its administration on any government agency and its enforcement therefore devolves upon the Department of Justice, an agency without any special facilities for the discovery of predatory dumping. As a criminal statute, it must be strictly construed, and the uncertainty as to when a price to or by an importer is "substantially less" than the foreign market value, and as to what constitutes "common and systematic importation," to say nothing of the difficulty of proving intent to injure or destroy an American industry or to establish a monopoly, would inevitably render it difficult to secure conviction in the typical case of predatory dumping.[2] An American manufacturer injured by such dumping would have

[1] Cf. Mr. Fordney, *Congressional Record*, December 9, 1919, p. 331.

[2] Cf. U.S. Tariff Commission, *Information concerning Dumping and Unfair Foreign Competition*, p. 33.

difficulty in recovering damages in a civil suit for the same reasons, magnified by the lack of means at his disposal for proof of systematic dumping and of predatory intent. An even more serious limitation on the effectiveness of the provision is the requirement that the predatory intent in connection with the dumping must be on the part of the importer if the penalties are to apply. To repeat what has already been said with reference to Section 73 of the Wilson Act of 1894, the importer of dumped goods rarely has any motive in his importation or sale of the goods other than the profit to be derived therefrom, and the predatory intent, if there is such, will normally be confined to the foreign exporter. Criminal antidumping statutes cannot be made effective unless some means is found of reaching the foreign offender.

The antidumping provision of the Act of 1916 has also been criticized on the ground that in confining its penalties to the common and systematic practice of predatory dumping it fails to provide remedies against sporadic dumping even though predatory in character and against other types of dumping which may be injurious to American industry though not predatory in intent or not provable to be so.[2] But these are not so much criticisms of the effectiveness of the measure in attaining its objectives as of the limited character of these objectives. It was intended to reach only predatory dumping and the failure to penalize sporadic dumping was therefore well-advised. Sporadic dumping cannot result in an appreciable restraint of competition or monopolization of commerce. It is necessary, moreover, under the American law of unfair competition, to demonstrate that there is sustained practice of unfair methods, to establish intent to restrain commerce or to gain monopoly control. A

[1] Cf. *ibid.*, p. 18.

[2] Cf. *ibid.*, p. 33; W. C. Culbertson, *Commercial Policy in War Time and After*, New York, 1919, pp. 152 ff.

single instance or a few scattered instances of such practice will not secure conviction.[1]

Section 316, Fordney-McCumber Tariff Act of 1922.—Section 316 of the Fordney-McCumber Tariff Act of 1922 adds a third to the series of measures specifically attempting to restrain unfair competition in import trade. This section was substituted by the Finance Committee of the Senate for a comprehensive antidumping bill of an elaborate character passed by the House. It declares unlawful unfair methods of competition and unfair acts in the importation of articles into the United States or their sale by the owner, importer, consignee, or the agent of one of these, if their effect or tendency is to destroy or substantially injure an industry efficiently and economically operated in the United States, or to prevent the establishment of such an industry, or to restrain or monopolize trade and commerce in the United States. The Tariff Commission is instructed to investigate any alleged violation of this provision on complaint under oath or on its own initiative, under such rules as it may prescribe. Its findings, *if supported by evidence*, are to be conclusive except that it may grant a rehearing and that an appeal may be taken from its findings to the United States Court of Customs Appeals upon a question of law only. This court may upon such appeal order the Tariff Commission to hold further hearings and take further evidence, and the Tariff Commission may thereupon modify its findings as to the facts or make new findings, which shall be conclusive as to the facts, *if supported by "the evidence,"* except that another appeal will lie to the Court of Customs Appeals on a question of law only. The judgment of the court shall be final except that it shall be subject to review upon certiorari by the United States Supreme Court. The final findings of the Tariff Commission are to be transmitted with the record of proceedings to the president, who

[1] Cf. H. C. Emery, "The Problem of Anti-Dumping Legislation," *Report of Third National Foreign Trade Convention*, 1916, p. 78.

shall, if satisfied that the existence of unfair methods or acts has been established, determine the rate of additional duty, not exceeding 50 per cent nor less than 10 per cent of the value of the imported articles as determined for the purpose of assessment of ordinary duties, "which will offset such method or act." In extreme cases of unfair methods he shall direct that such articles as he shall deem the interests of the United States shall require, imported by any person violating the provisions of the Act, shall be excluded·from entry into the United States.

The form of this provision follows in general the recommendations made to Congress by the Tariff Commission in connection with its criticism of the antidumping provision in the Revenue Act of 1916.[1] Its sponsors in the Senate claimed for it that it was broad enough to prevent every type and form of unfair practice and was therefore a more adequate protection to American industry than any antidumping statute the country has ever had.[2] It is clear, however, that this provision will not apply to dumping unless predatory intent or some unfair act is connected with it, for there is nothing in the meaning which has been given to the term "unfair competition" in American statutes or judicial decisions which will make it apply to ordinary non-predatory dumping.[3] The significance of this provision as an antidumping measure depends therefore on the additional safeguards which it establishes against predatory dumping. Does it establish any such safeguards additional to and superior to those already established by previously enacted measures?

[1] Cf. U.S. Tariff Commission, *Information concerning Dumping and Unfair Foreign Competition*, pp. 33, 34; *Sixth Annual Report*, 1922, pp. 3, 4.

[2] Finance Committee of the Senate, *Majority Report on H.R. 7456*, 67th Cong., 2d Sess., *Sen. Rept.* 595, p. 3. When this Act was passed there was already on the statute books, in addition to Section 73 of the Wilson Act of 1894 and the antidumping provision of the Revenue Act of 1916, the excellent antidumping law enacted in 1921 as part of the Emergency Tariff Act. See *infra*, pp. 258 ff.

[3] Except that the determination of the "fairness" of a competitive act is sometimes based on the probable results of the act, whatever its intent may have been.

Section 73 of the Wilson Tariff Act of 1894 and the anti-dumping provision of the Revenue Act of 1916 proved ineffective mainly because they were criminal statutes providing judicial remedies and therefore subject to strict construction, and because they could not be made to reach the offender if he were a foreigner operating in a foreign country. Also contributory to their ineffectiveness was, perhaps, the failure to assign to some government agency the special task of seeing to their enforcement. Section 316 is apparently regarded in official quarters as providing an administrative rather than a judicial remedy against unfair competition in import trade, but the prescribed procedure for its enforcement is at least quasi-judicial in character, and the requirement that there must be an act of unfair competition before the penalties can be applied will, in the absence of a precise legal definition of what is unfair competition, open the way to judicial review in every attempted instance of the imposition of the penalties. Although the appeal to the Court of Customs Appeals can be made in the first instance only on a question of law, it may develop in practice that the importer against whom proceedings have been instituted can obtain a judicial review even as to the facts by first appealing on any question of law which can be raised, if the Court thereupon orders a rehearing by the Tariff Commission. On a rehearing the findings of the Tariff Commission as to the facts are conclusive only "if supported by *the* evidence," and the Court might conceivably hold that it had the right of review as to the sufficiency of the evidence.[1] Moreover, the great measure of discretion allowed to the president as to the penalties to be imposed in case of an unfair act will raise a constitutional question if an important case should arise under this provision.

[1] There is reason to suppose, however, that the inclusion of the word "the" was an unintentional slip in draftsmanship and therefore should not be permitted to affect the interpretation of the provision.

The constitutional question involved is, of course, whether the grant to the president of authority to fix the rates of additional duty is an invalid delegation of legislative (or judicial?) power. The same question is involved in Sections 315 and 317 of the Fordney-McCumber Tariff Act. The famous *Field* v. *Clark* case[1] is commonly cited in support of the constitutionality of such tariff provisions. In this case the Supreme Court held that the power granted by Section 3 of the Tariff Act of 1890 to impose certain duties on five commodities specified in the Act when imported from countries whose duties on American products he deemed to be "reciprocally unequal and unreasonable" did not involve a delegation of legislative power because it gave no discretion to the president as to the commodities to be taxed, the rates at which they were to be taxed, or the countries whose products were to be taxed.[2] Section 316 attempts to conceal the wide grant of discretionary power to the president by stating that the president is to determine the penalty "which will offset such [unfair] method or act," but there is no genuine limitation in these words since his decision is made conclusive and in most instances of unfair competitive acts there is no possible method of determining even approximately what penalty will "offset" any such act. Within the maximum and minimum limits set by the law the president will in practice have complete discretion. Moreover, in extreme cases he may prohibit the importation of the commodities in question, and the law throws no light on what are extreme cases. There is no close parallel therefore between Section 3 of the Tariff Act of 1890, as the Supreme Court interpreted it in *Field* v. *Clark*, and Section 316 of the Fordney-

[1] 143 U.S. 649.

[2] As a matter of fact, President Harrison exercised considerable discretion in his choice of the countries to be penalized, and took steps only against three Caribbean countries which were not in a position to inflict substantial injury on American commerce by retaliatory measures. (Cf. U.S. Tariff Commission, *Reciprocity and Commercial Treaties*, 1919, pp. 156 ff.)

McCumber Act.[1] But the trend of judicial interpretation of the constitutional prohibition against delegation of powers has since *Field* v. *Clark* been decidedly in the direction of greater leniency, on the ground, mainly, that otherwise the plenary power of Congress to regulate foreign commerce and to perform its other functions could not be effectively exercised.[2] It is nevertheless doubtful whether this provision will be less impaired in effectiveness by the necessity of judicial interpretation and enforcement than the 1894 and 1916 measures against unfair competition in the import trade.

Section 316 does, however, assign to a government agency, the Tariff Commission, the special task of investigating alleged violations of its provisions, and in this respect it adds something to the 1894 and 1916 measures. But the Federal Trade Commission Act had already declared unlawful "unfair methods of competition in commerce" and had assigned to that Commission the duty of investigating alleged instances of unfair competition and of securing through the courts the enforcement of the prohibition thereof. Aside from any superiority which may rest in the Tariff Commission as the investigating agent as compared to the Federal Trade Commission and in the procedure

---

[1] Cf. the comment of Senator Walsh of Montana in the Senate when this section was under discussion: "I dare say that the President of the United States is as accomplished a mathematician as the ordinary Member of this body; but how he is going to convert into a rate of duty the offense committed by importers or dealers in imported articles so as to offset by his rate of duty the evil that is thus perpetrated is a problem which I shall not undertake to solve. I merely call attention to this matter in passing.

"He may not only impose this speculative duty which is thus arrived at, however, but in extreme cases he may declare that the merchandise shall be excluded from the United States entirely. Just exactly what is an extreme case, or a moderate case, or a mild case, we are left merely to speculate. Of course, this gives to the President the power to impose any duty he sees fit, or to exclude the merchandise altogether if he sees fit. In other words, the discretion vested in the President . . . . is made perfectly obvious and indisputable under the provisions of section 316" (*Congressional Record*, August 11, 1922, p. 12,274).

[2] Cf. e.g., *Buttfield* v. *Stranahan*, 192 U.S 470.

and the quasi-judicial nature of the penalties prescribed under Section 316 as compared to the procedure and the necessity of resort to the courts to enforce the penalties provided for by the Federal Trade Commission Act, there is not evident so far any substantial contribution by Section 316 to the already existent safeguards against predatory dumping and against unfair competition in general in the import trade.[1]

Such being the conclusion in regard to the procedure and the penalties under Section 316, it follows that that section, unless it reaches acts which are not reached under previous legislation, adds little or nothing to the existing body of law. Section 316 declares unlawful and provides penalties for "unfair methods of competition and unfair acts in the importation of articles into the United States, or in their sale by the owner, importer, consignee, or agent of either, the effect or tendency of which is to destroy or substantially injure an industry, efficiently and economically operated, in the United States, or to prevent the establishment of such an industry, or to restrain or monopolize trade and commerce in the United States." But the Federal Trade Commission Act had already declared unlawful, and without any stated limitations or provisos, unfair methods of competition in commerce, and had so defined commerce as to include import and export trade as well as interstate trade.[2]

The earlier measures restraining unfair competition in the import trade have been ineffective because of their failure to reach, directly or indirectly, unfair acts done outside the territorial jurisdiction of the United States. If Section 316 provides a means of reaching such acts it succeeds, therefore,

[1] The antidumping provisions of the Emergency Tariff act of 1921 still await consideration. An examination of its provisions affords still further support for this conclusion.

[2] Sec. 4. Cf., however, U.S. Tariff Commission, *Sixth Annual Report*, p. 4; "Section 316 extends to import trade practically the same prohibition against unfair methods of competition which the Federal Trade Commission act provides against unfair methods of competition in interstate trade."

in filling a gap in·American legislation and has some degree of potential utility. But the courts have made it clear that a federal statute will be given extraterritorial application only if its language clearly indicates such an intent.[1] To meet this situation in so far as the export trade was concerned, the Webb-Pomerene Act extended the prohibition by the Federal Trade Commission Act of unfair methods of competition in commerce so that it now applies to methods of competition in the export trade unfair to American competitors, even though the acts constituting such unfair methods are done without the territorial jurisdiction of the United States.[2] If Section 316 is to have extraterritorial jurisdiction it would seem, therefore, that there must be a clear indication in the statute itself, or at least in the Congressional discussions thereof, that such is its intent.

There was but perfunctory discussion of Section 316 in the Senate, none at all in the House. The Senate discussion throws but little light on the intent of the provision, but it does indicate that the section was intended to apply only to unfair acts done by importers in the United States. In the original draft the penalties were applicable—or appeared to the Senate to be applicable—to all imports of a kind in connection with which unfair acts were being done by the "owner, importer, consignee, or agent of either." The Senate, by general consent, amended the phraseology so as to make it clear that innocent importers were not to be penalized because other importers of the same

---

[1] Cf. p. 240, *supra*. Cf. also, *Sandberg* v. *McDonald*, 248 U.S. 185: "Legislation is presumptively territorial and confined to limits over which the law-making power has jurisdiction."

[2] Sec. 4: "That the prohibition against 'unfair methods of competition' and the remedies provided for enforcing said prohibition contained in the Act entitled 'An Act to create a Federal Trade Commission, to define its powers and duties, and for other purposes,' approved September twenty-sixth, nineteen hundred and fourteen, shall be construed as extending to unfair methods of competition used in export trade against competitors engaged in export trade, even though the acts constituting such unfair methods are done without the territorial jurisdiction of the United States."

kind of commodity were committing unfair acts. The implication of this discussion was clearly that the section was
directed only against unfair acts by importers, and no mention
was made of unfair acts by foreign exporters to the United
States. In the process of amending the section the Senate so
phrased the penalty clause as to make the additional duties
applicable only to articles *"imported* in violation of this Act"
and to make the prohibition of import applicable only to articles
"imported by any person violating the provisions of this Act,"[1]
and these changes are incorporated in the section as finally
enacted. The section fails, therefore, to reach unfair acts in
connection with the *exportation* of the goods to the United States.
Even if the goods are exported prior to sale so that the exporter
is also the "owner" thereof, the section may make unfair acts
on his part unlawful, but its penalties will not reach him because
they apply only to the importer. Since the unfair acts are
almost always on the part of the exporter or seller rather than
on the part of the importer or purchaser, Section 316 appears,
therefore, to have the same shortcoming which has rendered
ineffective previous American legislation against unfair competition in the import trade, namely, the failure to reach the foreign
exporter. The Tariff Commission, however, interprets Section
316 as giving jurisdiction over acts done outside the United States.
"These provisions," it declares, "make it possible for the
President to prevent unfair practices, even when engaged in
by individuals residing outside the jurisdiction of the United
States."[2] Unless the innocent purchase by an American of goods
sold by a foreign exporter with unfair intent is also unfair, or
unless it is immaterial under the law of unfair competition who
does the unfair act or where it is done and the section con-
templates action against the goods rather than the person, it is
difficult to see how the section can be so construed. Nor does

[1] *Congressional Record*, August 11, 1922, pp. 12,277 ff.
[2] *Sixth Annual Report*, p. 4.

there appear to be any indication in the statute itself that such a construction was intended.

American Participation in the International Union for the Protection of Industrial Property.—The difficulty, in most cases the impossibility, of establishing an effective system of control of unfair competition through criminal penalties which will reach the offender even if he is a foreigner operating from a foreign country has given rise to the suggestion that the problem of unfair competition in international economic relations should be met either through the establishment of an international commerce court or by international agreement whereby each country would pledge itself to extend to the nationals of every other country which was a party to the agreement the same measure of protection against unfair competition which it gives to its own nationals.[1] There has already been achieved a substantial measure of success in establishing such international control of the problem of unfair competition,[2] the most important forward step in this direction having been the establishment at Paris in 1883 of the International Union for the Protection of Industrial Property and the subsequent extension of its powers at later conferences and especially at the Washington Conference of 1911. This Union is primarily concerned with the protection of patent and trade-mark rights, but it deals also with the general problem of unfair competition in its international aspects. The agreement as revised at Washington in 1911 and signed by the representatives of twenty-one countries, including the United States, contained the two following provisions:

ART. 2. The subjects or citizens of each of the contracting parties shall enjoy in all other countries of the Union, with regard to patents of invention, models of utility, industrial designs or models, trade-marks, trade names, the statements of place of origin, suppression of unfair compe-

[1] Cf. Federal Trade Commission, *Annual Report*, 1919, pp. 91 ff., 388; W. S. Culbertson, *Commercial Policy in War Time and After*, chap. xii, "Where National Control Breaks Down."

[2] Cf. *Trust Laws and Unfair Competition*, pp. 697–704.

tition, the advantages which the respective laws now grant or may hereafter grant to the citizens of that country.   Consequently, they shall have the same protection as the latter and the same legal remedies against any infringements of their rights, provided they comply with the formalities and requirements imposed by the National laws of each State upon its own citizens.   Any obligation of domicile or of establishment in the country where the protection is claimed shall not be imposed on the members of the Union.

ART. 10bis. All the contracting countries agree to assure to the members of the Union an effective protection against unfair competition.

If the words "unfair competition" in these pledges can properly be given their American interpretation, the faithful execution of this agreement by its signatories would give to the citizens of each of the signatory countries, including the United States, an effective protection against predatory dumping on the part of the citizens of any of the other signatory countries. The official reports of the proceedings of the Conference indicate, however, that "unfair competition" is an inexact rendering into English of what was intended by the Conference.   "Dishonest competition" signifies more accurately the type of practice which the signatories pledged themselves to suppress.   There are few, if any, countries other than the United States which prohibit either under the civil or under the criminal code price-discrimination in domestic commerce with the intent or result of restraining competition or injuring competitors.   The laws of those foreign countries which have legislated against certain methods of competition confine themselves with almost no exception to the prohibition of practices into which there enters fraud or lying or deceit or breach of promise or some other morally reprehensible element.[1]   The term "unfair competition" in the

[1] For the laws of foreign countries dealing with unfair competition, cf.: *Report of United States Industrial Commission*, 1901, XVIII; Great Britain, Ministry of Reconstruction, *Report of Committee on Trusts*, 1919, p. 33; *Trust Laws and Unfair Competition*, chap. x; U.S. Library of Congress, *Guide to the Law and Legal Literature of Germany*, 1912, pp. 94 ff.; Francis Walker, "Policies of Germany, England, Canada and the United States Towards Combinations," *Annals*, XLII, 185.

Washington Agreement must be interpreted to apply to such practices alone. The basic French text of the Agreement reads "concurrence déloyale" where the English text reads "unfair competition" and that this was understood to mean "dishonest competition" is shown by the report of the British delegates to the Conference at whose suggestion Art 10bis was added and Article 2 was strengthened. In their report the British delegates speak only of "dishonest competition" and they make clear that the Conference understood the term in the narrower sense.[1]

That this is the interpretation adopted by the United States is indicated by the passage in 1918 of the Webb-Pomerene Act, which permits Americans engaged in the export trade to combine in restraint of export trade and prohibits unfair acts in export trade only if they are injurious to competing *American* exporters or to American consumers.[2] The International Union for the Protection of Industrial Property cannot be regarded, therefore, as providing a remedy against predatory dumping in international trade, nor is it likely, notwithstanding the precedent of the Brussels Sugar Convention, that any international agreement to suppress predatory dumping can be reached until most of the important commercial countries make unlawful analogous practices in domestic trade. But for those countries which do

[1] Great Britain, *Parliamentary Papers*, Cd. 5842 (1911). E.g., "We were successful in obtaining a new Article binding the contracting countries to give effective protection against dishonest competition" (p. 95). "Article 2.—This Article . . . . was amended to include indications of origin, and the repression of dishonest competition" (p. 96).

[2] Cf. Eliot Jones, *The Trust Problem in the United States*, p. 384; W. S. Notz and R. S. Harvey, *American Foreign Trade*, p. 241. Cf. also, *Report from the House Committee on the Judiciary on the Webb Bill*, 1916 (64th Cong., 1st Sess., *House Rept.* 1118), p. 3: "Few, if any, foreign countries compel their exporters to observe the business standards prescribed by our antitrust laws, then why should we require our exporters to observe a higher and stricter standard of conduct than their foreign competitors are required to observe? In other words, by this bill we permit our American exporters to meet their foreign rivals on foreign soil on equal terms."

not wish to adopt ordinary antidumping legislation, the establishment of an effective international control of price-practices in international commerce or reconciliation to the continuance of predatory dumping are the only practical alternatives.

ADMINISTRATIVE REMEDIES AGAINST DUMPING

Antidumping provision proposed in 1913.—The Underwood Tariff Bill of 1913 as passed by the House contained a provision for the imposition of additional duties on foreign goods of a kind produced in the United States if exported to the United States at a price less than the fair market value of the goods in the country of exportation at the time of exportation. These dumping-duties were to equal the difference between the export price and the fair market value for home consumption, provided, however, that the dumping-duty was not to exceed 15 per cent ad valorem in any case and that goods whereon the ordinary duties were equal to 50 per cent ad valorem were to be exempt from the dumping duty. The Secretary of the Treasury was to make the rules and regulations for the administration of the provision.[1]

In its provisions and even in its phraseology this proposed antidumping measure was almost an exact duplicate of the Canadian antidumping law, with the important exception, however, that most of the qualifications in the Canadian law modifying, or authorizing the customs authorities to modify, the severity of the penalizing clause were omitted. The Underwood Tariff Bill proposed to make important reductions in the rates of the ordinary Tariff. The Ways and Means Committee of the House, in reporting the bill, explained that the ordinary duties were designed to be low enough to permit "reasonable and fair competition at normal prices" of foreign with American goods, and that the antidumping provision was added to protect

[1] The text of the proposal is given in 63d Cong., 1st Sess., *House Rept.* 2, p. 455.

American industry from demoralization by abnormal foreign competition.[1] The dumping-duties, it was explained by the Committee, were to apply to goods dutiable under the ordinary tariff,[2] and two unsuccessful attempts were made in the House to extend their application to free goods of a kind produced in the United States.[3]

The Senate Finance Committee struck out the antidumping provision from the bill on the grounds: that if applied at all, it should not be restricted to dutiable goods; that it was capable of being used by an "unfriendly administration" as a means of increasing by 15 per cent ad valorem the duties on imported articles; and that the provisions in the existing law penalizing undervaluation were "a very good antidumping provision, and as we are informed and believe immediately stopped dumping in the American market, and this too, without making it discretionary with any executive officer (to be exercised in a broad way) to raise the duty."[4] In conference the House receded, and in the Underwood Tariff as enacted into law there was no antidumping provision.

Antidumping Act, 1921.—The Emergency Tariff Act of 1921 contained as Title II an important antidumping measure to be known, according to the Act, as the Antidumping Act, 1921. This measure had a long and complex legislative history going back to the autumn of 1919, of which only the barest outline need be presented here. In 1919 several proposals for antidumping legislation were presented to the House of which one introduced by Representative Fordney was passed by the House on December 11, 1919.[5] Mr. Fordney claimed that there was need for such legislation because of the ineffectiveness and the

---

[1] *Ibid.*, p. liii.

[2] This is not obvious from the text of the proposal, and there was some confusion in the House with respect to this point.

[3] *Congressional Record*, May 6, 1913, pp. 1235, 1366.

[4] 63d Cong., 1st Sess., *Sen. Rept.* 80, p. 31.   On the last point see p. 268, *infra*.

[5] 66th Cong., 2d Sess., *House Rept.* 10918.

inadequacy of the antidumping provision in the Revenue Act of 1916.[1] The bill passed by the House provided for the imposition, on all imported merchandise sold by the exporter at a price less than the foreign home value and of a class or kind produced in the United States or competing with American products, of dumping-duties equal to the difference between the foreign home value and the export price. The dumping-duties were to be administered by the Treasury.

In the Senate the Finance Committee substituted for the House provisions another antidumping measure which provided that the dumping-duties should apply in case of merchandise sold to the United States at less than the foreign home value only after an investigation by the Secretary of the Treasury and the publication by him of a finding that an industry in the United States was being or was likely to be injured or was prevented from being established by such dumping. A minority report of the Finance Committee recommended against the adoption of either of the proposals on the grounds that either of them would entail serious administrative difficulty and expense, that it might serve completely or partially to destroy the free list in the ordinary tariff, and that by raising the prices of imported goods it would perpetuate the high cost of living.[2]

The antidumping measure made no further progress at this stage, but in the next session of Congress the antidumping provision passed by the House in 1919 was, with slight alterations, incorporated in the Emergency Tariff Bill and again passed by the House. The Senate Finance Committee again substituted for the House proposal its own measure as presented in the previous session, and this was passed by the Senate.[3] In conference the House

[1] 66th Cong., 2d Sess., *House Rept.* 479.

[2] 66th Cong., 2d Sess., *Sen. Rept.* 510.

[3] An amendment proposed in the Senate by Senator Reed to the effect that when commodities were commonly being sold abroad by American exporters at dumping prices the importation into the United States of similar commodities should not be subject to duty was rejected by a moderate margin of votes. (*Congressional Record*, May 11, 1921, pp. 1296, 1306.)

accepted the Senate proposal[1] and it was contained in the Emergency Tariff Act as finally passed.

The substance of the antidumping provision of the Emergency Tariff Act is as follows: whenever the Secretary of the Treasury finds that an industry in the United States is being or is likely to be injured, or is prevented from being established, by reason of the importation into the United States of foreign merchandise, and that merchandise of such class or kind is being sold or is likely to be sold in the United States or elsewhere at less than its fair value, he shall make public a finding to this effect; in the case of all imported merchandise of a class or kind as to which the Secretary has made public a finding (provided that the customs appraiser had not already made an appraisal report thereon to the collector of customs), if the "purchase price" or the "exporter's sale price" is less than the "foreign market value," there shall be imposed thereon, in addition to the ordinary duties if any, a special dumping-duty in an amount equal to such difference.

The "foreign market price" is defined in the customary way as the price at which the goods are sold in the usual wholesale quantities to all purchasers in the principal markets of the exporting country at the time of exportation. The appraising officers are instructed, however, to make due allowance, in comparing foreign market value with the exporter's sale price or the purchase price, for differences in price wholly or partly due to differences in quantities sold. There is also a provision that where the purchase or agreement to purchase was made prior to the time of exportation, the foreign market value shall be taken as of the date of such purchase or agreement to purchase.

The "purchase price" is defined as the price to the importer at the time of sale prior to the time of importation less the various costs incidental to bringing the goods to the place of delivery

[1] 67th Cong., 1st Sess., *House Rept.* 79, p. 11.

if these were covered by the sale price, plus (1) if not included in the sale price, the amount of any export tax imposed by the country of exportation, and (2) the amount of remission of drawback of any import duties and the amount of remission or rebate of any internal taxes in the exporting country on goods exported to the United States.

The provision relating to the difference between the "exporter's sale price" and the foreign market value is intended to cover cases where foreign goods are sold to American purchasers *after* exportation on consignment or to an agent in the United States. The exporter's sale price is defined as the price at which the goods are sold in the United States delivered to the purchaser by or for the account of the exporter before or after the time of importation: *minus* (1) the various costs, including ordinary customs duty if any, incidental to bringing the goods to the place of delivery in the United States, (2) the commissions and the expenses connected with selling the goods in the United States, and (3) the amount of any export tax imposed by the country of exportation; *plus* the amounts of any drawbacks or remissions of import duty and of any rebates or remissions of internal taxes on goods exported to the United States. The definitions of purchase price and exporter's sale price eliminate from the price to the American purchaser all charges connected with the shipment of the goods after they leave the point of exportation and establish, as the basis for the determination of the existence of dumping, the comparison between the foreign market value and the price to the American exporter at its f.o.b. factory or point of exportation equivalent, but with allowances for any excess of foreign market value over the price to the American purchaser due to remissions or refunds on exports of foreign import duties or internal taxes.

Additional sections provide: for the use of the foreign cost of production, including a reasonable profit, instead of the foreign market value where the latter is not ascertainable; for insistence upon a genuine and not a fixed or artificially established foreign market value; and for bonding goods of a kind as to which the Secretary of the Treasury had made a finding if these are entered for customs on behalf of the exporter, in order to safeguard the collection of the dumping-duty in case of their later sale or delivery at an exporter's sale price less than the foreign market value. The customs appraisers are instructed to assist in the administration of the antidumping law by withholding their appraisal report to the collector of customs (which opens the way to clearance of the goods through the customs) if they have reason to suspect that goods as to which no finding has been made are being dumped in the United States, such report to be withheld until further orders from the Secretary or until the Secretary has made a finding. The appraisers are also required to secure the information with respect to prices necessary for the administration of the law. The special dumping-duties are made subject to drawback upon re-exportation of the goods upon which they have been levied in the same manner as ordinary customs duties.

This measure is in almost all respects a model of draftsmanship in so far as antidumping legislation is concerned, and has a number of points of superiority over the Canadian measure.[1] The requirement that a finding be made public before goods become subject to the dumping-duty has distinct merit. It frees the customs service from the necessity of investigating every shipment, large or small, for evidence of dumping. It makes the measure a preventive rather than a punitive one, since the publication of a finding gives notice to all concerned that imports of the kind designated in the finding will be closely scrutinized for evidence of dumping and penalized if dumping is discovered, and thus is equivalent to an order to cease dumping. It will

[1] A great deal of the credit for the excellent draftsmanship appears to be due to John E. Walker, Chief of the Legislative Drafting Service of the Senate. Cf. *Emergency Tariff and Antidumping, Hearing before the Committee on Finance, United States Senate, on H. R. 2435*, April 18, 1921, pp. 9 ff.

probably leave sporadic instances of dumping free from penalty in most cases. The limitation of the dumping-duties to dumping which injures or is likely to injure an American industry leaves it open to a wise customs administration to refrain from interfering with all dumping whose benefit to the American consumer is not clearly offset in part at least by an injury, actual or prospective, to American industry. The administrative procedure is simple and is intrusted wholly to a single department and to that department which is probably best equipped to handle it. The definition of dumping is as precise and as free from ambiguities and uncertainties as it appears possible to make it, and it is such as to bring all types of genuine dumping within reach of the penalties, if they are injurious to, or are likely to be injurious to, an American industry, and to leave free from penalty all types of spurious dumping. Some of the provisions which contribute most to protect the importer and the foreign exporter from the unfair operation of the Act, such as the requirement that in case of purchase prior to exportation the existence of dumping is to be determined by comparison of the purchase price with the foreign market value as of the date of purchase instead of as of the date of exportation, and the provisions for allowances for remissions of foreign taxes on exports and for differences in price due to differences in the quantities sold, were inserted only after lengthy consideration and in several instances in spite of opposition from customs experts who did not wish to see administrative facility or additional protection to American producers against low foreign prices sacrificed to what they apparently regarded as an excessive zeal for equity.[1]

In some minor details the antidumping law is, however, open to criticism. There is something to be said for provisions such as those in the Canadian law limiting the maximum amount of

[1] Cf. *Anti-Dumping Legislation, Hearings before the Committee on Ways and Means, House of Representatives, on H.R. 9983 and H.R. 10071*, October 22, 1919, pp. 15 ff.; *Emergency Tariff and Antidumping, Hearing before the Committee on Finance, United States Senate, on H.R. 2435*, April 18–22, 1921, pp. 69 ff.

dumping-duty which can be assessed and exempting from dumping-duty those imports which are already subject to a very high import duty.[1] The provision for the addition to the purchase price, if not already included in the price, of any export tax levied by the exporting country is a slip in draftsmanship. The purpose of the provisions with respect to export taxes, as is shown by the requirement that the amount of any export tax be *subtracted* from the price to the American purchaser in determining the exporter's sale price, is to identify as dumping the sale for export at a price which is not higher than the foreign market value by the amount of the tax. The law should have required, for the purpose of determining the existence of dumping, the subtraction of the export tax from, instead of its addition to, the purchase price, i.e., the sale price to the importer. As it now stands, goods sold for export at a price lower than the foreign market value plus the export tax by twice the amount of the export tax are free from the dumping-duty.[2]

Up to the end of 1922 the Secretary of the Treasury had made findings with respect to some twenty commodities. The findings are all uniform in phrasing and merely state that a specified commodity imported from a specified source is sold or is likely to be sold in the United States at less than its fair value and that a specified industry in the United States is being or is likely to be injured thereby. In one case, that of cotton embroideries known as "Hamburgs," the finding referred to such goods manufactured by a specified concern either in Italy or Switzerland.[3]

---

[1] Cf. p. 194 *supra*. Cf. also, Merchants' Association of New York, *Recommendations Relative to H.R. 10918* (Anti-Dumping Bill), 1921, pp. 53 ff. (Printed also in *Hearings on General Tariff Revision, before the Committee on Ways and Means, House of Representatives, 1921*, p. 4233.)

[2] Suppose that the foreign market value is $30 and the export tax $10. Sale for export at a price lower than $40 should be regarded as dumping. But under the law, sale for export at any price over $20 will not be subject to the dumping-duty.

[3] *Treasury Decisions*, 39025.

Findings with respect to Canadian products sometimes specify imports from Canada as a whole, at other times specify imports from one of the provinces. The most important finding specified wheat flour imported from Canada. Up to April 1, 1923, no dumping-duties had been collected under the findings issued to date. The provision in the law making the dumping-duties subject to drawback upon re-exportation of the goods upon which they have been levied will probably result in the re-exportation of such goods in cases where heavy additional duties had been assessed thereon and may thus impair the effectiveness of the provision as a warning to prospective dumpers. In this respect the Canadian law, which provides that the dumping-duties shall not be subject to drawback,[1] appears to be preferable.

ADMINISTRATION OF ANTIDUMPING LAW

The American system of administration of the ordinary import duties facilitates the operation of an antidumping law such as the one contained in the Emergency Tariff Act. Goods sold to American purchasers prior to exportation must be accompanied by an invoice upon entry for customs which states in full detail the actual price at which the goods were sold. If the goods are shipped other than by purchase, i.e., on consignment or to an agent for subsequent sale, the invoice must state the foreign market value. In addition the invoices must be certified before the American consular officer located nearest the point of exportation, and it is the duty of this officer to note on the invoice the foreign market value if he can ascertain it. If the goods are subject to ad valorem duties, the duties are assessed on the foreign market value or the invoice value, whichever is higher. If goods are entered for customs at a value less than the foreign market value, they become subject to an additional undervaluation duty of 1 per cent of the value as appraised by the customs authorities for each 1 per cent that

[1] *Customs Tariff, 1907.* Schedule B.

such final appraised value exceeds the value declared in the entry, but limited to a maximum of 75 per cent. If the appraised value exceeds the entered value by more than 100 per cent the goods are subject to forfeiture. If an exporter fails upon request to open his books and papers to inspection by an accredited officer of the Treasury, the Secretary of the Treasury is required to prohibit the importation into the United States of goods produced, sold, shipped, or consigned by such person. If an importer under similar circumstances refuses to open his books and papers to inspection, the Secretary of the Treasury is required to prohibit the importation of foreign goods into the United States by or for the account of such person. As a further check on values, the Treasury maintains a number of experts in foreign countries whose duty it is to ascertain foreign market values.[1]

It might seem that these requirements for the administration of the ordinary customs duties would make it a simple matter to administer also the antidumping law, and that all the information necessary for the application of the dumping-duties would automatically have been made available beforehand for the assessment of the ordinary duties. The penalties for undervaluation, moreover, serve also as penalties for attempts to conceal dumping by minimizing the foreign market values. But the matter is not so simple. The enactment of antidumping legislation creates an incentive to *overvaluation* of the purchase or invoice price as a means of concealing dumping, and the undervaluation penalties will not reach this practice. But the main difficulty in the administration both of the ordinary ad valorem customs duties and the dumping-duties arises from the necessity of determining foreign market values. There is general agreement among customs officials that the information given in the

---

[1] This is an account of present customs procedure in its broad outlines. In some important particulars the procedure as here described dates only from the passage of the Emergency Tariff Act of 1921 and the Fordney-McCumber Act of 1922.

invoices although certified to before an American consul is not dependable, and that the consuls furnish little or no assistance in the verification of invoice values and foreign market values. The main reliance is upon the information secured through the special agents of the Treasury stationed in the exporting countries. But the United States, with its much greater volume of imports, its higher duties, and the wider distribution of the sources of importation, is faced with a much more difficult problem in this regard than is Canada, over 90 per cent of whose imports come from the United States and Great Britain, countries with a common language and closely similar commercial methods. Canada nevertheless maintains as large a force of investigators abroad (chiefly in the United States) as does the United States, and the American staff of investigators is wholly inadequate even for the protection of the operation of the ordinary ad valorem import duties.[1]

The enactment of antidumping legislation, in addition to increasing the importance of ascertaining the actual purchase prices and foreign market values for goods subject to ordinary ad valorem import duties, makes it essential for the first time that these values be accurately determined also for goods subject to ordinary specific duties and, in the case of goods of a kind produced in the United States, for goods free of duty under the ordinary tariff. The substantial character of this additional administrative burden is made clear by the Tariff Commission's analysis of the imports for the calendar year 1920, which shows that of the total imports in that year about 61 per cent were admitted free, 26.5 per cent paid specific duties, *and only 12 per cent paid ad valorem duties*.[2] The passage of the Fordney-

[1] On these matters, cf. *Emergency Tariff and Antidumping, (Senate) Hearing*, April 18–21, 1921, pp. 36 ff.; *Anti-Dumping Legislation, Hearings* (House of Representatives), October 22, 1919, pp. 9 ff.

[2] U.S. Tariff Commission, *Information concerning American Valuation as the Basis for Assessing Duties Ad Valorem*, 1921, p. 38. It is rather surprising that this should have been the first published study of this kind.

McCumber Tariff Act and the fact that a large fraction of the specific duties is collected on a few important commodities, especially sugar and tobacco, may somewhat modify the conclusions to be drawn from these figures, but it remains true that the antidumping law, if strictly and comprehensively enforced, will add substantially to the burdens of the customs service, and will require, above all other things, an increase in the staff of foreign investigators.

In this connection it should be pointed out that the frequently expressed opinion that the undervaluation provisions of the customs administrative law operate as an antidumping measure in themselves is erroneous.[1] The undervaluation provisions, until their revision in the Fordney-McCumber Act, penalized the entry of goods for customs at less than their foreign market value on the date of exportation, even if the entry was made in good faith through ignorance of what the foreign market value was on the date of exportation. They now penalize such entry only if there is intent to deceive or defraud the customs. But an importer who purchases foreign goods at a dumping price is at liberty to escape the undervaluation penalties by adding to the invoice price at the time of entry for customs a sufficient amount to bring it up to the foreign market value. What is penalized by the undervaluation provision is not the purchase of foreign goods at dumping prices, but the entry for customs at such prices.

Section 303, Fordney-McCumber Tariff Act, 1922.—Section 303 of the Fordney-McCumber Tariff Act of 1922, which imposes countervailing duties on imports of bounty-fed commodities, at first glance appears to be identical with the clause providing for the imposition of countervailing duties on imports of commodities

---

[1] I have been myself guilty of this error, and have even criticized Professor T. E. G. Gregory, author of *Tariffs: a Study in Method*, for his failure to commit the same error (*Journal of the American Statistical Association*, XVIII (1922), 130. I hereby make the *amende honorable*.

from countries which granted official export bounties on such commodities, which was contained in the Tariff Acts of 1897, 1909, and 1913. But without any emphasis in the various committee reports on the bill while in progress and without any mention in the Congressional debates the clause was modified by the insertion of a few additional words so as to make the penalties apply not only to imports of goods from countries which grant export bounties thereon, but also to imports of goods from countries which grant bounties on production and to imports of goods from countries wherein production or export bounties are granted by any "person, partnership, association, cartel, or corporation." There follows a comparison in parallel columns of the text of the bounty-countervailing clauses in the 1913 and 1922 acts:

Tariff Act of 1913, Sec. IV, Par. E.	*Tariff Act of 1922, Sec. 303.*
That whenever any country, dependency, colony, province, or other political subdivision of government shall pay or bestow, directly or indirectly, any bounty or grant upon the exportation of any article or merchandise from	That whenever any country, dependency, colony, province, or other political subdivision of government, *person, partnership, association, cartel, or corporation* shall pay or bestow, directly or indirectly, any bounty or grant upon the *manufacture or production or* export of any article or merchandise *manufactured or produced in*

such country, dependency, colony, province, or other political subdivision of government, and such article or merchandise is dutiable under the provisions of this Act, then upon the importation of any such article or merchandise into the United States, whether the same shall be imported directly from the country of production or otherwise, and whether such article or merchandise is imported in the same condition as when exported from the country of production or has been changed in condition by remanufacture or otherwise, there shall be levied and paid, in all such cases, in addition to the duties otherwise imposed by this Act, an additional duty equal to the net amount of such bounty or grant, however the same be paid or bestowed. The net amount of all such bounties or grants shall be from time to time ascertained, determined, and declared by the Secretary of the Treasury, who shall make all needful regulations for the identification of such articles and merchandise and for the assessment and collection of such additional duties.

The grant of unofficial bounties on production has rarely, if ever, occurred, and it is altogether unlikely that it should ever attain importance as a factor in international competition. The chief significance of the extension of the bounty-countervailing clause to private bounties relates therefore to its bearing on export bounties. But export bounties can give cause for complaint to importing countries only as they result in a reduction in the export price of the bounty-fed commodities. The normal effect of the grant of an export bounty, official or unofficial, is to make the export price lower than the domestic price by the amount of the bounty, in other words, to result in dumping. But bounty-dumping is no more objectionable and no more likely to injure competing industries in the importing country than dumping which does not arise from the grant of export bounties. The antidumping provisions of the Emergency Tariff Act had already provided an adequate remedy against all dumping which injures, or is likely to injure, American industry. Section 303 of the Fordney-McCumber Tariff Act makes it mandatory on the part of the Treasury to impose countervailing duties on imports of commodities which had received unofficial export bounties, regardless of whether such bounties are absorbed by the foreign exporter, and regardless of whether the grant of such bounties results in injury to American industry. It is now possible for a double penalty to be imposed on imports of dumped commodities if such commodities have received an export bounty, official or unofficial, one penalty because they have been sold to American purchasers at a price lower than the foreign home price and another penalty because they have received a bounty. The extension of the bounty-countervailing provision to unofficial bounties was unnecessary and even undesirable because of the extra duties it throws on the customs authorities and the possible clash with the antidumping law.

Section 303 in its present form will inevitably create serious administrative difficulties if an attempt is made vigorously to enforce it, and if it is interpreted in conformity with the established interpretation of the countervailing provisions in previous American tariff laws. The countervailing duties, according to the letter of the law as hitherto read by Treasury officials and by the courts in connection with the corresponding provisions in previous tariff acts, are applicable to *imports of goods from countries in which bounties are granted on that kind or class of goods*, whether or not the particular shipment has received such a bounty.[1] In the case of official bounties this reading of the law gives rise to no serious administrative difficulties, although it works harshly in special cases; there is usually only one official bounty-granting authority in one political unit and one uniform schedule of rates of bounty. But suppose that there is occasion to apply the present provision to imports from a country in which there are ten producers in a given industry, that nine of these producers grant export bounties varying in amount from producer to producer, and that the tenth grants no export bounties, will the established rule in connection with official bounties, of applying to all shipments of the commodity in question coming from the country in which bounties are granted a countervailing duty equal to the highest bounty which is granted on any shipment, be followed also in connection with unofficial bounties? Or suppose that only one of the ten producers grants an export bounty, will all imports of the commodity in question from that country be subjected to the additional duty? Or suppose, as is frequently the case with respect to unofficial export bounties, that the amount of the bounty varies for different export markets; there is nothing in the law itself which prescribes that the bounty paid on exports

[1] Cf. p. 173, *supra*. The bounty-countervailing clause in the Tariff Act of 1894, however, is an exception to the rule, since it made specific provision for the exemption from the additional duties of goods which had received no bounty, even though imported from a country in which ordinarily such goods would have been bountied. See. p. 169, *supra*.

to the United States be taken as the basis for the assessment of the countervailing duty; will, it therefore, be the highest bounty paid on exports to any country which will be used as the basis for determining the amount of additional duty to be imposed? How will the customs authorities determine the amount of a cumulative bounty, increasing at every successive stage of the productive process, and subject to complex and frequently revised adjustments at each stage? There has been complaint that the Court of Customs Appeals has not had sufficiently extensive duties to keep it occupied.[1] If this situation still prevails, Section 303 may have been intended to remedy it.

Miscellaneous provisions.—Section 322 of the United States (Fordney-McCumber) Tariff Act of 1922 imposes a duty of 90 per cent ad valorem on the original value of such articles in the United States, on automobiles and parts exported from the United States prior to February 11, 1919, for use by the United States or one of the Allies in the war against the Central Powers, and sold or delivered by the United States to a foreign government. The purpose of this provision is to protect American manufactures from the competition of returned American surplus supplies which had been disposed of to foreign governments at sharply reduced prices. A duty of 90 per cent ad valorem on the original value of such articles in the United States is probably in excess of their present American value, and is undoubtedly equivalent to an absolute prohibition of their reimport. An antidumping provision of the usual type based on current foreign market value would clearly fail to afford a sufficient remedy against such imports, as their value for export to the United States would in many cases be even higher than their value for domestic consumption in the re-exporting country.

A proposed amendment to the Emergency Tariff Act of 1921, which failed however, of enactment, provided that where the foreign market value of airplanes, parts, or accessories, was

---

[1] *Tariff Hearings before the Committee on Ways and Means,* 1913, p. 6183.

abnormally low because of the accumulation of excess stocks resulting from artificial or abnormal conditions, then, for the purpose of the antidumping section, the foreign market value should be taken to be not less than the cost of production.[1]

These provisions are significant as indications of the general tendency in recent years to broaden the scope and modify the provisions of antidumping legislation so as both to give the officials intrusted with its administration a greater degree of discretion in enforcing the special duties and to make the special duties reach imports at prices which are not technically dumping prices but which are nevertheless abnormally or artificially low.

[1] "(d) If it is established to the satisfaction of the appraising officers, under regulations established by the Secretary, that the foreign market value of airplanes, or airplane motors, parts, and accessories therefor, is wholly or partly based not upon cost of production or ordinary trade conditions of supply and demand, but is based upon unusual excess stocks procured or accumulated through artificial or abnormal conditions, then the foreign market value of such airplanes or airplane motors, parts, or accessories for the purposes of this section shall not be less than the cost of production" (*Congressional Record*, May 11, 1921, p. 1295).

CHAPTER XIV

COMPARATIVE ANALYSIS OF ANTIDUMPING LAWS

Seven countries have enacted laws which specifically provide for the imposition of additional duties on imports sold at dumping prices. These countries, and the dates of original enactment of their laws, are as follows: Canada, 1904; British South Africa, 1914; Great Britain, Australia, New Zealand, Newfoundland, United States, 1921. The Canadian law was amended in 1907 and again in 1921. The British South African law was amended in 1922. The bulk of this legislation has, therefore, been enacted within the last two years, and all of it is still in effect. Another group of laws also in effect at present consists of the Australian Industries Preservation Act of 1906-10 and several American laws which deal with predatory dumping as a phase of the problem of unfair competition. Not clearly belonging to either of these two groups are: the Japanese law of 1920, providing for the imposition of additional duties on foreign goods sold at unreasonably low prices; the Canadian law of 1922 authorizing the arbitrary valuation for assessment of customs duties of natural products imported into Canada under such conditions as prejudicially to affect the interests of Canadian producers; and the provision of the New Zealand law of 1921 authorizing the governor-general in special cases to change the tariff treatment of any class of imports when the existing tariff provisions operate injuriously.

To aid in the attempt made in this chapter to discover and formulate the principles which should govern the drafting of the detailed provisions of antidumping legislation, there will be presented in connection with each topic a summarized comparison of the relevant provisions contained in the existing body of antidumping legislation. The laws belonging to the last two of the groups as classified in the preceding paragraph differ so radically in their provisions as to defy detailed comparison; they are much more restricted in the scope of their possible application than the more general measures of the first group; and they are not nearly as likely to prove to be of substantial importance as the laws in the first group. For these reasons there will be only occasional reference to the provisions of the laws in the last two groups and attention will be mainly directed to the provisions of the laws in the first group.

TYPE OF IMPORT PRACTICE PENALIZED

All of the laws in the first group except the British, if allowance is made for verbal differences of minor, if any, significance, provide for the imposition of penalties on imports in case they are sold for export at f.o.b. prices or their equivalent which are lower than the current fair market values for domestic sale in the country of export. The British law restricts the scope of the dumping penalty by making it applicable only in case foreign goods are sold in Great Britain, c.i.f., at prices lower than the fair market value in the country of export. All of the laws in the second group apply to dumping only if some unfair act or unfair intent is connected therewith. The laws in the third group give to the appropriate officials the authority to levy additional duties on imports which have been sold at low prices, without reference to whether these low prices are dumping prices.

Provided adequate provision is made for reaching cases of concealed dumping and for exempting from the penalties instances of spurious dumping, the definition of dumping in the laws of the first group, with the exception of the British, is in accord with that laid down at the beginning of this study. The British law exempts from the penalty imports which are sold in Great Britain at what is strictly speaking a dumping price, if the difference between the foreign market value and the foreign f.o.b. export price does not exceed the various costs, including the ordinary British customs duties, incidental to delivering the goods to the British purchaser.   The laws in the first group, again with the exception of the British, make subject to the dumping penalties goods sold for export at a price lower than the foreign market value, without allowance for the possibility that a particular exporter may sell in his domestic market at a price lower than the generally current foreign market value or may make no sales at any price in his domestic market. Strictly speaking, dumping does not occur unless there is a difference between the export and the domestic price of the foreign exporter, but if the dumping penalties were restricted to such instances, there would be opened a path to technical avoidance of dumping and of the penalties directed against it by making some sales in the domestic market at artificially low prices or by refraining from selling in the domestic market commodities identical in kind with those exported.   The British law makes provision for the last eventuality by specifying that in case goods identical with those exported are not sold by the exporter to domestic purchasers, comparison of his price to British purchasers shall be made with his price to domestic purchasers of goods as nearly similar as possible to those exported.

DATE OF PRICE-COMPARISON

The British and the American laws provide that the date of sale be taken as the time-basis for the comparison of prices to determine the existence of dumping.   The other laws in the first group provide that comparison of prices be made as of the date of exportation or shipment.   A Canadian customs regulation provides, however, that the amount of any advance in the foreign market value between the date of sale and the date of exportation shall not be subject to the dumping-duty, and the Australian law contains a similar provision which is limited, however, to goods bought within six months of the date of exportation.

The only time basis for comparison of prices to determine the existence of dumping which will reach all cases of genuine dumping, and which will exempt from penalty all cases of spurious dumping resulting from variations in the foreign market value between the date of sale and the date of exportation, and therefore the only time-basis which is fair to the importer without impairing the protection to domestic producers against genuine dumping, is as of the date of sale.   If date of exportation is taken, a special and unwarranted hazard is attached to the purchase of foreign goods for later delivery during a rising market, since an increase in the foreign market value in the interval between sale and shipment will result in making the foreign goods subject to the dumping-duty even though they were sold for export at the same price as that current for domestic sales at the time of sale. Where the foreign market value falls between the date of sale and the date of exportation, the use of the date of exportation basis to determine the existence of dumping frees dumping from penalization to the extent of the fall in the foreign market value. The Canadian and Australian provisions for the use of the date of sale if the foreign market value rises in the interval between sale and exportation are satisfactory, therefore, from the point of view of the importer.   From the point of view of the producer who wants effective protection against foreign dumping, it is important that the date of sale basis be used during a period of falling prices, which is the period during which dumping is most likely to be prevalent.

From the administrative point of view, however, the date of exportation basis is preferable to the date of sale basis.   The date of exportation is a certain and readily ascertainable date, but the actual date of sale is a matter of record only to the participants in the transaction and can easily be kept secret.   During a period of rising prices it would be in the interest of the exporter and the importer of dumped goods, if they seek to conceal the fact of dumping in order to evade the dumping-penalty, to report the date of sale to the authorities as having been earlier than the true date.   Conversely, during a period of falling prices, it would be to their interest to report the date of sale as having

been later than the true date.   The adoption by Great Britain
and the United States of the date of sale method involves,
therefore, the assumption of the difficult administrative problem
of discovering the true date of sale.

MARGINAL ALLOWANCE BEFORE THE DUMPING-DUTY BECOMES APPLICABLE

Most of the laws in the first group contain provisions whereby the dumping-duty does not become applicable unless the
margin between the foreign market value and the export price
exceeds a. stated percentage or is substantial in amount.   The
Canadian law authorizes the customs authorities to exempt from
the dumping-duty foreign goods sold for export at a price which
is not lower than the foreign market value by more than a small
percentage, and an identical provision is contained in the Newfoundland law.   By regulation the Canadian customs authorities
exempt imports dutiable under the ordinary tariff from the
dumping-duty if the difference between the foreign market
value and the export price does not exceed 5 per cent of the
former.   The Australian law permits the making of regulations
which exempt from the dumping-duty imports sold for export
at a price lower than the foreign market value by not more than
5 per cent of the latter, or not more than 10 per cent of the latter
if the Tariff Board reports that such exemption would not be
detrimental to any Australian industry.   In the British law the
dumping-duty is not applicable to imports sold at dumping
prices unless the foreign market value minus 5 per cent thereof
exceeds the price delivered to the British purchaser.   The South
African and the American laws contain no provisions of this kind.

Of the laws dealing with predatory dumping as a phase of
unfair competition, imports sold at dumping prices with unfair
intent are subject to penalty under the Australian law of 1906
only if the goods were sold for export at a price "greatly below"
their foreign market value and under the American law of 1916

only if they were imported or sold in the United States at a price "substantially less than" the foreign market value.

Provision for the exemption from the dumping-duty of goods sold at an export price which is less than the foreign market value by only a small percentage is commendable on grounds of administrative expediency. It probably results in a substantial reduction in the burden of administering the dumping-duty provisions by making it unnecessary to investigate and to apply the duties in a great number of instances where there are trifling differences between foreign market values and export prices. It gives to the importer a margin of protection against penalization resulting from slight errors on his part or on the part of the customs authorities in determining foreign market values. It permits an importer to retain some of the advantage which may accrue to him as a result of good merchandising on his part. Antidumping legislation tends to put all importers on a parity and to prevent any of them from deriving any advantage from their superior buying ability in so far as prices are concerned. There is no reason, however, why the ability of a buyer to make his purchases, whether in the domestic or in the foreign market, at a shade under the prices paid by most buyers should if exercised in his foreign purchases make him subject to the dumping penalty. The allowance of a small margin of difference between the current foreign market value and the export price before the dumping-duty becomes applicable permits the importer to utilize his buying skill within limits without losing all advantage therefrom through making himself liable to additional duty.

ALLOWANCE FOR REMISSION OF FOREIGN TAXES

Of the laws in the first group, the American, Australian, New Zealand, and British laws require, and the Canadian law authorizes the customs officials to permit, the deduction of foreign excise taxes from foreign market values in determining the existence of dumping. Canadian customs regulations have been issued which provide for such deduction. The American and the New Zealand laws also require the deduction of foreign drawbacks of import duties from foreign market values for the purpose of assessing dumping-duties. The South African and the Newfoundland laws do not contain provisions for the deduction either of foreign excises or of drawbacks for the purpose of assessing dumping-duties.

All remissions or refunds of foreign taxes on commodities upon their export should be allowed as a deduction from foreign market values in comparing them with export prices to determine the existence of dumping. The remission of such taxes enables the foreign exporter to make his export price lower than his domestic price by the amount of such taxes and nevertheless make as high a rate of profit on his export as on his domestic sales. Such remission of taxes does not give the foreign exporter a special advantage in his competition outside his own market with the producers of other countries, but merely frees him from a special handicap in such competition. There is no difference of principle in this connection between excise taxes and import duties. The fact that five of the antidumping laws of the first group provide for the deduction of foreign excises from foreign market values in the assessment of the dumping-duties while only two of them make similar provision for the deduction of drawbacks of foreign import duties is probably to be explained by the greater difficulty which customs authorities ordinarily encounter in determining the amount of drawback of import duties which foreign commodities had received upon export than in determining the amount of excise to which such commodities would have been subject in the foreign country if they had been sold for domestic consumption. The problem of determining accurately the amount of foreign drawbacks of import duty could be easily solved, however, if provisions for the deduction of such drawbacks from foreign market values for the purpose of determining the existence of dumping were made conditional upon the presentation by the foreign exporter—or the importer—claiming such deduction of a certificate from the government of the exporting country stating the amount of drawback which had actually been granted for the particular shipment of goods under consideration.

ALLOWANCE FOR DIFFERENCES IN CONDITIONS AND TERMS OF SALE

Specific provision is made in the Canadian regulations for a limited allowance for differences in foreign domestic and foreign export prices due to differences in credit terms in domestic as compared to export sales, and the American antidumping law of 1921 specifies that allowance be made in determining the existence of dumping for differences in price between domestic and export sales due to differences in the quantities sold. All of the laws in the first group except the British require more or less specifically that comparison between foreign domestic values and foreign export prices for the purpose of determining the existence of dumping be made on the basis of prices f.o.b. the point of exportation, thus preventing the concealment of dumping by including in the price to the foreign purchaser the charges for extra export packing, freight, and other costs incidental to the delivery of export goods. In general, however, the full allowance for differences between foreign market values and export prices which are due to differences in conditions and terms of sale is either not provided for under the antidumping laws or is impliedly within the discretion of the officials charged with the administration of these laws.

The methods whereby dumping may be concealed so that a mere comparison of foreign market values and export prices will not reveal its occurrence, and the ways in which such a comparison may appear to disclose the existence of dumping whereas in reality dumping is not being practiced, are so numerous as to make it impracticable to attempt to define in an antidumping law with precision and certainty the circumstances which shall make imports subject to the dumping-duties, if it is desired to prevent evasion of the law through concealment of dumping and likewise to leave free from penalization imports which are only in appearance but not in reality being sold at dumping prices. The most satisfactory method of handling the problem is unquestionably to leave to the administrative officials a considerable measure of discretion in determining in each case whether dumping is being practiced, and if so to what extent, but subject to the general rule that dumping shall be interpreted to mean the sale for export at prices lower than foreign market values, and that in comparing prices proper allowance shall be made for differences in price which make a reasonable adjustment for differences in conditions and terms surrounding export as compared to domestic sales. A literal enforcement of the provisions of any of the laws in the first group would result in numerous instances in the penalization of spurious dumping and in failure to reach genuine dumping because concealed by either inadequate or excessive adjustments of export prices to the different conditions and terms surrounding export, as compared to domestic sales.

SPECIAL STATUTORY EXEMPTIONS OF COMMODITIES FROM DUMPING-DUTIES

All of the laws in the three groups either specifically or by implication make subject to the dumping-duties only goods of a kind or class produced in the importing country.[1] Most of the laws contain further limiting provisions. The British dumping-duties are applicable only to goods whose importation at dumping prices would seriously affect employment in a British

---

[1] The New Zealand law of 1921, which extends the protection of the dumping penalties to industries in other parts of the British Empire which are injured by non-British dumping into New Zealand, is a partial exception.

industry which is operated with reasonable efficiency and economy, and before the duties can be applied, consideration must be given to the effect of their application on any British industry using the imported goods as materials for further manufacture; the Australian law makes the dumping-duties applicable only where detriment may result from the dumping to an Australian industry; the American law applies only to goods whose importation at dumping prices injures, or is likely to injure, or prevents the establishment of an American industry; the New Zealand law authorizes the exemption from the dumping-duties of goods whose importation would not be injurious to any industry in New Zealand or in any other part of the British Empire; the laws in the second group apply only to instances of dumping with intent to injure a domestic industry, or restrain competition, or establish a monopoly: of the laws in the third group, the Japanese law makes the additional duties apply only to goods whose importation threatens staple Japanese industries, and the Canadian law of 1922 applies only to natural products whose importation prejudicially affects the interests of Canadian producers. The Canadian, Newfoundland, and Australian laws authorize the temporary exemption by regulation from the dumping-duties of articles of a class or kind not made or sold in the importing country in substantial quantities and offered for sale to all purchasers on equal terms under like conditions. The Canadian law exempts from the dumping-duties goods whereon the ordinary duties equal 50 per cent ad valorem, goods subject to excise tax in Canada, binder twine, sugar refined in Great Britain, and by recent amendment, sugar imported from any country when the price in Canada rises above a specified level. The British law does not apply to articles of food or drink. The Australian law exempts samples.

There is an obvious case for exempting from the dumping-duties imports at dumping prices of commodities of a kind not produced in the importing country, unless it is clearly evident that the dumping is intended to etablish a monopoly able to exact monopoly prices in the future. With the same reservation, it is desirable to limit the application of the dumping-duties to goods whose importation at dumping prices is, or is likely to prove, injurious to a domestic industry. Such a limitation generally involves a preliminary investigation by the officials charged with the administration of the dumping law before the duties can be applied. Dumping may be injurious to the country dumped on even if the dumping is not predatory, so that a limitation of the penalties to predatory dumping leaves domestic industries inadequately safeguarded against the dumping menace. The exemption from dumping-duties of goods subject to a very high rate of import duty under the ordinary tariff is logically defensible on the ground that an industry which is receiving a generous measure of ordinary tariff protection has no valid claim for further assistance in maintaining itself. A provision exempting from the dumping-duty goods of a kind not produced on a substantial scale in the importing country and sold on equal terms to all purchasers, such as that contained in the Canadian law and copied from it in the Newfoundland, New Zealand, and Australian laws, has two objects: to make unnecessary the imposition of dumping-duties on goods of a kind produced only in trifling amounts in the importing country so that no serious injury to the industry of that country can ordinarily result from their being dumped, and to prevent the antidumping legislation through its restriction of imports, from aiding a domestic concern in exploiting its monopoly of the domestic market. The provisions contained in several of the laws for the exemption from the dumping-duties of specified commodities are generally to be explained by special circumstances, usually political in character, which make expedient the specially favorable treatment of certain importing or consuming interests.

All of the laws in the first group except the British make provision for the assessment of dumping-duty where goods are sold after exportation at a price delivered which would indicate dumping if reduced to its f.o.b. point of exportation equivalent. Since the British law does not make goods subject to the dumping-duty unless the price to the first British purchaser after importation is less than the foreign market value, it has no need for such a provision. Under the British law, however, the special problem arises of how to treat imports sold to a British importer at a substantial margin below the foreign market value, in case this importer does not resell them but uses them in the manufacture of his own products. The British law provides that in such cases the goods shall be subject to dumping-duty if the price to the British importer, including freight and other delivery costs and ordinary import duty if any, is less than the foreign market value. The Australian, American, and South African laws—the last by an amendment enacted in 1922—provide that where sale by an exporter in a foreign country is made on consignment, or through an agent in the importing country, or generally in such a way as not to permit of immediate comparison between the foreign market value and an f.o.b. export price, the sale is to be reduced, for the purposes of the antidumping law, to its f.o.b. equivalent by subtraction therefrom of freight, insurance, and other costs involved in its shipment to the importing country and delivery to the purchaser. The Canadian, Newfoundland, and New Zealand laws authorize the administrative authorities to guard against evasion of the dumping-duty through consignment sales or other methods of sale after exportation by determining as best they can the equivalent f.o.b. point of exportation price.

If the antidumping laws did not provide for such contingencies, it would be easy for a foreign exporter to evade the dumping-duties by shipping his goods on consignment or to an agent at a price equal to the foreign market value and permitting the consignee or agent to sell the goods to purchasers in the importing country at prices which after deduction of the costs of shipment, ordinary duties, commissions, etc., were lower than the foreign market value. Instances have been reported of attempts to evade the full ordinary duties even when sales were made prior to exportation by requiring the purchaser to accept delivery from, and to make payment for, the goods to an agent of the exporter in the importing country. This device made it possible for the exporter to bill his goods at a price *lower* than the true selling price and thus to reduce the amount of duty payable under ad valorem rates. The same device could be used to evade dumping-duties by invoicing the goods to the agent in the importing country at a price *higher* than the true selling price. The proper basis for determination of the existence of dumping in the case of goods shipped prior to sale, or, if sold prior to exportation, delivered via an agent in the importing country who enters the goods for customs, is to compare with the foreign market value of such goods the price to the first purchaser in the importing country who has no business connection with the exporter, after deduction from this price of all costs incidental to the transfer of the goods from the exporting country to the point of delivery to this purchaser.

A more difficult problem in the detection of dumping is presented where a manufacturing concern in one country has a branch plant in another country and ships to that plant partly manufactured goods, to be there completed, or assembled, for sale in the country in which the plant is situated. By the establishment of such branches in its export markets, a concern can readily evade the dumping-duties of these countries. Suppose, for example, that an American automobile manufacturing concern which finds that it cannot sell its cars in Canada at the full American prices and is prevented from dumping them in Canada by the Canadian antidumping law establishes an assembling plant in Canada and invoices the parts to this plant at their full American values. The Canadian branch then sells the assembled car at what is virtually a dumping price. Such dumping could be reached in at least its extreme manifestations by the incorporation in the Canadian antidumping law of a provision that where the Canadian branch of a foreign concern obtains its materials in whole or in substantial part from the head plant, the sale of its product in Canada at a price which fails to cover the full book costs to the branch shall be held to constitute dumping and shall be subject to the dumping-duties. With the scores of branch plants in Canada which are finishing or assembling plants for American products, it is conceivable that there is sufficient evasion or possibility of evasion in this manner of the Canadian antidumping law to warrant the enactment by Canada of such a provision. For other countries the problem can scarcely be present to a sufficient degree to justify special legislation to meet it

METHODS OF DETERMINATION OF RATES OF DUMPING-DUTIES

The laws in the first group all provide for the imposition of additional duties as penalties against dumping, and none of them authorizes the absolute prohibition of importation of dumped goods. All in the first group except the British and the New Zealand laws require that the dumping-duty where applied shall be equal to the difference between the foreign market value and the export price. The British law provides for the imposition on dumped goods of additional duties at a flat rate of $33\frac{1}{3}$ per cent of the value in bond at the point of importation. The New Zealand law leaves to the discretion of the Minister of Customs the amount of dumping-duty to be imposed, but with the proviso that it must not exceed the difference between the foreign market value and the export price. The Canadian, South African, and Australian laws limit the additional duties to 15 per cent of the foreign market value; the

Newfoundland law limits them to 25 per cent of the foreign market value; the New Zealand and the American laws set no maximum limits other than those automatically resulting from the requirement that the duties do not exceed the difference between the foreign market value and the export price.

Of the laws in the other two groups: the American laws of 1894 and 1916 provide for fine or imprisonment, to be imposed by the courts; the American law of 1922 (Section 316 of the Fordney-McCumber Act) authorizes the president to impose such additional duties, not to be less than 10 per cent nor to exceed 50 per cent of the foreign market value, as will offset the unfair method or act in connection with the importation of foreign goods, or, in extreme cases, absolutely to prohibit the importation of the goods; the Australian law of 1906 authorizes the courts to impose absolute prohibition of import or such other restrictions on unfair importation as it sees fit; the Japanese law of 1920 authorizes the government to impose additional duties on imports sold at reasonably low prices, provided, however, that the additional duty must not in any instance exceed the value of the imported article; the Canadian law of 1922, which authorizes the Minister of Customs to value for customs natural products whose importation prejudicially affects the interests of Canadian producers without regard to the valuation provisions of other Canadian legislation and the provision in the New Zealand law of 1921 which authorizes the governor-general in special cases to alter the tariff treatment of any class of imported goods make possible the assessment of additional duties on such imports virtually without limit.

Antidumping laws should require that the dumping-duty be equal to the difference between the foreign market value and the export price. Such a provision makes possible the exact offsetting of the effect of foreign dumping without further restricting importation where the foreign market value is low enough to permit the making of sales for export at the full foreign price. Domestic producers can demand of antidumping legislation only that it shall offset any advantage in making sales in their market which accrues to foreign competitors from cutting their export prices below the level current in their home markets, due allowance being made for differences in conditions and terms of sale as between domestic and export sales. Beyond this, antidumping legislation should not go, except perhaps in the case of predatory dumping. Absolute prohibition of import of dumped goods and the imposition of dumping-duties exceeding the amount of difference between the foreign market value and the export price cannot be defended on economic grounds, unless the dumping is actuated by predatory motives. It is ordinarily not desirable to leave to the officers charged with the administration of customs or other laws the decision as to what duties or penalties shall be imposed under such laws, except as such decision is merely the application to a particular case of a general rule laid down in the law. Otherwise the importer is exposed to the danger of arbitrary, unequal, and harsh penalties, especially if the officials have a protectionist or fiscal bias. Since the injury which may result to a domestic industry from the importation of foreign goods at dumping prices is offset, in part at least, by the gain to the consumer of the foreign goods, and since the greater the amount by which the export price falls below the foreign market value, the more likely is the gain to the consumer from the importation of the dumped goods to offset the loss to the domestic producer, a provision limiting the amount of dumping-duty which can be imposed to a stated moderate percentage of the foreign market value of the dumped goods is a desirable feature in an antidumping law, especially in countries whose domestic producers already receive a substantial amount of ordinary tariff protection against foreign competition.

NOTICE BEFORE APPLICATION OF DUMPING-DUTIES

The South African law requires that notice be given by proclamation at least six weeks before the duties on any specific class of goods are to take effect. The British law provides that before the dumping-duties can be imposed an order must be issued specifying the goods which are to be subjected to the dumping-duties, and it exempts from the duties goods which leave the point of consignment within fourteen days of the date of the order. A customs notice issued in explanation of the New Zealand law announces that as far as practicable three months' notice will be given before the duties are applied on any particular class of goods, and that the duties will not be applied without previous notice except in emergency cases. The Australian and the American laws require that an order be issued, designating the goods to be subjected to dumping-duty, before the duties can be applied. Under the British and Australian laws the requirement that before a dumping order can be issued a report must be made recommending the application of the dumping-duties by a board independent of the customs departments will operate to give warning to those concerned even before an order is issued that the application of the dumping-duties is under consideration. The Canadian and the Newfoundland laws do not require that notice be given before the dumping-duties are imposed, and provide for the execution of the dumping provisions in the same manner as the ordinary tariff duties.

A requirement that notice be given before goods of a specified kind can be subjected to the dumping-duties if imported at dumping prices is desirable for several reasons. It operates in effect to exempt sporadic dumping from the dumping-duties, and the menace to domestic industries of such dumping is rarely great enough to offset the benefit to the consumer therefrom and to warrant the administrative cost and difficulty of discovering and penalizing instances thereof. The issuance of a notice that goods of a certain kind will thereafter, or after a specified interval, be subject to the dumping-duties if imported at dumping prices, gives warning to the importer of such goods that he must ascertain the foreign market value of such goods if he is to guard himself against liability to payment of heavy penalties on subsequent purchases. In the absence of such notice an importer who was unaware of the fact that the goods he was importing were being sold to him at dumping prices would be subject to penalization even though he was innocent of any intent to facilitate the introduction into the country of dumped goods. If he is given notice, he can reasonably be expected to inform himself as to the true foreign market values of the goods specified in the notice. Moreover, the primary object of antidumping legislation should be to stop dumping rather than to collect additional duties on dumped imports, and an antidumping law will accomplish its purpose if notice that dumping-duties will be imposed in case of the continuance of dumping operates to bring its practice to an end. In the existing body of antidumping legislation, the requirement that notice be given before the dumping-duties can be applied is, with the exception of the American law of 1921, contained only in the laws which leave it to the discretion of the officials charged with their administration whether or not the duties shall be applied. Where application of the dumping-duties is discretionary with the customs officials, it is especially desirable that notice be given of the intention to apply them.

COST OF PRODUCTION PROVISIONS IN ANTIDUMPING LAWS

The Canadian law, by amendment in 1921, provides that the foreign market value for the purpose of assessment of both ordinary and dumping-duties shall in no case be less than the actual cost of production of similar goods plus a reasonable profit thereon, and thus makes subject to the dumping-duties goods sold for export to Canada at a price less than cost of production even though the goods are being sold to domestic purchasers in the exporting country at as low a price. The New Zealand law provides that the dumping-duties shall apply to goods sold at dumping-prices as here defined and also to goods sold to New Zealand purchasers at a price which is less than their cost of production, including a reasonable profit, in the country of origin or the country of exportation. A provision in the Australian law makes subject to a "dumping below cost duty" goods sold to an Australian importer at an export price less than their cost of production plus 5 per cent plus free on board charges. The British law nominally provides for the determination of the existence of dumping by comparison of the price of the imported goods at their first sale in Great Britain with the foreign cost of production, but cost of production is defined in the law as the wholesale price at the foreign works less 5 per cent. The American law provides that where the foreign market value is not ascertainable, or where there is no foreign market value, cost of production, including a reasonable profit, is to be substituted for foreign market value in determining the existence of dumping. The Newfoundland and British South African laws make no mention of cost of production.

There is on theoretical grounds which have already been presented even a stronger case for the penalization of imports sold at a price below cost of production than for the penalization of imports sold at dumping prices which may or may not be below the cost of production. But the administrative problems which would be presented by a law requiring the determination of foreign costs on a comprehensive scale and with any degree of precision would be almost insuperable. Even in so relatively simple a case as that presented by a small industry producing goods of only one kind and grade, and even with full access to all the books and records and all the information possessed by the owners of this industry, the determination of cost of production is scarcely possible of accomplishment with the degree of precision and certainty which is desirable, if not essential, for the purpose of uniform and equitable assessment of duties. Above all, it is impossible for the officials of a foreign government without means of obtaining access to secret records. Such problems arise as the necessity of distinguishing between genuine salary payments and distribution of profits; the determination of what is a proper depreciation allowance; the inclusion or exclusion from costs of interest on borrowed and on invested capital, respectively; and variations in the cost of production of different portions of the output. In the case of an industry producing from the same plant and equipment a variety of kinds and grades of products, the exact determination of costs of production is impossible. All that is possible under such circumstances, and all that is attained in ordinary business practice is the reaching of an estimate resting on theoretical assumptions of necessarily disputable validity with respect to what are the proper items to include in cost, and what are the most satisfactory bases of apportionment of joint costs to the different products from the point of view of guidance of price-policy and of future production. Even if the customs officials could discover in every case the figures of cost of production of foreign products as ascertained for their own purposes by foreign producers, it would by no means necessarily follow that these figures would afford a satisfactory basis for the assessment of import duties, whether of the ordinary kind or additional duties based on the difference between foreign costs of production and export prices. Accountants' costs of production are estimates intended to provide a basis for the comparison of the efficiency of different departments of a given industry, or to guide in the direction of future production, or to aid in the determination of selling prices, or to serve other purposes. What from the accounting point of view may be a satisfactory basis for estimating costs for one purpose may not be satisfactory for another. The development of comprehensive tariff legislation dependent upon the accurate determination of costs of production, whether foreign or domestic, for its administration is a dream incapable of even partial realization.

The only practical scope for the application of provisions for the penalization of imports sold below their cost of production is where the difference between the export price and the cost of production is so great that the existence of an excess of cost over price, even though not the exact determination of the amount of such excess, can readily be ascertained. Such provisions, however, should leave to the discretion of the officials charged with their administration the occasion for their application and the amount of additional duty to be imposed. A provision which would make it mandatory upon the customs officials to penalize every instance of the importation of goods sold at export prices less than their cost of production by the imposition of duties equal to the excess of cost of production over export price would necessarily be largely inoperative or else would result in harsh, arbitrary, and inequitable administration.

METHODS OF ADMINISTRATION

The Canadian, Newfoundland, and American laws are essentially mandatory in character; in general they make it obligatory on the part of the customs officials to apply the dumping-duties in every instance in which goods are imported under circumstances which according to these laws make them subject to the duties. The only exceptions to this rule are the provisions in the Canadian and the Newfoundland laws which permit the exemption from the dumping-duties by customs regulations of: (a) imported goods of a class or kind not made or sold in these countries in substantial quantities and offered for sale to all purchasers on equal terms under like conditions; and (b) foreign goods sold for export to these countries at a price which is not lower than the foreign market value of these goods by more than a small percentage. The other laws of the first group, excepting the New Zealand law, are permissive or discretionary in character; they merely authorize the application of the dumping-duties to foreign goods imported under stated circumstances, and they leave wholly to the discretion of the officials concerned with the administration of the laws the decision as to whether or not the duties shall be applied when goods are imported under these circumstances. The New Zealand law uses the discretionary verb "may" instead of the mandatory verb "shall," but there is a provision in the law which states that in all cases where the dumping-duty *may* be levied under the law such duty *shall* be levied "save where the Minister may otherwise specially direct on the ground that the imposition of such duty is not required in the public interest."

Most of the laws of the first group assign the task of administration wholly or mainly to the government department charged with the administration of the ordinary tariff laws. The administration of the American law is wholly in charge of the Treasury Department, which administers the ordinary customs duties. In Canada, New Zealand, and Newfoundland the antidumping laws are administered by the respective customs departments of these countries, but with the following minor exceptions: in Canada and in Newfoundland the provision authorizing the special treatment of consignment sales to guard against evasion of the dumping-duties can be brought into operation only by order of the governor-general-in-council, i.e., the Cabinet; in New Zealand the authority to make administrative regulations rests with the governor-general, which in practice also means the Cabinet. The Australian law authorizes the Minister of Customs to apply the dumping-duties only after a report and recommendation by the Tariff Board, an independent bureau, and gives to the governor-general the authority to make the necessary administrative regulations. The administration of the British antidumping law requires the joint intervention of the Board of Trade, of special committees appointed by the Board of Trade from a panel of persons most of whom are not to be government officials, of Parliament, and of the commissioners of customs and excise; in case of dispute about the value of goods decision is to be made by referee to be appointed by the Lord Chancellor. The administration of the laws of the second group is generally left to the courts or to some quasi-judicial body. The Canadian law of 1922 concerning natural products imported under circumstances which prejudicially affect the interest of Canadian producers charges the Minister of Customs with its administration and the Japanese law of 1920 authorizing the imposition of additional duties on foreign products imported or sold at unreasonably cheap prices can be applied by the customs authorities only upon the issue of a government ordinance after investigation by a board of inquiry.

Each country must choose between mandatory and permissive antidumping legislation in the light of the constitutional requirements and the legislative and administrative traditions peculiar to it, and its decision should also depend on the extent to which its industries are, or are believed to be, facing the menace of foreign dumping. In general, a permissive antidumping law, other things being equal, may be expected to prove milder in operation than a mandatory law. There will be a tendency for permissive measures either to become wholly inoperative or to be held in reserve to be invoked only in extreme cases of dumping. These conclusions receive a measure of support from the history of bounty-countervailing legislation and also of antidumping legislation, recent in origin as it is. None of the many bounty-countervailing provisions with the exception of the American one, which alone was mandatory, has ever been applied except against imports of bounty-fed sugar, which presented an unusually serious menace to domestic industries. The antidumping provisions of the Canadian law of 1907 and the American law of 1921 (but only in so far as orders are concerned), both of which are mandatory, have alone been often applied. There have been few instances of the issue of orders and probably no instances of the actual application of dumping penalties under all the other antidumping laws, including those which deal with dumping as a phase of unfair competition. If the object of antidumping legislation is to provide a means of defense against foreign dumping, to be used only in case it becomes a serious menace to some domestic industry or industries, permissive legislation is clearly preferable to mandatory. If it is sought to put a stop to all dumping, or to all dumping which occurs under certain clearly defined circumstances, mandatory legislation appears to be essential. For countries which do not levy import duties on a wide range of commodities or whose ordinary duties are not predominantly of the ad valorem type, permissive legislation is to be preferred. For such countries the administrative burden of seeking to discover and to penalize every instance of dumping would be greater than the extent of the dumping menace would ordinarily warrant, and a permissive measure which would authorize the imposition of additional duties in case of extreme instances of dumping would best meet the situation.

From the point of view of administrative convenience and economy it would generally be desirable that the enforcement of the antidumping law should be assigned to one department and most appropriately to the department which administers the ordinary tariff. Where investigation of the effects of dumping on domestic industries is required as a preliminary to the application of the dumping-duties, it may be convenient, however, to assign the task of making such investigation to another government department or bureau better equipped for the task. Spreading the task of administration over a number of departments, as in the British law, must necessarily result in increasing the administrative burden of the law or in lessening the probability of its vigorous enforcement.

CHAPTER XV

TREATY OBLIGATIONS AND ANTIDUMPING MEASURES

The measures adopted to offset the effect of foreign bounties by the imposition of additional duties on bounty-fed imports resulted in the years from 1894 to 1903 in numerous protests from the bounty-granting countries on the ground that such additional duties were in violation of treaty pledges made by the countries levying such duties. A similar situation has not as yet arisen with respect to general antidumping measures and countervailing measures against foreign private bounties, but the principles involved are essentially the same, and in the absence as yet of a definitive juristic solution of the fundamental problem raised by these protests, it may be expected that, as the extent and importance of antidumping legislation increases, the question of its consistency with treaty obligations will also become a matter for diplomatic controversy.

THE COMPATIBILITY OF BOUNTY-COUNTERVAILING DUTIES WITH MOST-FAVORED-NATION OBLIGATIONS

The protests against bounty-countervailing duties have been based primarily on the claim that such duties are incompatible with the obligation to grant most-favored-nation treatment. For many years there has been an extensive network of commercial treaties containing the most-favored-nation clause. This clause appears in many forms and applies to many types of international economic relations. Its main purpose is to eliminate discriminations in the treatment by one country of the economic interests of other foreign countries. The most-favored-nation clause, in whatever form it appears, is essentially a pledge to grant to the co-contracting country as favorable treatment in the matters covered by the clause as is granted to any other foreign country.   There follow two examples of the pledge as applied to tariff matters, the first of which is couched in more specific terms than the second:

No higher or other duty shall be imposed on the importation into the United States of any article the growth, produce or manufacture of the Dominican Republic, or of her fisheries; and no higher or other duty shall be imposed on the importation into the Dominican Republic of any article the growth, produce or manufacture of the United States, or their fisheries, than are or shall be payable on the like articles the growth, produce or manufacture of any other foreign country, or its fisheries.[1]

The contracting powers agree that, in all matters relating to commerce and navigation, any privilege, favor, or immunity whatever, which either . . . . has actually granted or may hereafter grant to the subjects or citizens of any other State shall be extended immediately and unconditionally to the subjects or citizens of the other contracting party; it being their intention that the trade and navigation of each country shall be placed, in all respects, by the other on the footing of the most-favored-nation.[2]

Both of these forms are "unconditional."   In the "conditional" form, which is almost invariably used by the United States, each of the contracting countries becomes entitled to favors which the other country may grant to third countries for compensation only upon giving equivalent compensation. For the question at issue here, the difference between the conditional and the unconditional pledge is immaterial.   That question is: Is the application of additional duties on goods imported from a country granting an official export bounty on such goods compatible with the treaty obligation to grant that country most-favored-nation treatment in tariff matters?

If the most-favored-nation pledge, especially in the first of the forms cited above, is to be literally interpreted, the answer would appear to be necessarily in the negative.   The pledge not to impose higher or other duties on goods imported from the

---

[1] United States-Dominican Republic, October 24, 1867, Art. IX.

[2] Great Britain-Paraguay, October 16, 1884, Art. II.

treaty country than on like goods imported from any other country appears to be sufficiently clear and sufficiently definite to render invalid any claim that the imposition of higher duties is not in violation of the pledge.   Many countries have nevertheless asserted their right to impose additional duties on imports of articles from countries which grant bounties on such articles, even though these countries are entitled by treaty to most-favored-nation treatment, and some jurists have conceded the validity of such claims.   How explain this apparent conflict of interpretation and practice with the obligations imposed by the most-favored-nation pledge if literally construed ?

The letter of a treaty, as of a law, may not adequately reveal the spirit or the intent of the provisions it contains.   "Public treaties are to be interpreted like other laws and contracts. Such is the inevitable imperfection and ambiguity of all human language that the mere words alone of any writing, literally expounded, will go a very little way towards explaining its meaning."[1]   But if the text of a treaty provision does not unambiguously and clearly disclose its intent, the most appropriate source of additional light as to its meaning is the interpretation given to it by those who negotiated it and by those whose duty it was to carry it out.   No support can be derived from these sources by those who assert the compatibility of countervailing duties with most-favored-nation obligations.   The most-favored-nation pledge and export bounties both antedate the first bounty-countervailing measure by at least two centuries.   The first suggestion that countervailing duties might not be in violation of the most-favored-nation pledge was made in the 1860's and no government unreservedly committed itself even temporarily to this position until 1888.   The postponement until the 1890's of the first enactment of a bounty-countervailing duty was due primarily to the common belief that such duties would be in conflict with most favored-nation obligations.   If additional duties on

---

[1] Henry Wheaton, *Elements of International Law*, 6th ed., Boston, 1855, p. 355.

bounty-fed imports are compatible with the most-favored-nation obligation, the discovery of this compatibility came rather late to be convincing.

It is obvious from a reading of the most-favored-nation pledge, especially if it appears in the first of the forms cited above, that considerable dexterity of interpretation is required if it is to be held to admit of differential treatment of bounty- and non-bounty countries, and if no support for such a claim can be derived from the evidence as to the general interpretation of the clause in the period during which it became a common feature of commercial treaties. In so far as the United States is concerned, however, two Supreme Court decisions eliminate any difficulty in interpreting the most-favored-nation pledge as permitting countervailing duties which might appear to result from the appearance of the pledge in the "no higher or other duties shall be imposed" form. In *Bartram* v. *Robertson*,[1] the Court held that any right which the United States might possess to levy higher duties on imports from a treaty country under the general pledge to grant most-favored-nation treatment to such country was in no way impaired if the general pledge was also accompanied by the specific pledge not to levy higher duties. In *Whitney* v. *Robertson*,[2] the Court held that even if the specific pledge appeared alone in the treaty, it imposed no obligation on the United States which would not equally have been imposed under a pledge of most-favored-nation treatment couched in general terms. Neither of these cases directly involved the question of bounty-countervailing duties, but the effect of the decisions for the United States is to establish for the "no higher or other duties" pledge the same legal meaning as the pledge in general terms of most-favored-nation treatment. The Court based its decisions on what in the light of what the Court held to be the traditional American policy must have been the intent of the United States

[1] 122 U.S. (1887) 116.
[2] 124 U.S. (1888) 190.

when it entered into these pledges. It is doubtful whether the United States has had a traditional and uniform policy with regard to the interpretation of the most-favored-nation clause. It is even more doubtful whether the American participants in the negotiation of treaties have always been informed as to what that policy is.[1] It would appear to the layman in any case that when there is a conflict in traditional policies and interpretations as between two parties to a treaty and that when the form in which an international contract is put is the form appropriate to the foreign and not the American interpretation, refusal to give any consideration to the foreign interpretation is a decisive demonstration of the shortcomings of a system of international intercourse under which each country asserts the right to interpret wholly from its own point of view the extent of its contractual obligations to other countries and there is no higher authority to adjudicate the conflicting claims.

Supreme Court decisions, of course, are, or should be, accepted as binding by American diplomatic officials. To this extent, therefore, American officials are saved from embarrassment when they insist that a pledge not to impose higher duties, no conditions being stated, means a pledge not to impose them only under certain conditions defined by themselves. But foreign countries are not bound to accept the decisions of the United States Supreme Court as authoritative definitions of their rights in international law under treaty obligations of the United States, and foreign jurists have not been wholly convinced of the logic of these decisions.[2] Moreover, the force of these decisions as precedents in international law must have been greatly impaired by the failure of the American government to follow them in at least two later occasions when to have done so

[1] In so far as the interpretation of the "no higher duty" pledge is concerned, cf. p. 303, *infra*.

[2] Cf. Sir Thomas Barclay, "Effect of 'Most-Favored-Nation' Clause in Commercial Treaties," *Yale Law Journal*, XVII. 30.

would have operated adversely to the American commercial policy of the moment. On these occasions the United States insisted that it was entitled to equality of treatment under the "no higher or other duties" clause in commercial treaties even though the circumstances were such that it was admittedly not entitled to such treatment under the American interpretation of the general pledge of most-favored-nation treatment appearing in the same treaties.[1]

HISTORICAL PRECEDENTS

While the "no higher or other duty" pledge would appear to make it more difficult to reconcile countervailing duties with treaty obligations, officials seeking to establish the consistency of the two have found it sufficiently difficult to present a convincing argument even when the most-favored-nation pledge was phrased in less precise and unambiguous terms. Since the first introduction and enforcement of countervailing duties, the most effective defense of their juristic validity for countries imposing such duties has been the appeal to the example of other countries which did likewise. So many countries have levied countervailing duties on bounty-fed imports, or have claimed the right to do so, that the question of their compatibility with most-favored-nation obligations is regarded in some quarters as a closed question. A study of the precedents must consist in the main of an examination of the history of the sugar-bounty question and of the American application of bounty-countervailing duties, since these two phases of the problem have been almost the sole occasion for diplomatic discussion of the juristic questions raised by countervailing duties. In appraising the weight of the precedents, due consideration should be given to the fact that it was not until most-favored-nation treaties and export bounties had been in contemporaneous existence for at least

[1] Mr. Gresham, Secretary of State, to the Russian Minister (1895), *Foreign Relations*, 1895, II, 1119; Mr. Hay, Secretary of State, to Minister to Hayti (1901), *ibid.*, 1901, pp. 278, 279.

two centuries that the claim was made in any quarter that special measures directed against bounty-fed imports were compatible with most-favored-nation obligations.

The Brussels Sugar Convention, which was signed in 1902 by Great Britain, Germany, France, Austria-Hungary, Italy, Belgium, Holland, Spain, and Sweden, and upon its renewal in 1907 by Russia, pledged the signatory countries to levy .countervailing duties on or to prohibit the importation of bounty-fed sugar. Since all of these countries had a large number of most-favored-nation treaties in force at the time of their entrance into the Sugar Convention, their acceptance of the penal clause of the Convention involved either: (1) their acknowledgment of the compatibility of countervailing duties with most-favored-nation obligations; or (2) their assumption that all sugar-growing countries would eventually enter the Convention and that there would consequently be no occasion, once the Convention had become operative, to apply the counter-vailing duties to imports of bounty-fed sugar from non-signatory countries;[1] or (3) their deliberate determination in the face of a difficult situation to disregard their most-favored-nation obligations in so far as bounty-fed sugar was concerned; or some combination of these. If the first of these was dominant, it was not binding on the non-signatory countries as a definition of their rights under most-favored-nation treaties, but it established an important precedent. If the second consideration was most important, then the signature of the Convention had little or no bearing on the problem here under discussion, although the manner of operation of the Convention might have such a bearing. If the third consideration were known to have been the deciding one in leading to the adoption of the penal clause, this would support instead of weaken the claim that on juristic

[1] The signatory countries, by their acceptance of the terms of the Convention, virtually renounced any claim which they might have under most-favored-nation treaties to the non-discriminatory treatment of their sugar if it enjoyed a bounty.

grounds countervailing duties were not compatible with most-favored-nation obligations.[1] Examination of the history of the negotiations which finally culminated in the conclusion of the Brussels Sugar Convention justifies the conclusion that the second and the third considerations were paramount in leading to the acceptance of the penal clause of the Convention, and that although there was a *pro forma* assertion by the participants in the Convention of its legality, there was reasonable ground for doubt as to whether this assertion was made with full sincerity.

Sugar bounties first became an important international problem in the middle of the nineteenth century. In the early days of the sugar-bounty question it was frankly admitted in England and in other countries which were opposed to the bounty system that the imposition of bounty-countervailing duties would be in violation of most-favored-nation obligations.[2] The Sugar Convention of 1864, which was signed and ratified by Great Britain, France, Belgium, and The Netherlands, but was never made effective, provided that each signatory country was to be free to apply such additional duties as it deemed proper to imports of bounty-fed refined sugar from non-signatory countries.[3] This was clearly not to be regarded as an assertion of the compatibility of such additional duties with most-favored-nation obligations, since no obligation was placed on the signatory countries to impose such duties and any of them could theoretically regain the right to impose them, if they were contrary to

[1] Although allowance should be made for the fact that important or repeated violations of a law or compact tend to destroy its force; laws, in other words, may become inoperative even in the absence of their formal repeal.

[2] Cf. Wilhelm Kaufmann, *Welt-Zuckerindustrie*, p. 287.

[3] Art. XIX. "Les Hautes Parties Contractantes se réservent de se concerter sur les moyens d'obtenir l'adhésion des Gouvernements des autres pays aux dispositions de la présente Convention.

Dans les cas où des primes seraient accordées dans les dits pays à l'exportation des sucres raffinés, les Hautes Parties Contractantes pourront s'entendre sur les surtaxes à établir à l'importation des sucres raffinés des dites provenances" (*ibid.*, p. 569).

treaty obligations, by denouncing or obtaining a revision of the treaties.[1]

The unratified Sugar Convention of 1888 pledged each of the signatory countries to exclude from its territory either by prohibition of import or by countervailing duties sugar which had received a bounty from another country. It provided also that the most-favored-nation clause in other treaties should not be pleaded with a view to evading the consequences of the stipulation for the exclusion of bounty-fed sugar, even by countries which once having entered the Convention subsequently retired from it.[2] This last provision and the negotiations which preceded its adoption have been interpreted by Visser as showing that it was the intention of the Convention that the penal clause was to be applied only against signatory countries which failed to keep their pledge not to grant bounties. Visser concludes, therefore, that the 1888 Convention did not imply a recognition of harmony between countervailing duties and most-favored-nation obligations.[3] Whether or not this is a correct interpretation, of the countries represented at the Conference, six—Russia, Belgium, Denmark, Sweden, France, and The Netherlands—all maintained that countervailing duties would be in violation of their treaty obligations, and only four—Great Britain, Germany, Spain, and Austria—supported the contrary view.[4] The British govern-

---

[1] Cf. M. L. E. Visser, "La Clause de 'La Nation La Plus Favorisée' dans les Traités de Commerce," *Revue de Droit International et de Législation Comparée*, 2d ser., IV, 166, note.

[2] Art. VII. ". . . . Il est entendu que le bénéfice de la clause du traitement de la nation la plus favorisée inscrite dans d'autres Traités ne pourrait être réclamé pour se soustraire aux conséquences de l'application du deuxième alinéa du présent Article, même de la part des États Signataires qui viendraient à se retirer de la Convention" (Wilhelm Kaufmann, *op. cit.*, p. 573).

[3] M. L. E. Visser, *op. cit.*, pp. 168, 169.

[4] M. L. E. Visser, *op. cit.*, p. 167. Cf., however, Wilhelm Kaufmann, *op. cit.*, p. 141, who cites five countries, including those named above and also Russia, as supporting the compatibility of countervailing duties with most-favored-nation obligations, and only four countries, Belgium, Denmark, The Netherlands, and

ment later in the same year in effect repudiated the position taken by its representative at the Conference by declaring that it could not ratify the penal clause of the Convention without previously terminating or revising its most-favored-nation treaties.[1] Moreover, practically all the beet-sugar interests of the world and more than four-fifths of the cane-sugar interests were represented at the Conference,[2] and it was expected that all the parties interested in the sugar-bounty question would join the Convention and thereby surrender any right of protest they might have under most-favored-nation treaties against the application of the penal clause to their sugar. The failure of the Convention to obtain ratification was due in large part to the refusal of some countries to enter on the ground that the penal clause would clash with their treaty obligations and the refusal of other countries to enter unless the adherence of all the sugar-growing countries were obtained.[3]

All the countries which signed the Brussels Sugar Convention of 1902 thereby committed themselves to that extent to the position that the penal clause was not in violation of their treaty obligations to non-signatory countries. Since none of the signatory countries made any move toward revising or terminating its most-favored-nation treaties with non-signatory countries after its adherence to the Convention, it cannot be questioned that the 1902 Convention established an important precedent in favor of the compatibility of countervailing duties with most-favored-nation obligations. But as Visser points out with respect to the conclusions reached by the earlier sugar

---

France, as denying it. But according to Kaufmann's own evidence, Russia agreed merely that countervailing duties were justifiable, and stated that if the Convention was ratified she would take advantage of the delay before it was to come into operation to bring her commercial treaties into harmony with the penal clause thereof (*ibid.*, pp. 304, 305).

[1] *Ibid.*, p. 295.

[2] *Foreign Relations*, 1888, I, 689.

[3] Cf. Wilhelm Kaufmann, *op. cit.*, pp. 575, 576.

conferences, the position taken by the Convention rested primarily on economic rather than on juristic considerations.[1] It was the growing seriousness of the sugar-bounty problem to both the exporting and the importing countries and not any new arguments resting on principle instead of on expediency which induced those of the signatories which had hitherto denied the compatibility of countervailing duties with most-favored-nation obligations to recede from their original position.

In the case of Great Britain, the attitude taken toward the purely legal question of the consistency of countervailing duties with most-favored-nation obligations was unmistakably governed in large part by the views of the party in power at the moment as to the economic and political desirability of countervailing duties. The support of countervailing duties came almost wholly from the Conservatives, who leaned toward protection, whereas the Liberals, who were determined free traders, in general opposed countervailing duties as inconsistent with free trade principles or at least as an entering wedge for ordinary import duties. The Conservatives, moreover, were more inclined than the Liberals to consent to modifications in the commercial policy of the United Kingdom in the interests of the Colonies, and in the later years of the sugar-bounty question the British opposition to the bounties rested more on the injury which resulted from them to the cane-producing colonies than on any injury to British refiners. It is not surprising, therefore, to find that the official British pronouncements in favor of the compatibility of countervailing duties with most-favored-nation obligations have all been made during Conservative administrations. As late as 1897, the West India Royal Commission, which included as one of its members Sir Edward Grey, later Foreign Minister in the Asquith government, recommended against the enactment of countervailing duties on bounty-fed sugar in the interest of the West Indies on the ground that it

[1] *Op. cit.*, p. 171.

was inexpedient to raise questions connected with the interpretation of the most-favored-nation clause which might have the
effect of weakening its force.[1]

It was not until 1899, when India upon the insistence of
Joseph Chamberlain, the British Secretary of State for the
Colonies, enacted a bounty-countervailing provision, that the
British government definitely and unqualifiedly committed
itself, in reply to the Russian protests against the Indian duties,
to the position that countervailing duties were not in violation
of most-favored-nation obligations.   Chamberlain at this time
was a convert to Imperial Preference and was moving toward
support of outright tariff protection, and his urgent appeal to
the Indian government to enact the countervailing-duty measure
was motivated by the desire to help the sugar-producers of
Mauritius in their competition in the Indian market with the
bounty-fed beet sugar of Europe.   Chamberlain was now a
member of a Conservative (yclept Liberal-Unionist) Cabinet,
but in his earlier days he had been a Liberal and a convinced
free trader.   His views on the compatibility of countervailing
duties with most-favored-nation obligations had conveniently
changed with the change in his political and economic affiliations,
for in 1881, when he was president of the Board of Trade in a
Liberal Cabinet, he had regarded countervailing duties as
inconsistent with treaty obligations: "There are many ways,"
he had then declared, "besides bounties in which governments
can and do encourage or discourage particular industries.   None
of these have hitherto been thought to call for retaliation by
His Majesty's government, yet they are open to the same kind
of objection as sugar bounties."[2]

The Brussels Sugar Convention was signed by Great Britain
in 1902 while a Conservative administration was in power.

[1] Great Britain, *Report of the West Indian Royal Commission*, 1897 (C. 8655),
pp. 12, 13, 72, 74.

[2] Cited in *Parliamentary Debates, Commons*, June 15, 1899, col. 1219.

The Liberals were again in power in 1907, when the question of the renewal of the Convention was to be determined, and they had come into power on a platform which included a pledge to withdraw from the Convention. In response to the appeals made by the sugar-growing colonies, this pledge was not executed, but Great Britain did withdraw in 1907 from all obligations under the penal clause of the Convention. Evidence that the Liberals were not convinced of the consistency of countervailing duties with most-favored-nation obligations is further adduced by the fact that in the last years of the Asquith Ministry it introduced into new treaties containing the most-favored-nation pledge the provision that the obligation to grant most-favored-nation treatment should not apply to measures applicable in either country to articles enjoying a bounty in the other.[1]

That the position taken by the Brussels Sugar Convention with regard to the relation of countervailing duties to most-favored-nation obligations was the result of a special and extraordinarily pressing economic situation and was not necessarily indicative of the real attitude of the countries which were members of the Convention with respect to the juristic question is indicated by the fact that none of these countries has ever applied bounty-countervailing duties to any products other than sugar.[2] Moreover, two provisions of the Convention demand careful scrutiny before the Convention can be cited as establishing a precedent of juristic weight. By the "surtax" provision of the 1902 Convention the signatory countries were

[1] Cf. The Great Britain-Honduras Treaty of 1912, Art. VI. (*British and Foreign State Papers*, CVI, 788); and the Great Britain-Portugal Treaty of August 12, 1914, Art. VII (Sir Edward Hertslet, *Commercial Treaties*, XXVII, 1022).

[2] Several of the countries which joined the Brussels Sugar Convention in 1902 subsequently signed commercial treaties with Russia in which the most-favored-nation clause expressly stated that bounties were not to be made the pretext for differential treatment, thus in effect repudiating the principle upon which the validity of the penal clause of the Convention rests. Cf. Fabien Thibault, "Conflits entre la Convention Sucrière de Bruxelles et les Traités de Commerce," *Revue d'Économie Politique*, XXIII (1909), 509 ff.

obligated not only to restrict the importation of sugar which had received an official bounty but to impose similar restrictions on sugar coming from countries in which the taxes on foreign exceeded the taxes on domestic sugar by more than a stated moderate amount. In 1907 Russia was admitted into the Convention with the special concession that her bountied sugar should be free within specified limits as to quantity from countervailing duties upon exportation to member-countries. It is scarcely permissible to cite as authoritative the interpretation given by the Brussels Convention on one phase of most-favored-nation obligations and to reject as of no weight because erroneous its interpretation of other phases.

But the surtax provision would justify, in spite of most-favored-obligations to grant equality of treatment, discrimination in the tariff treatment of imports according to whether the exporting countries had high tariffs, on the one hand, or low or no tariffs on the other, a practice which would certainly be regarded by most countries with high tariffs as an invalid departure from the most-favored-nation principle. The United States, it is true, has operated to some extent on a somewhat similar basis, notably under Section 3 of the McKinley Tariff Act of 1890, where the relative severity on each other's products of the American and the foreign tariffs taken as a whole was made the basis for the application or the withholding of special duties,[1] and under the contingent duties in later tariff acts, and especially in the Fordney-McCumber Tariff Act of 1922,[2] whose application is dependent upon whether or not the country from which they are imported levies duties upon similar imports from the United States.

The contingent duties in recent American tariff laws have not received any attention from jurists and if they have been the occasion for protest by other countries such protests have not

[1] Cf. U.S. Tariff Commission, *Reciprocity and Commercial Treaties*, pp. 155 ff.

[2] See Pars. 369, 371, 1536, 1541, 1543, 1548, 1585, in the Tariff Act of 1922.

been made public. A contingent duty on salt in the Tariff
Act of 1894 elicited a formal protest by Germany.[1] The special
or penalty duties in the Tariff Act of 1890 brought vigorous
protests from the three countries—all small Latin-American
countries—on whose products they were imposed, and although
these protests were rather cavalierly handled by the State Department their justice was later conceded in Congress and by the
Tariff Commission.[2] The surtax provision in the Brussels Sugar
Convention appears to be the sole instance in which any country
other than the United States has asserted that its obligation to
maintain equality of import duties under a most-favored-nation
pledge is dependent upon the height of the duties of the other
contracting country. If the United States were willing, which
she undoubtedly is not, to accept the application of this interpretation to her own exports, it would deprive the most-favored-
nation treaties to which it is a party of a large part, probably the
major part, of their effectiveness as a guaranty against foreign
discriminations.

The special exemption from countervailing duties granted to
Russian exports of bounty-fed sugar by the Brussels Sugar
Convention of 1907 is also incompatible under any conceivable
construction with the principle of most-favored-nation treatment,
and therefore further detracts from the force of the Convention
as an authoritative precedent with respect to the proper interpretation of most-favored-nation treaty obligations.

[1] U.S. Tariff Commission, *Reciprocity and Commercial Treaties*, p. 428.

[2] Cf. Report of Committee on Ways and Means on tariff bill of 1894, which
provided for the repeal of the penalty duties: "Under the provisions of this section
presidential proclamations have been issued imposing retaliatory duties upon the
five above-mentioned articles . . . . when coming from certain countries. These
proclamations have naturally led . . . . to diplomatic correspondence, in which it
has been claimed with apparent justice that such discriminations were in violation
of our solemn treaty obligations" (53d Cong., 2d Sess. *House Rept.* 234, p. 11).
Cf. also, U.S. Tariff Commission, *Reciprocity and Commercial Treaties*, pp. 40,
421, 422.

The United States has since 1890 made imports of bounty-fed goods subject to countervailing duties, and has with one exception uniformly maintained that such action was not in violation of its most-favored-nation obligations.   In 1894 Secretary of State Gresham advised President Cleveland that the German position was well taken in protesting against the imposition of counter-vailing duties on its sugar as in contravention of the most-favored-nation pledge in the treaties of German states with the United States.   President Cleveland thereupon asked Congress to repeal the countervailing provision in the Tariff Act of 1894,[1] but Congress failed to do so.   With this exception, the American government has never varied from its position that countervailing duties were compatible with most-favored-nation obligations.

The decision of the Supreme Court in *Downs v. United States* is sometimes cited in connection with discussions of the compatibility of countervailing duties with most-favored-nation obligations in such a manner as to imply that it supported the position that the two are compatible.[2]   But the decision did not touch upon the question of treaty obligations, and confined itself to an examination of the two questions which were at issue: Did the Russian system of excise taxation result in effect in a bounty on exported sugar? and Was it constitutional for Congress to delegate to the Secretary of the Treasury the power to determine the existence and the amount of foreign bounties and to impose upon imports of bountied goods countervailing duties equal in amount to the bounties?   A most-favored-nation treaty, signed in 1832, was at this time still in effect between the United States and Russia, but there is no evidence that it was referred to in the Court proceedings.   Moreover the Court would have been powerless to declare invalid the countervailing duties even though it had regarded them as violating the treaty

[1] *Foreign Relations*, 1894, pp. ix, 236.

[2] Cf. S. K. Hornbeck, "The Most-Favored-Nation Clause in Commercial Treaties," *Bulletin of the University of Wisconsin*, VI (1910), 73; U.S. Tariff Commission, *Reciprocity and Commercial Treaties*, p. 434.

obligation, since the enactment of the countervailing provision was subsequent to the conclusion of the treaty and was therefore controlling under municipal law.

Germany, Austria-Hungary, Denmark, and Russia all protested against the countervailing duties as not being consistent with most-favored-nation treatment, but the protests were of no avail. Russia for a time retaliated against the countervailing duties by imposing discriminatory duties on American products and Germany retaliated by prohibiting the importation of American cattle.[1] It is significant as indicating the doubtful validity of the countervailing duties that two of the four countries which at the Sugar Conference of 1888 had supported the compatibility of countervailing duties with most-favored-nation obligations later reversed their positions.

Such in brief is the case in support of the legality of the imposition of bounty-countervailing duties on imports from countries entitled by treaty to most-favored-nation treatment, in so far as it rests on precedents. It cannot be regarded as a strong case. In no instance has there been a judicial or an arbitral decision of the issue. No country has maintained without exception the legality of countervailing duties. Many countries have conceded that countervailing duties were in violation of their most-favored-nation obligations even though they were otherwise in favor of such duties. No country has ever formally conceded that such duties were not in violation of its rights to most-favored-nation treatment when the duties were imposed by other countries on its own products.

OFFICIAL ARGUMENTS FOR THE VALIDITY OF COUNTERVAILING DUTIES

An examination of the reasoning which has been presented by government officials in support of the legality of the countervailing duties will demonstrate that there has been failure also in this direction to establish a convincing argument in their favor.

[1] Cf. U.S. Tariff Commission, *Reciprocity and Commercial Treaties*, pp. 160, 221.

The American official argument in defense of the compatibility of countervailing duties with most-favored-nation obligations has uniformly followed the line of reasoning presented in an opinion of Attorney-General Olney issued in 1894.[1] Olney held that countervailing duties could not be regarded as causing a discrimination which was in violation of the most-favored-nation clause because: (a) "the clause permits any internal regulations that a country may find necessary to give a preference to 'native merchants, vessels, and productions'" and (b) this interpretation was held by foreign powers, especially Germany and Great Britain. The clause does permit protection to domestic interests against foreign competition, but not in any form which involves discrimination between different foreign countries. If the clause did not apply to import duties, it would have little meaning since in so far as it deals with the treatment of international commerce its main purpose is to prevent discriminatory import duties. If the United States pledges itself in a reciprocal treaty to grant Germany most-favored-nation treatment, there is no obligation on the part of Germany except that of granting like treatment to the United States. If Germany by giving bounties to its exporters offsets the protective effect for American producers of the American tariff this is not of itself sufficient to release the United States from its obligation not to discriminate against German products in favor of the products of other countries. If equal treatment of the products of Germany and of other foreign countries is incompatible with the protection of American producers against foreign competition, there is always the alternative of terminating the treaty which obligates the United States not to depart from equality of treatment. There is nothing in the letter at least of the most-favored-nation pledge which provides that the pledge shall be binding only in so far as it does not conflict with the policy of protecting domestic

[1] 53d Cong., 3d Sess., *Sen. Misc. Doc.* 52, p. 6

industry.[1]   Nor should Olney's appeal to the interpretation of
the clause by other powers have brought conviction to anyone.
He cited in particular the position of Great Britain and Germany
at the Sugar Conference of 1888, but the British government
had shortly after in the same year reversed the position of its
representative at the Conference, and the occasion for Olney's
memorandum was in part the German protest that the American
countervailing duties were in violation of treaty obligations.

The British Foreign Office, in defending against Russian
protests the legality of the Indian countervailing duties and the
duties contemplated by the penal provisions of the Brussels
Sugar Convention, maintained that since the discrimination
against the sugar of bounty-granting countries was consequent
upon acts within the volition of those countries, Great Britain
was justified in protecting her industries against the artificial
preference to foreign producers resulting from the bounties,
notwithstanding her most-favored-nation obligations.   In such
a case a remedy against the countervailing duties was available
to the country whose goods were subjected to these duties,
namely, the discontinuance of the bounties.[2]   If the principle of

[1] It might be argued with some force that the conflict is not so much with
the *policy* of protection as with the *measures* determined upon to execute that
policy, and that a country in most-favored-nation relations with a bounty-granting
country can carry out its protective policy without violation of its treaty obligations
and without allowing it to be neutralized by foreign bounties simply by raising its
ordinary import duty whenever foreign countries are paying bounties.   But, as
has already been pointed out, ordinary import duties are unsatisfactory devices
for meeting the menace of bounty-fed or dumped imports, since in order to reach
a fraction of the imports they must be imposed on all alike.   There is a good economic case for bounty-countervailing duties.   All that is here claimed against them is
that their compatibility with most-favored-nation obligations is extremely doubtful.

[2] Marquess of Salisbury to Russian Minister, July 15, 1899: "When an artificial
preference of such a character is produced by the direct legislative act of the foreign
Government which is a party to a most-favored-nation stipulation, Her Majesty's
Government consider that it should be open to the other Contracting Party, if
such action should seem expedient, to redress the balance of trade which has
thus been artificially disturbed.   The remedy in such a case lies in the hands of

volenti non fit injuria is properly invoked here, undoubtedly a strong argument is presented for the validity of the counter-vailing duties. But as Russia pointed out in reply, if its grant of export bounties released Great Britain on this ground from its obligation to give equality of treatment to Russian imports, any advantage conferred upon its producers by the Russian government and within its power to withhold, such as efficient and economical government, low rates of taxation, low railroad rates on government railroads, low shipping freights on govern-ment-owned ships, etc., could with equal reason be made the basis for withholding equality of treatment from Russian goods. Such an interpretation would destroy the effectiveness of the most-favored-nation clause as a guaranty against discrimination, since it would always be possible to discover some particular in which foreign industries profited from the legislative action of their governments.[1]

Russia might have added that the argument that an "artifi-cial" disturbance of the balance of trade through legislative

---

the country granting the bounty, or by its legislative act producing the artificial stimulus, the discontinuance of which would cause the counteracting measures to be withdrawn" (Great Britain, *Commercial No. 1*, 1903 [Cd. 1401], p. 3).

Marquess of Lansdowne to Russian Minister, November 20, 1902: "It is precisely the fact that it is within the power of the Legislature in Russia to abolish the conditions which form the basis of the Russian system . . . . that deprives the Russian Government, notwithstanding the existence of a most-favored-nation clause, of any ground of complaint against the action of any other Government in endeavoring to free its own home market from the intrusion of goods sold in that market at less than cost price" (*ibid.*, p. 19).

[1] *Ibid.*, pp. 16 ff. Cf. *Geofry v. Riggs*, 133 U.S. (1890), 258: "It is a general principle of construction with respect to treaties that they shall be liberally con-strued, so as to carry out the apparent intention of the parties to secure equality and reciprocity between them. As they are contracts between independent nations, in their construction words are to be taken in their ordinary meaning, as understood in the public law of nations, *and not in any artificial or special sense impressed upon them by local law, unless such restricted sense is clearly intended.* And it has been held by this court that *where a treaty admits of two constructions, one restrictive of rights that may be claimed under it and the other favorable to them, the latter is to be preferred.*" (Italics mine.)

act of a foreign country suspended the obligation to grant such country equality of treatment, even if it had validity, could be invoked only by countries which did not themselves artificially disturb the balance of trade by protective duties.   This argument could be consistently used, therefore, by Great Britain while it still adhered to free trade, but not by protectionist countries.

Great Britain refused the Russian offer to submit the conflict in interpretation to impartial arbitration, but offered in return to terminate its most-favored-nation treaty with Russia:[1] Russia retaliated against the Indian countervailing duties by imposing a discriminatory duty on Indian tea.

THE OPINIONS OF JURISTS

Writers on international law have differed as much as governments in their views as to the compatibility of countervailing duties with most-favored-nation obligations. Most European jurists, however, have denied their compatibility and American jurists have taken a non-committal attitude.   Among American writers of note, S. K. Hornbeck appears to stand alone in support of the compatibility of countervailing duties with most-favored-nation obligations, and even he does not unqualifiedly commit himself;[2] C. C. Hyde has taken the contrary position;[3] the others

[1] Great Britain, *Commercial No. 1*, 1903, p. 19.

[2] "International law has not yet become so established that it may be cited as either affirming or denying the right in question; whatever appears the more practical and equitable interpretation will become the law.   At present, economic interests, the equities involved, and the tendency of international opinion (witness the Brussels Sugar Convention) certainly favor the attitude assumed by the United States and Great Britain" (*The Most-Favored-Nation Clause in Commercial Treaties*, p. 75.   See also the paragraph preceding the one here cited).

Hornbeck cites Herod as considering the countervailing duties "both equitable and legal" (*ibid.*, note).   But Herod merely affirms the economic merits and the legality in international law of countervailing duties of themselves.   He does not commit himself on the question here at issue of their compatibility with most-favored-nation obligations (cf. J. R. Herod, *Favored Nation Treatment*, New York, 1901, pp. 120 ff.).

[3] "Concerning the Interpretation of Treaties," *American Journal of International Law*, III (1909), 59.

confine themselves to stating the American official position, which may perhaps justify the inference that they accept it as juristically sound.

It has been argued in support of the validity of countervailing duties in relation to most-favored-nation obligations that to accept all imports of a given kind on equal terms is to discriminate "against countries which pay no bounties and those which pay less than the highest, to the advantage of those countries which pay the highest, and that this is contrary to the spirit of the clause."[1]   This differs from the official British and American arguments in that the countervailing duties are to be imposed in the interest of producers in non-bounty-granting countries entitled to most-favored-nation treatment rather than in the interest of domestic producers.   It would follow from the acceptance of this argument that a country *must*, instead of *may*, impose countervailing duties, and presumably also that these countervailing duties must be such as to leave all foreign countries entitled to most-favored-nation treatment as far as possible in the same position relative to each other as if no bounties were granted.   On this reasoning the action of Great Britain in making its restriction take the form of absolute prohibition of import of bounty-fed sugar, the action of the United States under the countervailing provisions of the Tariff Acts of 1890 and 1894 in penalizing only imports of bounty-fed sugar and in imposing on such sugar a flat-rate additional duty, and under later tariff acts of subjecting to countervailing duties only such bounty-fed goods as were dutiable under the ordinary tariff; and the action since 1903 of practically the entire world with the exception of the United States in permitting bounty-fed imports, sugar alone excluded, to enter on equal terms with imports which had received no bounty, have all fallen short of strict

[1] S. K. Hornbeck, *op. cit.*, p. 74.   Cf., also, J. B. Moore, *A Digest of International Law*, Washington, 1906, V, 282, for the citation of a similar opinion from the *Spectator* of August 21, 1880; and Wilhelm Kaufmann, *op. cit.*, p. 280.

regard for the obligations imposed by the most-favored-nation pledge.

But there is no historical basis for the position that a country is either obligated or permitted under its most-favored-nation pledges to redress the differences in the comparative situation of foreign countries, whether these differences are due to "artificial" or to "natural" causes, by discriminating in its tariff treatment of the products of these countries. Once the interpretation is established that the most-favored-nation pledge permits the classification of countries and the differential treatment of their commerce on any basis not explicitly provided for in the pledge, the way is open to the complete destruction of the efficacy of the clause by a process of gradual attrition. The possible bases of classification of countries are innumerable, and many of them are equally defensible with the classification according to whether they grant bounties. Germany, for instance, in its protest against the American countervailing duties under the Tariff Act of 1894 argued that the United States could with the same degree of justification assert that German manufacturers in any particular industry paid lower taxes than the manufacturers of other countries, "and then, in order to bring about a so-called equalization, levy a discriminating duty on the German product concerned, on its importation into an American port."[1] Once discrimination between countries on the basis of differences in political conditions in these countries is established as permissible under the most-favored-nation clause, why not also on the basis of differences in economic conditions whether or not due to political conditions? As Judge Marion De Vries, of the United States Court of Customs Appeals, has pointed out, "there is no difference in legal principle between economic conditions and other conditions" and he proceeds to present as not in violation

[1] *Foreign Relations*, 1894, p. 234. Secretary of State Gresham conceded the force of the German argument, *ibid.*, pp. 237, 238.

of the most-favored-nation principle a proposal which carries this reasoning to its appropriate *reductio ad absurdum:* namely that duties be levied on imports at different rates for different countries, the rates to be adjusted so as to equal the differences in cost of production between the United States and the respective foreign countries![1]

It should also be taken into consideration that if the most-favored-nation pledge permits or requires the equalization by differential duties of the differences in the comparative advantages in the export trade of different foreign countries, it does not follow that bounty-countervailing duties equal to the amounts of the foreign bounties will achieve such equalization of differences. The bounties may have been granted as an offset to disadvantages resulting to the producers in the bounty-granting country from natural causes or from legislative acts, and may be necessary to these producers if they are to be able to export their products.

The compatibility of countervailing duties with most-favored-nation obligations has been defended also on the ground that a country is required by its most-favored-nation pledge to grant equal treatment only "under like circumstances," and that the grant of a bounty in one country and its absence in another makes the circumstances unlike. But circumstances are never identical in every detail and this interpretation would always afford some pretext for justifying the departure from equality of treatment. If a most-favored-nation pledge were intended upon its inclusion in a treaty to apply only in cases where goods were imported under like circumstances, it is reasonable to expect that the pledge would have been so phrased as to make this clear and indisputable. A few treaties do specifically limit the application of the most-favored-nation pledge by the inclusion

[1] *Hearings on General Tariff Revision,* House Committee on Ways and Means, 1921, pp. 4308, 4330.

of the words "under like circumstances" or their equivalent.[1] It is unwarranted by any principle of interpretation or any precedent to read such a limitation into any treaty pledge which does not expressly reveal that such was the intent of the pledge.

A French jurist, Fabien Thibault, offers what is perhaps the most ingenious of the arguments presented in defense of the compatibility of bounty-countervailing duties with most-favored-nation obligations.[2] He argues that a country which has received a pledge of most-favored-nation treatment from another country is evading, if not violating, the spirit of the pledge if it grants an export bounty on goods shipped to that country, for it thereby destroys the equality of conditions which the most-favored-nation pledge was intended to maintain. His original contribution is not this argument, which had often before been presented, but his claim that *it was the common understanding* that the grant of bounties was virtually a violation of most-favored-nation obligations. That this was the general attitude, he argues, is shown by the inclusion in many commercial treaties containing the most-favored-nation clause of an additional provision prohibiting the grant of export bounties.[3] The absence from some treaties of the bounty clause he explains as due to the fact that its inclusion was demanded only in treaties with countries who were regarded as being likely to attempt the evasion of the spirit of their most-favored-nation pledges. In other words, where a country could be trusted to carry out its treaty

---

[1] E.g., the Great Britain-Mexico Treaty of November 27, 1888, Art. 3; the Argentina-Germany Treaty of November 19, 1857, Art. 3; the Austria-Hungary-Roumania Treaty of December 21, 1893, Art. 3. The limitation was inserted in these treaties merely to make clear that the right to apply differential treatment to direct and indirect imports, respectively, was not surrendered by the pledge of most-favored-nation treatment.

[2] "Conflits entre la Convention Sucrière de Bruxelles et les Traités de Commerce," *Revue d'Économie Politique*, XXIII (1909), 503 ff.

[3] For a discussion of bounty clauses in treaties, see pp. 166 ff., *supra*.

obligations honorably and without any attempt at evasion thereof, it was unnecessary to insert explanatory provisions as a safeguard against evasion. Export bounties, therefore, are themselves a violation of the most-favored-nation contract strictly interpreted, and as such may be penalized by counter-vailing duties without affording the bounty-granting country any ground for protest.[1]

The argument is ingenious, but its plausibility vanishes upon an examination of the facts. The evidence which Thibault presents purporting to show that countries omitted the bounty clause from treaties pledging most-favored-nation treatment only when they were dealing with countries which could be trusted not to evade their obligations actually shows merely that in the one or two cited instances a pledge not to grant bounties was demanded of a country which had been habitually granting bounties and was not demanded of another country in which the bounty system was absent. No bounty clause is to be found in any of the commercial treaties of some important countries, including the United States, Great Britain, and Russia.[2] Is it to be inferred that these countries felt assured that no country with which they negotiated a most-favored-nation treaty would depart from the spirit of its pledge by granting export bounties? Only a cursory comparison of the treaties which do contain the bounty clause with the treaties from which it is absent is necessary to demonstrate that the inclusions and the omissions follow no one principle and cannot be explained by any simple formula. There is not a shred of evidence to support the theory that the bounty clause was regarded by the countries using it as merely an explanatory or precautionary addendum to the most-favored-nation pledge, instead of as an independent and additional pledge.

---

[1] Thibault concedes, however, that the surtax provision of the Brussels Sugar Convention was not compatible with the most-favored-nation obligations of member- to non-member countries (*op. cit.*, p. 517).

[2] Cf. *supra*, p. 166 n.

The plea for such an interpretation of the most-favored-nation pledge as will permit bounty-countervailing duties on the ground that bounties are economically objectionable and that a country should be free for economic reasons to take measures to protect its domestic producers against foreign subsidized competition or to discriminate in favor of non-bountied imports would have weight if the only alternatives were either acknowledgment of incapacity to provide remedies against the bounty evil or insistence upon the right to levy countervailing duties, treaty obligations to the contrary notwithstanding. But the most-favored-nation pledges in commercial treaties are terminable by either party thereto. The way to secure freedom from the obligations of a terminable contract which have become burdensome is not to violate the contract but to terminate it or to obtain by mutual consent a revision thereof which eliminates the objectionable features. The proper solution of the problem is the inclusion in the most-favored-nation pledge of a provision such as that contained in recent British treaties which exempts measures taken against bounties from the obligations of the pledge, or a provision such as that contained in a Roumanian treaty, which specifically declares countervailing duties to be consistent with the pledge.[1]

It has been a regrettable feature of the bounty controversy that—with one exception, the Germany-Switzerland Treaty of 1904—none of the treaties which were made the basis for protest against countervailing duties contained a provision requiring the reference to impartial arbitration of disputed points of interpretation, and that none of the countries claiming the right to impose countervailing duties has consented to submit the

---

[1] Belgium-Roumania, May 28, 1906, Art. 4: "Il est entendu que la clause du traitement de la nation la plus favorisée stipulée par la présente convention . . . . n'exclut pas . . . . la perception de droits supplémentaires en compensation de primes d'exportation ou de production." (*Martens, N.R.G. XXXV*, 267.)

issue to arbitration.[1]   As many commercial treaties contain an arbitration provision, a recurrence of controversy as to the legality of countervailing duties might serve to bring about a definitive judicial determination of the issue, under circumstances more favorable to impartial and reasoned decisions than the *ad hoc* pronouncements of government officials primarily concerned with the successful execution of their governments' policies.   It is desirable that countries be free to take effective action toward the discouragement of the bounty system, but it is even more important that the value of the most-favored-nation clause as an instrument for the elimination of discriminatory legislation be not destroyed by interpretation.

THE GERMAN-SWISS FLOUR DUTY CONTROVERSY

The most recent of the diplomatic controversies arising out of the conflicting interpretations of the relationship between countervailing duties and treaty obligations presents a somewhat different problem than the one so far discussed.   Switzerland in its tariff revision of 1902 enacted a provision authorizing the government to take such measures as it deemed appropriate in case foreign countries neutralized the effect of Swiss import duties by granting bounties on exports.   In 1904 a treaty was signed by Switzerland and Germany which in addition to a reciprocal pledge for most-favored-nation treatment specified the rates of duty which the products of each country should pay upon importation into the other.   By an act of May 1, 1906, Germany established a system of drawbacks upon exported

---

[1] Cf. the resolution which Sir Thomas Barclay recommended for adoption to the International Law Association: "Whereas any varying interpretation of the most-favored-nation clause gives rise to instability in the trade relations of co-contracting countries, it is suggested that any state holding itself to be aggrieved by any such varying interpretation should be entitled to cite the co-contracting party before the Hague Court, and that the jurisdiction of the said Hague Court in all such matters should be accepted without reservation" (*Yale Law Journal*, XVII [1907], 32).

flour which the Swiss millers claimed was in excess of the German import duties on the amount of grain necessary for the milling of a given amount of flour of the higher grades and in effect constituted a substantial export bounty. In 1907 the Swiss millers urged the Swiss government to apply to German flour the provision in the tariff law authorizing countervailing measures against bounty-fed goods. The Swiss government notified the German government that it was contemplating the application of countervailing duties to German flour. The German government replied that Switzerland was bound by its treaty with Germany not to levy duties on German flour higher than 2.50 francs per 100 kilograms and that she would be held to the strict execution of the treaty. Switzerland thereupon replied that the treaty provided for the submission to arbitration upon the request of either country of conflicts of interpretation of its provisions, and requested that the dispute be referred to arbitration. Germany, however, feared that an unfavorable decision would result in similar protests by other countries and would destroy the effectiveness of its drawback system as an important phase of its policy of encouraging its agrarians, and therefore refused the Swiss request. Switzerland was too weak either to impose the countervailing duties in defiance of the German warning, or to insist upon reference of the controversy to arbitration.[1]

This controversy involved not only the question of the compatibility of bounty-countervailing duties with most-favored-nation obligations, but also the question of the bearing on the validity of countervailing duties of the "binding" of import duties by treaty. Granting that a country may consistently with its most-favored-nation obligations impose countervailing duties on bounty-fed imports, does it retain this right after it has agreed by treaty not to levy a duty on the product in question higher than a specified amount? The German refusal to

[1] For an account of the controversy, see Sigmund Schilder, "Der Deutsch-Schweizerische Mehlkonflikt," *Das Handelsmuseum*, XXIV (1909), 29 ff.

acknowledge the right of Switzerland to impose the countervailing duties on German flour cannot be cited with much effect as a precedent affirming the negative. Germany based her refusal in part on the claim that her drawback system did not conceal a bounty. Moreover, the disparity of political and military power between Germany and Switzerland undoubtedly lessened the influence of juristic considerations in determining the German attitude. The problem must be regarded, therefore, as still an unsettled one, and as the binding of tariff rates by treaty is common, the revival of export bounties on an extensive scale would make it acquire considerable practical significance.

THE COMPATIBILITY OF GENERAL ANTIDUMPING DUTIES WITH MOST-FAVORED-NATION OBLIGATIONS

The question of the compatibility of antidumping duties with treaty obligations either of the most-favored-nation type or of the tariff treaty type providing for maximum specified rates of duty has never as yet been the subject of diplomatic discussion. Russia in 1903 believed that she would have to obtain a revision of her most-favored-nation treaty with Germany in order to acquire the right to levy additional duties on German products which had received a private export bounty or had been sold for export at dumping prices.[1] The British Safeguarding of Industries Act of 1921 provides that the dumping-duties must not be applied in any case in which they would be in conflict with treaty obligations, but it is apparently the position of the British government that the dumping-duties proper are unquestionably not in conflict with most-favored-nation obligations, whereas the "exchange-dumping" provisions are.[2] The Canadian dumping-duties are the only ones which had been applied prior to 1921, and these were applied almost solely to imports from

[1] Wilhelm Kaufman, *op. cit.*, pp. 341, note; 545, note.

[2] *Parliamentary Debates, Commons*, July 6, 1921, col. 395; July 13, 1921, col. 1315; August 10, 1921, col. 557.

the United States, which has no most-favored-nation treaty with Canada. Since 1921, however, antidumping orders have been issued by the United States Treasury specifying imports from several countries entitled to most-favored-nation treatment, but there has not been reported any instance of an official foreign protest against the orders. As yet, however, no duties have actually been imposed under these orders.

The compatibility of dumping-duties with most-favored-nation obligations is probably less open to question than in the case of countervailing duties against official bounties. The dumping-duties are ordinarily applicable to imports which have been sold at dumping prices, regardless of their country of origin. There does not, therefore, result from the application of these duties any classification of countries, but only a classification of goods without differentiation of countries. In many cases dumped and non-dumped articles of a given kind or class will both come from the same countries, so that if a classification of imports according to whether they have been sold at the full foreign prices or at dumping prices does happen to correspond to a classification of countries, this will be accidental and not the result of the intent or the necessary mode of operation of the antidumping provision.

Where the antidumping law requires or permits the designation of commodities by their country of origin or exportation, and the dumping-duties become applicable only on goods of a given kind or class imported at dumping prices from the country or countries specified in the order, there results not merely a classification of commodities according to whether or not they had been sold at dumping prices but a classification of commodities sold at dumping prices according to their countries of origin or exportation. Under the American antidumping law of 1921, for instance, the dumping-duties become applicable to dumped imports only if these imports are of a kind *and are imported from a country* specified in an order issued by the Secretary of the

Treasury. When an antidumping law is administered in this manner, the country specified in an antidumping order has clear ground for protest that its treaty rights to equality of treatment are being violated. It is not a sufficient answer if it be replied that the discrimination in treatment is merely a discrimination in form and not in actuality since the order specifies by name all the countries from which imports have been coming in at dumping prices, since if this be the case the discrimination in form will become a discrimination in fact as soon as there is an importation of goods from a non-specified country at dumping prices. Moreover, in this case there cannot be pleaded in defense of the classification of countries the principle of *volenti non fit injuria*. Treaty contracts are made between governments, and governments are ordinarily not responsible for the dumping practiced by their citizens. In the interest of scrupulous regard for treaty obligations and to avoid the danger of diplomatic controversy, it would seem desirable to sacrifice a measure of administrative expediency and to make orders issued under antidumping legislation apply to imports of the specified kind or class regardless of their place of origin or exportation.

SELECTED BIBLIOGRAPHY

AFTALION, ALBERT
"Les Kartells dans la Région du Nord de la France," *Revue Économique Internationale*, I (1908), 107–65; II (1911), 274–308.

ALFASSA, M. MAURICE
"L'Impérialisme Économique en Grand-Bretagne," *Bulletin de la Société d'Encouragement pour l'Industrie Nationale*, CXII (1909), 152–62; 377–98.

ASHLEY, W. J.
The Tariff Problem. 3d ed. London, 1911.

BEETON, MAYSON M.
The Truth about the Foreign Sugar Bounties. London, 1898.

BENN, WEDGWOOD.
"The Safeguarding of Industries Act: Orders under Part II," *Economic Journal*, XXXII (1922), 408–14.

BERGLUND, ABRAHAM.
"The Ferroalloy Industries and Tariff Legislation," *Political Science Quarterly*, XXXVI (1921), 245–73.

CABIATI, A., JANNACCONE, P., LORIA, A., RIDOLFI, R.
[A Symposium on Dumping], *Riforma Sociale*, XXV (1914), 193–291.

CANADA.
Report of the Board of Inquiry into the Cost of Living, 1915, I, 750–59.

CHOMLEY, C. H.
Protection in Canada and Australasia. London, 1904.

COSOIU, MIHAIL N.
Die belgische Handelspolitik der letzten 40 Jahre. Stuttgart, 1914.

CROHN-WOLFGANG, H. F.
"Zur Frage des 'dumping,'" *Jahrbücher für Nationalökonomie und Statistik*, 3d Ser. LVII 1 (1919), 177-80.

CULBERTSON, W. C.
Commercial Policy in War Time and After. New York, 1919.
"The Making of Tariffs," *Yale Review*, XII (1923), 255–74.

CURTISS, G. B.
Protection and Prosperity. New York, 1896.

DE LAVISON, A.
La Protection par les Primes. Paris, 1900.

DE LEENER, G.
L'Organisation Syndicale des Chefs d'Industrie. Brussels, 1909.
DE ROUSIERS, PAUL.
Les Syndicats Industriels de Producteurs en France et à l'Étranger.
2d ed. Paris, 1912.
DIEPENHORST, F.
Die handelspolitische Bedeutung der Ausfuhrunterstützungen der Kartelle.
Leipzig, 1908.
DIETZEL H.
"Depression und 'Exportdusel,'" *Nation* (Berlin), 1902, No. 11.
"Free Trade and the Labour Market," *Economic Journal*, XV (1905),
1–11.
DONALD, W. J. A.
The Canadian Iron and Steel Industry. Boston, 1915.
ELLIOTT, O. L.
The Tariff Controversy in the United States, 1789–1833. Palo Alto, 1892.
EMERY, H. C.
"The Problem of Anti-Dumping Legislation," *Report of Third National
Foreign Trade Convention,* 1916.
FEER, EDUARD.
*Die Ausfuhrpolitik der deutschen Eisenkartelle und ihre Wirkungen in
der Schweiz.* Zürich, 1918.
FELD, WILHELM.
"Anti-Dumping, Prämienklausel und Ausgleichzölle," *Archiv für
Sozialwissenschaft und Sozialpolitik*, XLIV (1917–18), 456–86.
FISK, G. M.
International Commercial Policies. New York, 1907.
FONTANO-RUSSO, L.
Traité de Politique Commerciale (translated from the Italian). Paris,
1908.
FRANCE.
Chambre des Députés, Commission des Douanes. *Rapport Général*,
1908.
FUCHS, C. J.
The Trade Policy of Great Britain and Her Colonies since 1860. London,
1905.
GLOWACKI, MARYAN.
Die Ausfuhrunterstützungspolitik der Kartelle. Posen, 1909.
GOETTLING, W.
"Anti-Dumping, Japan," *Trans-Pacific*, October, 1920, pp. 43–48.

GOTHEIN, GEORG.
"La Réglementation Internationale des Droits de Douane sur les Fers," *Revue Économique Internationale*, II (1904), 483–527.

GREAT BRITAIN.
Report of the Commissioner . . . . to Inquire into . . . . the State of the Population in the Mining Districts. 1854.
Commission on the Depression of Trade and Industry, 1886; *Second Report, Minutes of Evidence*, Part I (C. 4715); *Final Report* (C. 4893).
Board of Trade: *Report on British and Foreign Trade and Industrial Combinations*, 1903. (Cd. 1761).
Report of H.M. Representatives Abroad on Bounties, 1904 (Cd. 1946).
Board of Trade: *Report of the Committee on the Iron and Steel Trades after the War*, 1918 (Cd. 9071).
Committee on Commercial and Industrial Policy after the War: *Final Report*, 1918. (Cd. 9035).
Trading with the Enemy Committee: *Report*, 1918. (Cd. 9059).
Board of Trade: *Summary Statement of Legislative Provisions for the Prevention of Dumping*, 1919 (Cmd. 265).
Ministry of Reconstruction: *Report of Committee on Trusts*, 1919 (Cd. 9236).
Ministry of Reconstruction: *Final Report on Anti-Dumping Legislation*, 1919. (Cmd. 455).

GREGORY, T. E. G.
Tariffs: a Study in Method. London, 1921.

GRIFFIN, C. S.
"The Sugar Industry and Legislation in Europe," *Quarterly Journal of Economics*, XVII (1902), 1–43.

GRILLI, CARLO.
"Il Protezionismo dopo la Guerra," *Rivista Internazionale*, XC (1920), 289–96; XCI (1920), 12–32; 252–83.

GRUNZEL, JOSEF.
Economic Protectionism. London, 1916.

HAMILTON, ALEXANDER.
Report on the Subject of Manufactures, 1791, in F. W. Taussig (editor), *State Papers and Speeches on the Tariff.* Cambridge, 1893.

HAUSER, HENRI.
Germany's Commercial Grip on the World (translated from the French). New York, 1917.

HERINGA, A.
Free Trade and Protectionism in Holland. London, 1914.

HINCKES, R. T.
Seven Years of the Sugar Convention, 1903–1910. London, 1910.
HIRST, F. W.
Monopolies, Trusts and Kartells. New York, 1906.
HOBSON, J. A.
International Trade: an Application of Economic Theory. London, 1904.
HOLT, BYRON W.
Home and Foreign Price of American-made Goods, 1906. (New York Tariff Reform Club pamphlet reprinted in *Congressional Record,* XL [1906], 8024–33.)
HORNBECK, S. K.
"The Most-Favored-Nation Clause in Commercial Treaties," *Bulletin of the University of Wisconsin,* VI (1910), No. 2.
HUFNAGEL, G. E.
"Fighting Dumping in Holland," *Commercial Holland,* December, 1919, pp. 53–56; February, 1920, pp. 42–44.
HYDE, C. C.
"Concerning the Interpretation of Treaties," *American Journal of International Law,* III (1909), 46–61.
KAUFMAN, WILHELM.
Welt-Zuckerindustrie und Internationales und Koloniales Recht. Berlin, 1904.
LEVY, HERMANN.
Monopoly and Competition. London, 1911.
LIEFMANN, ROBERT.
Cartells et Trusts. (Translated from 2d German edition.) Paris, 1914.
MARSHALL, ALFRED.
"Fiscal Policy of International Trade," Great Britain: *House of Commons Papers,* 321 (1908).
Industry and Trade. London, 1919.
MARTINEAU, GEORGE.
"The Brussels Sugar Convention," *Economic Journal,* XIV (1904), 34–46.
McLAREN, A. D.
Peaceful Penetration. New York, 1917.
MÉNY, MARC.
Le Dumping. Paris, 1909.
MEREDITH, H. O.
Protection in France. London, 1904.

MORGENROTH, WILLI.
Die Exportpolitik der Kartelle. Leipzig, 1907.
NOTZ, WILLIAM.
"International Private Agreements in the Form of Cartels, Syndicates, and Other Combinations," *Journal of Political Economy*, XXVIII (1920), 658–79.
NOTZ, WILLIAM, and HARVEY, R. S.
American Foreign Trade. Indianapolis, 1921.
PAGE, T. W.
"Difficulties of Tariff Revision," *Journal of the American Bankers' Association*, XIII (1921), 653–56.
PARSONS, J. G.
Protection's Favors to Foreigners, 1909. Printed as government document, 61st Cong., 1st Sess., *Sen. Doc.* 54.
PESL, LUDWIG DAN.
Das Dumping, Preis-Unterbietungen im Welthandel. Munich, 1921.
PIGOU, A. C.
"Professor Dietzel on Dumping and Retaliation," *Economic Journal*, XV (1905), 436–43.
Protective and Preferential Import Duties. London, 1906.
"Pure Theory and the Fiscal Controversy," *Economic Journal*, XIV (1904), 29–33.
PLAUTT, THEODORE.
"Die Bedeutung des Dumping für die gegenwärtige englische Handelspolitik," *Weltwirtschaftliches Archiv*, XVI (1921), 389–412.
PORRITT, EDWARD.
Sixty Years of Protection in Canada. London, 1908.
The Fiscal and Diplomatic Freedom of the British Overseas Dominions. Oxford, 1922.
The Revolt in Canada against the New Feudalism. London, 1911.
RAFFALOVICH, ARTHUR.
Les Coalitions de Producteurs et le Protectionnisme. Paris, 1889.
RIST, CHARLES.
"L'Exportation Américaine, et les Lois sur les Trusts," *Revue d'Économie Politique*, XXXIII (1919), 78–82.
SAYOUS, ANDRÉ.
La Crise Allemande de 1900–1902. Paris, 1903.
SCHILDER, SIGMUND.
"Der deutsch-schweizerische Mehlkonflikt," *Das Handelsmuseum*, XXIV (1909), 29–32.

Scholefield, G. H.
  New Zealand in Evolution. London, 1909.
Shaw, Leslie M.
  Current Issues. New York, 1908.
Shepheard, W. P. B.
  "The Most Favoured Nation Article," *Journal of Comparative Legislation*, N.S., III (1901), 231–37.
Shortt, Adam.
  "The Anti-Dumping Feature of the Canadian Tariff," *Quarterly Journal of Economics*, XX (1906), 250–58.
Smart, William.
  The Return to Protection. London, 1904.
Stanwood, Edward.
  American Tariff Controversies in the Nineteenth Century. Boston, 1903.
Taussig, F. W.
  Free Trade, the Tariff and Reciprocity. New York, 1920.
  Some Aspects of the Tariff Question. Cambridge, 1915.
Thibault, Fabien.
  "Conflits entre la Convention Sucrière de Bruxelles et les Traités de Commerce," *Revue d'Économie Politique*, XXIII (1909), 497–515.
Tosdal, H. R.
  "The Kartell Movement in the German Potash Industry," *Quarterly Journal of Economics*, XXVIII (1913), 140–90.
United States:
  Alien Property Custodian:
    Report. 1919.
  Department of Commerce:
    Trust Laws and Unfair Competition. 1916.
    Special Agents' Series, No. 86 (1914), "Cotton Goods in Japan."
  Federal Trade Commission:
    Report on Cooperation in American Export Trade. 1916.
  Industrial Commission:
    Report, 1901, I, XIII, XVII, XVIII.
  Merchant Marine Commission:
    Report and Hearings. 1905. (58th Cong., 3d. Sess., *Sen. Rept.* 2755.)
  State Department:
    Selling Foreign Manufactures in United States at Prices Lower than the Domestic Prices. 1909. (61st Cong., 1st Sess., *Sen. Doc.* 16.)

Tariff Commission:
  Colonial Tariff Policies. 1922.
  Information concerning Dumping and Unfair Foreign Competition in the United States. 1919.
  Reciprocity and Commercial Treaties. 1919.
  Sixth Annual Report. 1922.
Hearings before the [House] Committee on Investigation of United States Steel Corporation. 1912.
Tariff Schedules, Hearings before the Committee on Ways and Means, House of Representatives, 1913, VI.
Anti-Dumping Legislation, Hearings before the Committee on Ways and Means, House of Representatives, on H.R. 9983 and H.R. 10071, October 22, 1919.
Emergency Tariff and Antidumping, Hearing before the Committee on Finance, United States Senate, on H.R. 2435, April 18–22, 1921.
Hearings on General Tariff Revision, before the Committee on Ways and Means, House of Representatives, 1921.
Report of the Commissioner of Corporations on the Petroleum Industry, 1907, Part II, pp. 316–425.
Testimony in U.S.A. vs. U.S. Steel Corporation and Others, District Court of the United States for the District of New Jersey, 1913.

VAN ISEGEHM, L.
  "Le 'Dumping' et les Mesures Prises ou Préconisées pour en Combattre les Effets," *Revue Économique Internationale,* 1921, No. 3, 327–40.

VISSER, M. L. E.
  "La Clause de 'La Nation La Plus Favorisée' dans les Traités de Commerce," *Revue de Droit International et de Législation Comparée,* 2d Ser., IV (1902), 66–87; 159–77; 270–80.

WALKER, FRANCIS.
  Monopolistic Combinations in the German Coal Industry. Publications of the American Economic Association, 3d Ser., V (1904), No. 3.
  "Policies of Germany, England, Canada and the United States towards Combinations," *Annals of the American Academy of Political and Social Science,* XLII (1912), 183–201.
  "The German Steel Syndicate," *Quarterly Journal of Economics,* XX (1906), 353–98.

INDEX

Adams, 45

Aftalion, 70 n.

Airplanes, 272

American Banana Co. v. *United Fruit Co.*, 240, 241

Antidumping legislation, chaps. xi–xiv, 327 ff.

Armitage Smith, 113 n.

Artificial prices, 19

Asquith, 222 n.

Auction sales, 41

Australia: antidumping legislation, 89, 206 ff., 227 ff.; dumping in, 49, 89; official bounties, 91

Austria: bounty-clauses in treaties, 166 n., 167; dumping by, 70 ff.

Automobiles, 272

Balfour, 218

Barclay, 302 n., 325 n.

Bartram v. *Robertson*, 301

Belgium: countervailing duty, 160 n., 169; dumping by, 5, 19, 66 ff.

Berglund, 7 n.

Binder twine, 190, 196

Bismarck, 49

Bounties: official export, 29, 36, 37, 50, 90 ff., 128, chap. x., 211, 232, 298 ff.; private export, 36, 50, 54 ff., 67, 70, 71, 73, 84 ff., 88, 106, 126 ff., 269 ff.; production, 72, 127 ff., 170, 171, 178, 182

Bounty-clauses in treaties. *See* Treaties

Branch plants and technical avoidance of dumping, 33, 287

British South Africa: antidumping legislation, 209 ff.; countervailing duty, 170 ff., 211

Brougham, 41 ff.

Brussels Sugar Convention, 91, 175, 178 ff., 304 ff.

Buttfield v. *Stranahan*, 250 n.

Canada: antidumping legislation, 86, 140 n., 192 ff., 223 n., 237, 267; dumping by, 6, 71 ff.; dumping in, 48, 86, 193, 196 n., 202 n.; production bounties, 92, 190

Canadian Manufacturers Association, 203

Carey, 43 n.

Carver, 128 n.

Chamberlain, 89, 309

Chamberlain Tariff Commission, 78

Chapman, 44, 76 n.

Chemicals, 26 n., 63

Chomley, 49

Clay, Henry, 45

Coffee valorization, 241

Colson, 185 n.

Concealed dumping, 17, 266, 281 ff.

Conditions and terms of sale, 8, 17, 260, 281 ff.

Consignment sales, 20, 25, 41 n., 211, 229, 233, 261, 285 ff.

Contingent duties in American tariffs, 311 ff.

Cordage, 190

Cosoiu, 160 n.

Cost of production: and dumping, 4, 32, 33, 146, 199, 207, 222, 228, 231, 273, 291 ff.; and tariffs, 162, 261, 292

Cottons, 72

Countervailing duties, 91, 163 ff., 168 ff., 211, 213, 231, 268 ff., 298 ff.

Credit terms, 11, 18, 65, 198

Culbertson, 189, 245 n., 254 n.

Customs procedure, 200 ff., 214 ff., 265 ff.

Date of price-comparison, 12, 197, 199, 228, 260, 276 ff.

De Leener, 67 n.

Democratic Party, 81, 82

Depreciated currency. *See* Exchange dumping

De Vries, 320

Dietzel, 119 n., 138 n., 148 ff.

Downs v. *U.S.*, 173, 175, 313

Drawbacks, 13, 91 ff., 162 ff., 197, 234, 262, 263, 265, 279 ff., 325 ff.

Dyestuffs, 26 n., 63

Economies of large-scale production, 28, 123 ff., 127

Emergency Tariff Act, 258 ff., 272, 328

Entrepôt trade, 136

Evarts, 49

Exchange dumping, 15, 219, 229, 235

Excise taxes, 14, 91, 173 ff., 197, 198, 212, 234, 263, 279 ff.

Export bounties. *See* Bounties, Export

Export tax, 64

Fair trade, 49

Farrell, 29 n., 85 n., 116, 118 n., 202 n.

Federal Trade Commission, 85 n., 95 n., 100, 250, 254 n.

Federal Trade Commission Act, 244, 250, 251

Federated Malay States: preferential export tax on tin, 189

Feer, 64

Feld, 167 n., 185 n.

Ferrosilicon, 7

Field v. *Clark*, 249

Fielding, 193, 196

Fisk, 77 n.

Flexible tariff provisions, 235 ff., 288

Flour, 6, 72, 165, 265, 325 ff.

F.o.b. prices, 11 n., 17, 19, 275, 281, 285

Fordney, 244 n.

Fordney-McCumber Tariff Act: under-valuation provisions, 8, 12 n., 268; countervailing duty, 169, 187 ff., 268 ff.; unfair competition provision, 246 ff.; contingent duties, 311 ff.; customs procedure, 265 ff.; returned automobile, 272

France: antidumping legislation, 212 ff.; countervailing duty, 171, 172; drawbacks, 164; dumping by, 49, 68 ff.; official bounties, 91, 164; preferential export duties, 189

Free trade and dumping, 75 ff., 144 ff., 180

Freight dumping, 16, 187, 229, 231

Fuchs, 50 n., 179 n., 180 n.

Full line forcing, 243

Gallatin, 38

Gallinger, 87 n.

Gary, 25 n., 29 n., 78 n., 87 n.

Geofry v. *Riggs*, 317 n.

Germany: bounty-clause in treaties, 166, 167; controversy with Switzerland, 325 ff.; controversy with U.S., 312, 314 ff.; and countervailing duties, 185, 304, 306, 313 ff., 320; credit methods, 18, 65; drawbacks, 164, 325 ff.; dumping by, 18, 26 n., 49, 51 ff, 65; official bounties, 50, 91, 325; potash law, 7, 98 n.

Glass, 5, 68

Goluchowski, 89

Gothein, 57 n., 89, 185 n.

Graham, 243 n.

Great Britain: antidumping legislation, 216 ff., 327; bounty-clauses in treaties, 166 n., 310, 323, 324; and Brussels Sugar Convention, 178 ff., 308 ff., 316 ff.; dumping by, 24 n., 26 n., 27 n., 37 ff., 74 ff., 165 n.; dumping in, 135; official bounties in, 37, 165 n.

Gregory, 3, 149 n., 268 n.

Gresham, 303 n., 313, 320 n.

Grey, 308

Grunzel, 58 n., 60 n., 71 n.

Hamilton, 37

Hardware, 63

Harvester Trust, 80, 89, 204

Hauser, 61 n.

Hay, John, 303 n.

Herod, 318 n.

Hides, 189

Hills v. *U.S.*, 173

Hirst, 75 n.

Holland: dumping in, 57, 135

Holt, 80 n., 83 n., 88 n.

Hornbeck, 318, 319

Hyde, 318

Import duties and export dumping, 57, 62, 75, 82, 259 n.

India: countervailing duty, 170, 172, 309; preferential export tax, 189

Intermittent dumping. *See* Short-run dumping, 99

International combinations, 99

International control of dumping, 185, 254

International Union for the Protection of Industrial Property, 254 ff.

Italy: bounty-clauses in treaties, 166 n.; dumping in, 64; dumping by, 71; preferential export taxes, 189

Japan: antidumping legislation, 236; countervailing duty, 171; dumping by, 72 ff.

Jones, 117 n., 256 n.

Kartells, 51 ff., 71, 84

Kaufmann, 179 n., 319 n.

Liefmann, 56 n., 62 n., 110 n.

List, 143 n.

Lister, 116

Local price-cutting, 3

Long-run dumping, 30, 31, 122 ff., 138 ff., 146

Longuet, 69

Lottery, Japanese export, 73

Luzzati, 89

Macrosty, 113 n.

Mandatory antidumping legislation, 294 ff.

Mandatory countervailing duties, 171 ff.

Marshall, 43 n., 47, 48, 62, 118, 128 n., 148 n., 156 n.

McLaren, 64 n.

Mercantilistic dumping, 28

Merchant Marine Commission, 87, 90

Meredith, 68 n.

Mill, 159

Mond, 226

Monopolies and dumping, 75 ff., 93 ff., 120 ff.

Morel, 69, 214

Morgenroth, 53 n., 59 n., 62 n.

Most-favored-nation pledge, 190 n., 297 ff.

Newfoundland: antidumping legislation, 212

New Zealand: antidumping legislation, 89, 204 ff., 231 ff., 237; countervailing duty, 171, 237

Nicholas & Co. v. *U.S.*, 174

Notz, 185 n., 256 n.

Olney, 315

Overvaluation, 266

Packing charges, 11

Page, 62 n.

Palmer, 63

Paris Conference, 216

Parsons, 83 n., 87 n.

Permanent dumping. *See* Long-run dumping

Permissive antidumping legislation, 294 ff.

Permissive countervailing duties, 171 ff.

Philippines, preferential export tax, 190

Phillips, 81 n., 82 n.

Pig-iron, 58, 70

Pigou, 114 n., 119, 148 ff.

Poland, dumping by, 71

Porritt, 48 n., 72 n., 193 n., 195 n.

Portugal: countervailing duty, 171; preferential export taxes, 189

Posadowsky, 89

Potash, 7, 98

Predatory dumping, 26, 37 ff., 61 ff., 79, 101, 111, 120, 133, 207, 239 ff.

Preferences in antidumping legislation, 197, 204 ff., 231 ff.

Preferential export taxes, 187 ff.

Preferential freight rates. *See* Freight dumping

Price-discrimination, 3, 8

Profitability of dumping, 32, chap. vii

Protection and dumping, 36, 47, 49, 148

Quantity orders, 9, 260

Rabbeno, 43 n.
Raffalovich, 53 n.
Redfield, 243 n.
Reed, 259 n.
Reimportation of dumped goods, 75 ff., 272
Republican Party, 83
Retaliatory dumping, 27
Revenue Act of 1916, 242 ff.
Reverse dumping, 5 ff.
Ridolfi, 64 n.
Roscher, 43 n.
Rusk, 80
Russia: bounty-clauses in treaties, 166 n.; and Brussels Sugar Convention, 181, 311; and countervailing duties, 309; dumping by, 71

Sandberg v. McDonald, 252
Schilder, 326 n.
Scholefield, 205 n.
Schwab, 85 n., 86 n.
Secrecy of export prices, 18, 80
Selling expenses, 11
Servia, countervailing duty, 171
Shaw, 13 n., 83 n.
Sherman Antitrust Act, 239
Shipbuilding materials, 87, 108
Short-run dumping, 30, 31, 111 ff., 115, 140 ff.
Shortt, 202 n.
Smart, 26 n., 61 n., 123 n., 135 n., 140, 143 n., 160 n.
Smith, 36
Spain: countervailing duty, 171; dumping by, 71; preferential export taxes, 189
Sporadic dumping, 23, 30, 61, 69, 74, 101, 110, 139, 245, 290
Spurious dumping, 8, 275 ff.
Stabilization of industry, 116 ff.
Stahlwerksverband, 55 n., 57, 60 n., 64, 78 n., 98
Standard Oil Co., 88, 90
Stanwood, 40 n., 42 n., 43 n., 44 n.

Steel, 57, 71, 72, 78
Sugar, 134, 165, 178 ff., 305 ff.
Switzerland: bounty-clauses in treaties, 166 n.; countervailing duty, 171, 325 ff.; dumping in, 64

Taussig, 4 n., 43 n., 105, 116, 123, 130 n., 138 n.
Technical avoidance of dumping, 20, 33, 276, 287
Thibault, 310, 322 ff.
Thompson, 43 n.
Tin, 189
Tin plate, 86, 88, 108, 135, 196 n.
Toronto Board of Trade, 203
Tosdal, 7 n., 98 n.
Treaties: bounty-clauses in, 166 ff., 322, 324; most-favored-nation pledge in, 190 n., 297 ff.; treaty-obligations, 167 ff., chap. xv
Turkey, dumping in, 63, 79

Undervaluation provisions, 12, 258, 265, 268
Underwood Tariff Bill, 257 ff.
Unfair competition, 2, 8, 34, 61 ff., 142, 147, 204 ff., 239, 255
Unintentional dumping, 25, 40
United States: antidumping legislation, chap. xiii; and bounty-clauses in treaties, 167 n.; cases cited: American Banana Co. v. United Fruit Co., 240, 241; Bartram v. Robertson, 301; Buttfield v. Stranahan, 250 n.; Downs v. U.S., 173, 175, 313; Field v. Clark, 249; Geofry v. Riggs, 317 n.; Hills v. U.S., 173; Nicholas & Co. v. U.S., 174; Sandberg v. McDonald, 252 n; Whitney v. Robertson, 301; contingent duties in tariffs, 311 ff.; countervailing duties, 168 ff., 173 ff., 187 ff., 313 ff.; dumping by, 48, 49, 63, 80 ff., 165 n., 195, 231 n; official export bounties, 92, 165 n.
United States Gold Leaf Manufacturers Association, 85 n., 107
United States Industrial Commission, 81, 90
United States Steel Corporation, 29 n., 78 n., 85 ff., 117 n., 135, 196 n., 201

United States Tariff Commission, 2 n.,
21, 72, 188 ff., 245, 246, 248, 250,
251 n., 253, 312

Villain, 70 n.
Visser, 306, 307

Walker, F., 53 n., 56
Walker, J. E., 262 n.

Walsh, 250 n.
Webb-Pomerene Act, 99, 252, 256
Wheaton, 300
Whiskey pool, 50, 107
Whitney v. *Robertson*, 301
Wilson Tariff Act, 240 ff.
Wire nails, 63
Witte, 89